CPCU 510 Course Guide

Foundations of Risk Management, Insurance, and Professionalism

4th Edition

American Institute for Chartered Property Casualty Underwriters/Insurance Institute of America

720 Providence Road • Suite 100 • Malvern, PA 19355

Table of Contents

Study Materials Available for CPCU 510

Charles M. Nyce, *Foundations of Risk Management and Insurance,* 2nd ed., 2006, AICPCU/IIA.

Code of Professional Ethics of the American Institute for Chartered Property Casualty Underwriters, 7th ed., 2002, AICPCU/IIA.

CPCU 510 *Course Guide,* 4th ed., 2006, AICPCU/IIA.

SMART Practice Exam CD-ROM, Eff. Date 08.06

CPCU 510 SMART Study Aids—Review Notes and Flash Cards, 3rd ed.

Student Resources

Catalog A complete listing of our offerings can be found in *Succeed*, the Institutes' professional development catalog, including information about:

- Current programs and courses

- Current textbooks, course guides, and SMART Study Aids

- Program completion requirements

- Exam registration

To obtain a copy of the catalog, visit our Web site at www.aicpcu.org or contact Customer Support at (800) 644-2101.

How To Pass Institute Exams! This free handbook, printable from the Student Services Center on the Institutes' Web site at www.aicpcu.org, or available by calling Customer Support at (800) 644-2101, is designed to help you by:

- Giving you ideas on how to use textbooks and course guides as effective learning tools

- Providing steps for answering exam questions effectively

- Recommending exam-day strategies

Institutes Online Forums Do you wish you could talk with people around the country about course questions and share information with others who have similar professional interests? We host forums at our Web site, where you can do just that. To access our forums:

- Go to the Institutes' Web site at www.aicpcu.org

- Click on the "Log on. Learn." link

- Scroll down and click on "Forums"

- Read the instructions, and you're ready to go!

Educational Counseling Services To ensure that you take courses matching both your needs and your skills, you can obtain free counseling from the Institutes by:

- E-mailing your questions to edserv@cpcuiia.org

- Calling an Institutes' counselor directly at (610) 644-2100, ext. 7630 or ext. 7633

- Obtaining and completing a self-inventory form, available on our Web site at www.aicpcu.org or by contacting Customer Support at (800) 644-2101

Exam Registration Information As you proceed with your studies, be sure to arrange for your exam.

- Consult the registration booklet that accompanied this course guide for complete information regarding exam dates and fees worldwide. Plan to register with the Institutes well in advance of your exam.

- If your registration booklet does not include exam dates for the current year, you can obtain up-to-date exam information by visiting the Institutes' Web site at www.aicpcu.org, sending an e-mail to customersupport@cpcuiia.org, or calling the Institutes at (800) 644-2101.

How to Contact the Institutes For more information on any of these publications and services:

- Visit our Web site at www.aicpcu.org

- Telephone us at (800) 644-2101 or (610) 644-2100 outside the U.S.

- E-mail us at customersupport@cpcuiia.org

- Fax us at (610) 640-9576

- Write us at AICPCU/IIA, Customer Support, 720 Providence Road, Suite 100, Malvern, PA 19355-3433

Using This Course Guide

This course guide will help you learn the course content and pass the exam.

Each assignment in this course guide typically includes the following components:

Educational Objectives These are the most important study tools in the course guide. Because all of the questions on the exam are based on the Educational Objectives, the best way to study for the exam is to focus on these objectives.

Each educational objective typically begins with one of the following action words, which indicate the level of understanding required for the exam:

Analyze—Determine the nature and the relationship of the parts.

Apply—Put to use for a practical purpose.

Calculate—Determine numeric values by mathematical process.

Classify—Arrange or organize according to class or category.

Compare—Show similarities and differences.

Contrast—Show only differences.

Define—Give a clear, concise meaning.

Describe—Represent or give an account.

Evaluate—Determine the value or merit.

Explain—Relate the importance or application.

Identify or list—Name or make a list.

Illustrate—Give an example.

Justify—Show to be right or reasonable.

Paraphrase—Restate in your own words.

Summarize—Concisely state the main points.

Required Reading The items listed in this section indicate what portion of the study materials (the textbook chapter(s), course guide readings, or other assigned materials) correspond to the assignment.

Outline The outline lists the topics in the assignment. Read the outline before the required reading to become familiar with the assignment content and the relationships of topics.

Key Words and Phrases These words and phrases are fundamental to understanding the assignment and have a common meaning for those working in insurance. After completing the required reading, test your understanding of the assignment's key words and phrases by writing their definitions. For help, refer to the page numbers that appear in parentheses after each key word and phrase.

Review Questions The review questions test your understanding of what you have read. Review the educational objectives and required reading, then answer the questions to the best of your ability. When you are finished, check the answers at the end of the assignment to evaluate your comprehension.

Application Questions These questions continue to test your knowledge of the required reading by applying what you've studied to real-life situations. Again, check the suggested answers at the end of the assignment to review your progress.

Sample Exam The sample exam helps you test your knowledge of the material. Use the sample exam at the back of the course guide or on the SMART practice exam CD-ROM (if it accompanies this course guide) to become familiar with the test format.

More Study Aids

The Institutes also produce supplemental study tools, called SMART Study Aids, for many of their courses. When SMART Study Aids are available for a course, they are listed on both page iii of this course guide and on the first page of each assignment. SMART Study Aids include review notes and flash cards and are excellent tools to help you learn and retain the information contained in each assignment.

CPCU Advisory Committee

The following individuals were instrumental in helping to analyze the audience for the CPCU program and to design the revisions and updates of the study materials for CPCU 510 that took effect in 2006.

F. Scott Addis, CPCU
The Addis Group

Chris Amrhein, AAI
Amrhein & Associates, Inc.

Richard L. Bennett, CPCU, ARM, ARe
St. John's University

Mark J. Browne, PhD
University of Wisconsin–Madison School of Business

Stephanie Colegrove, CPCU
State Farm Mutual Insurance

Michele F. Davis
The New School

Richard A. Derrig, PhD, CFE
OPAL Consulting

Elise M. Farnham, CPCU, ARM, AIM
Illumine Consulting

Harold J. Fink III, CPCU
NJM Insurance Group

Eric A. Fitzgerald, Esq., CPCU, ARe
Marshall, Dennehey, Warner, Coleman & Goggin

Steven A. George, CPCU, CLU
USAA

Joseph A. Gerber, Esq.
Cozen O'Connor

Joseph S. Harrington, CPCU, ARP
American Association of Insurance Services

Frederick P. Hessenthaler, CPCU
Chubb & Son

Steven M. Horner, CPCU, CLU, ARM
Horner & Associates, LLC

Robert E. Hoyt, PhD, CLU, ChFC
University of Georgia
Terry College of Business

John J. Kelly, CPCU, CLU, ARM
CPCU Society

Stanley L. Lipshultz, Esq., CPCU
Lipshultz & Hone Chartered & Interisk Ltd.

Dennis F. Mahoney, CEBS, CFP
The Wharton School, University of Pennsylvania

Gregory J. Massey, CPCU, CIC, CRM
Selective Insurance Group, Inc.

Ronald M. Metcho, CPCU, ARM, AAI
Saul-Metcho Insurance

Teresa A. Pavlin, CPCU, ARM, APA
ACE USA

Kent Schaum, CPCU, AIC
McNamara Insurance Services, Inc.

James A. Sherlock, CPCU, CLU, ARM
ACE INA

Stephen J. Trecker, CPCU, AIM
XL Insurance

Risk; Code of Ethics Introduction

Direct Direct Your Learning

Educational Objectives

After learning the content of this assignment, you should be able to:

1. Describe each of the following in the context of risk:
   - Uncertainty
   - Possibility
   - Possibility compared with probability

2. Explain the following elements for property, liability, personnel, and net income loss exposures:
   - Assets exposed to loss
   - Causes of loss, including associated hazards
   - Financial consequences of loss

3. Classify a given risk within the following categories:
   - Pure or speculative
   - Subjective or objective
   - Diversifiable or nondiversifiable

4. Describe the three financial consequences of risk.

5. Explain the purpose of the Code of Professional Ethics of the American Institute for CPCU (the Code).

6. Identify parties affected by the Code.

7. Describe the distinctive roles of the Code's Canons, Rules, and Guidelines.

8. Briefly summarize the Code's disciplinary process.

9. Describe the sanctions and penalties under the Code that may be applied to CPCU applicants, CPCU candidates, and CPCUs.

10. Define or describe each of the Key Words and Phrases for this assignment.

Study Materials

Required Reading:

- Foundations of Risk Management and Insurance
  - Chapter 1
- Code of Professional Ethics
  - Introduction (pages 1.1–1.11)

Study Aids:

- SMART Practice Exam CD-ROM
- SMART Study Aids Review Notes and Flash Cards— Assignment 1

Outline

- **Understanding and Quantifying Risk**

- **Loss Exposures**
  - A. Elements of Loss Exposures
    1. Asset Exposed to Loss
    2. Cause of Loss
    3. Financial Consequences of Loss
  - B. Types of Loss Exposures
    1. Property Loss Exposures
    2. Liability Loss Exposures
    3. Personnel Loss Exposures
    4. Net Income Loss Exposures

- **Classifications of Risk**
  - A. Pure and Speculative Risk
  - B. Subjective and Objective Risk
  - C. Diversifiable and Nondiversifiable Risk

- **Financial Consequences of Risk**
  - A. Expected Cost of Losses or Gains
  - B. Expenditures on Risk Management
  - C. Cost of Residual Uncertainty

- **Summary**

- **Introduction to the Code of Professional Ethics (Code)**
  - A. Purpose of the Code of Professional Ethics
  - B. Requirements for Earning the CPCU Designation
    1. Education Requirement
    2. Experience Requirement
    3. Ethics Requirement
  - C. Parties Affected by the Code
    1. Applicants
    2. CPCU Candidates
    3. CPCUs
  - D. Components of the Code
    1. Canons, Rules, and Guidelines
    2. Hypothetical Case Studies (HCSs)
    3. Advisory Opinions
    4. Disciplinary Rules, Procedures, and Penalties
  - E. Support of the Code of Professional Ethics

Key Words and Phrases

Define or describe each of the words and phrases listed below.

Risk (p. 1.4)

Probability (p. 1.5)

Loss exposure (p. 1.6)

Hazard (p. 1.8)

Moral hazard (p. 1.8)

Morale hazard (p. 1.8)

Physical hazard (p. 1.8)

Legal hazard (p. 1.9)

Property loss exposure (p. 1.11)

Tangible property (p. 1.11)

Intangible property (p. 1.11)

Real property (p. 1.11)

Personal property (p. 1.11)

Liability loss exposure (p. 1.12)

Personnel loss exposure (p. 1.14)

Personal loss exposure (p. 1.14)

Net income loss exposure (p. 1.15)

Pure risk (p. 1.18)

Speculative risk (p. 1.18)

Subjective risk (p. 1.20)

Objective risk (p. 1.20)

Diversifiable risk (p. 1.22)

Nondiversifiable risk (p. 1.22)

Code of Professional Ethics of the American Institute for CPCU
(*Code*, p. 1.1)

Matriculation (*Code*, p. 1.4)

Applicant (*Code*, p. 1.4)

Candidate (*Code*, p. 1.4)

Designee (*Code*, p. 1.4)

New designee (*Code*, p. 1.5)

CPCU (*Code*, p. 1.5)

Canon (*Code*, p. 1.6)

Rule (*Code*, p. 1.6)

Guideline (*Code*, p. 1.6)

Hypothetical Case Study (*Code*, p. 1.7)

Advisory Opinion (*Code*, p. 1.7)

Board of Ethical Inquiry (*Code*, p. 1.7)

Ethics Counsel (*Code*, p. 1.7)

Unpublished advisory opinion (*Code*, p. 1.8)

Published advisory opinion (*Code*, p. 1.8)

Disciplinary Rules, Procedures, and Penalties (*Code*, p. 1.8)

Review Questions

1. Describe the two elements of risk. (p. 1.5)

2. Describe the difference between possibility and probability.
    (p. 1.5)

3. Explain how understanding various outcome probabilities can aid
   an organization in its risk management efforts. (p. 1.6)

4. List three elements necessary to describe a loss exposure. (p. 1.6)

5. Identify types of assets that could be loss exposures for the
   following entities. (p. 1.7)

   a.   Organization's assets

   b.   Individual's assets

6. Describe the four classifications of hazards. (pp. 1.8–1.9)

7. Identify three factors that affect the financial consequences of a loss. (pp. 1.10–1.11)

8. Distinguish between the following types of property. (p. 1.11)

   a. Tangible property

   b. Intangible property

   c. Real property

   d. Personal property

9. Explain how an organization or individual might experience a financial loss from the following type of loss exposures. (pp. 1.11–1.15)

   a.   Property loss exposure

   b.   Liability loss exposure

   c.   Personnel loss exposure

   d.   Net income loss exposure

10. Describe how classifying risk helps an organization's risk management process. (p. 1.17)

11. Explain why it is important to distinguish between speculative risks and pure risks when making risk management decisions. (p. 1.19)

12. Explain reasons why the assessment of subjective and objective risk might differ. (pp. 1.21–1.22)

13. Identify three components that comprise the financial consequences of risk faced by individuals or organizations. (p. 1.23)

14. List hidden costs that can affect an organization's calculation of expected costs of loss. (p. 1.24)

15. Describe the costs of residual uncertainty. (p. 1.25)

16. Briefly describe each of the three requirements for earning the CPCU designation. (*Code*, pp. 1.2–1.4)

17. Which CPCUs are not subject to the Code of Professional Ethics? (*Code*, pp. 1.5–1.6)

18. Is a CPCU subject to discipline for violating a Canon of the Code? Explain. (*Code*, p. 1.7)

19. What sanctions may be applied to CPCU applicants and candidates? (*Code*, p. 1.10)

20. What sanctions may be imposed on a CPCU who is subject to the Code and is found guilty of a Rules violation? (*Code*, pp. 1.10–1.11)

Application Questions

1. Atwell Bus Company, Inc. (Atwell), is a corporation providing bus transportation to public and private schools in Midland County. Atwell owns 200 new school buses. Its major competitors are two larger bus companies that operate in the same general area. School districts and private schools generally award annual contracts to the lowest bidder from among the bus companies, but they also consider overall performance and level of service in their evaluations. Explain how the following elements apply to Atwell's risks. (p. 1.5)

   a. Uncertainty

   b. Possibility

   c. Probability

2. ABC's Used Cars, Inc., (ABC) has applied for property and liability insurance. Describe a possible hazard that ABC might face in each of the following categories. (pp. 1.8–1.9)

   a. Moral hazard

b. Morale hazard

c. Physical hazard

d. Legal hazard

3. Classify each of the following risks as pure or speculative, subjective or objective, and diversifiable or nondiversifiable. (pp. 1.18–1.23)

  a. Damage to an office building resulting from a hurricane

  b. Reduction in value of retirement savings

  c. Products liability claim against a manufacturer

4. Mary has purchased a vacation home located in a coastal
   region of South Florida. Give examples of each of the three
   financial consequences of risk that Mary is now exposed to with
   this purchase. (pp. 1.23–1.25)

If you are not sure that you have the current edition of the textbook(s), course guide, or registration booklet for the exam you plan to take, please contact the Institutes (see page iv).

Answers to Assignment 1 Questions

NOTE: These answers are provided to give students a basic understanding of acceptable types of responses. They often are not the only valid answers and are not intended to provide an exhaustive response to the questions.

Review Questions

1. The following are the two elements of risk:

   (1) Uncertainty of outcomes—Risk involves uncertainty about the type of outcome, the timing of the outcome, or both the type and timing of the outcome.

   (2) Possibility of a negative outcome—At least one of the potential outcomes is negative, which means a loss or reduction in value.

2. Possibility means that an outcome or event may or may not occur. It does not quantify risk; it only verifies that risk is present.

   Probability, the likelihood that an outcome or event will occur, quantifies risk. It is measurable and has a value between zero and one.

3. With an understanding of various outcome probabilities, an organization can focus its risk management efforts on risks that can be appropriately managed. The organization can also use probabilities to decide which activities (and associated risks) to undertake and which risk management techniques to use.

4. Elements necessary to describe a loss exposure include the following three:

   (1) An asset exposed to loss

   (2) Cause of loss (also called a peril)

   (3) Financial consequences of that loss

5. Assets exposed to loss can include the following:

   a. Organization's assets—property, investments, money that is owed to the organization, cash, intangible assets, and human resources

   b. Individual's assets—property, investments, money that is owed to the individual, cash, professional qualifications, a unique skill set, and valuable experience

6. Insurers typically define hazards according to the following four classifications:

   (1) Moral hazard—a condition that increases the frequency and/or severity of loss resulting from a person acting dishonestly, such as exaggerating a loss

   (2) Morale hazard—a condition that increases the frequency and/or severity of loss resulting from careless or indifferent behavior, such as failing to lock a vehicle

   (3) Physical hazard—a condition of property, persons, or operations that increases the frequency and/or severity of loss, such as an icy sidewalk

   (4) Legal hazard—a condition of the legal environment that increases the frequency or severity of loss, such as the fact that courts in certain districts are more likely to award large liability settlements

7. Three factors that affect the financial consequences of a loss include the type of loss exposure, the cause of loss, and the loss frequency and severity.

8. Types of property that can be exposed to loss include the following:

   a. Tangible property—property that has a physical form, such as a piece of equipment

   b. Intangible property—property that has no physical form, such as a patent or copyright

   c. Real property—tangible property consisting of land, all structures permanently attached to the land, and whatever is growing on the land

   d. Personal property—all tangible property other than real property

9. An organization might experience a financial loss from the following types of loss exposures:

   a. Property loss exposure—A loss can result from damage (including destruction, taking, or loss of use) to property in which the person or organization has a financial interest.

   b. Liability loss exposure—A loss can result from a claim alleging that the person or organization is legally responsible for bodily injury and /or property damage.

   c. Personnel loss exposure—A loss can result from a key person's death, disability, retirement, or resignation that deprives an organization of that person's special skill or knowledge.

   d. Net income loss exposure—A loss can result from a reduction in net income, often the result of property, liability, or personnel loss.

10. Classifying risk helps an organization assess, control, and finance risk as a part of its risk management process. Classifying risk also helps with the administrative function of risk management by helping to ensure that risks in the same classifications are less likely to be overlooked.

11. It is important for an organization to distinguish between speculative risks and pure risks when making risk management decisions because the two types of risk are often managed differently. For example, most insurance policies are not designed to handle speculative risks.

12. The assessment of subjective and objective risk may differ for the following reasons:

   • Familiarity and control—Perception of a particular risk is influenced by a person's level of familiarity with that risk and the control the person may be able to exert over it. If individuals are often exposed to a risk they believe they can control, their subjective assessment of the risk will often understate the objective frequency or severity of potential losses.

   • Severity over frequency—If the effect of a particular event can be severe, an individual's subjective perception of the frequency of deaths resulting from such an event may overstate the objective frequency or severity of potential losses.

13. Three components that comprise the financial consequences of risk faced by individuals or organizations are the following:

   (1) Expected cost of losses or gains

   (2) Expenditures on risk management

   (3) Cost of residual uncertainty

14. The following hidden costs can affect an organization's expected loss costs calculation:

   • Time lost by the injured employee

   • Time lost by other employees who stop work

   • Time lost by foremen, supervisors, or other executives

   • Time spent on the case by first-aid attendants and hospital department staff (when not paid by the insurer)

   • Damage to the machine, tools, or other property or the spoilage of material

   • Interference with production, failure to fill orders on time, loss of bonuses, payment of forfeits, and other similar causes of loss

- Continuation of the injured employee's wages after the employee returns to work even though the employee's services may temporarily be worth less than normal value
- Loss of profit on the injured employee's productivity and on the idle machines
- Lost productivity because of employees' excitement or weakened morale resulting from the accident
- Overhead per injured employee that continues while the employee is not productive

15. Residual uncertainty is the level of risk that remains after individuals or organizations implement their risk management programs. The cost of this uncertainty is difficult to measure but still may significantly affect the individual or organization. For individuals, the cost of residual uncertainty may include lost salary or forgone investment opportunities. For organizations, the cost of residual uncertainty includes the effect that uncertainty has on consumers, investors, and suppliers. For example, suppliers may be less willing to sell supplies on credit to organizations with large amounts of residual uncertainty.

16. Requirements for earning the CPCU designation are the following:
    - The *education* requirement, which is met by passing a prescribed series of exams.
    - The *experience* requirement, three years of insurance experience that may include work in related fields such as law, teaching, and providing services to the insurance industry. Candidates need not have met this requirement to begin CPCU studies, but they must meet it before earning the CPCU designation.
    - The *ethics* requirement, adherence to the *Code of Professional Ethics of the American Institute for CPCU.*

17. Those who became CPCUs before 1976 and did not voluntarily choose to be bound by the Code of Professional Ethics are not subject to the Code.

18. No, a CPCU is not subject to discipline for violating a Canon of the Code. Only Rules are directly enforceable.

19. The following sanctions may be applied to CPCU applicants and candidates: They may be denied admission to CPCU exams, either indefinitely or for a specified period. Award of the CPCU designation may be withheld pending proof of a candidate's rehabilitation. Furthermore, candidates may be subject to admonition, reprimand, or censure.

20. The following sanctions may be imposed on a CPCU who is subject to the Code and is found guilty of a Rules violation: private admonition, reprimand given limited publication, censure given wide publication, suspension of the CPCU indefinitely or for a specified period, or revocation of the CPCU.

Application Questions

1. The elements apply to Atwell's risks as follows:
   a. Uncertainty—Atwell faces uncertainty regarding which contracts it will win (what will occur) or what its risk for next year will be (when it will occur).
   b. Possibility—Atwell faces the possibility (may or may not happen) of a collision between two loaded school buses.
   c. Probability—Because Atwell has a new fleet of buses, the probability (likelihood) of mechanical breakdown is low.

2. The following are hazards an insurer might consider regarding property-casualty insurance for ABC's Used Cars.

   a. Moral hazard—ABC's employees may intentionally cause a loss or exaggerate a loss that has occurred, thinking that insurance will pay for it.

   b. Morale (attitudinal) hazard—ABC's employees might drive carelessly, fail to lock an unattended building, or fail to clear an icy sidewalk to protect pedestrians.

   c. Physical hazard—ABC's employees might increase the likelihood of an accident by failing to correct defects in used cars, putting an excessive number of cars on the lot, or reducing the lighting on the lot.

   d. Legal hazard—People living in ABC's geographic area might be more litigious than those in other areas, or the local courts might be considered more likely to deliver adverse verdicts or to grant large damage awards in liability suits than those in other areas.

3. The following are the classifications of risk examples:

   a. The risk of hurricane damage to an office building is a pure risk in that there is no chance of gain from the damage. The risk is both subjective and objective. The building owner may have his/her own idea about the frequency or severity of loss (subjective), and there are objective measures of frequency and severity based on historical data or catastrophe modeling. Hurricane damage to an office building is usually non-diversifiable because hurricanes affect many properties simultaneously.

   b. The reduction in value to retirement savings is a speculative risk because there is a chance of loss, no loss, or gain on retirement savings. The risk is both subjective and objective. The investor may have his/her own expectations of retirement investments (subjective) as well as historical data (objective) on investment returns. The risk is diversifiable because the investor has many investment options to offset the risk of a reduction in retirement savings.

   c. The risk of products liability claims against a manufacturer is a pure risk, is both subjective and objective, and is diversifiable. The manufacturer can diversify into other products or services to reduce its exposure to products liability claims.

4. Examples of each of the three financial consequences of risk that Mary now faces include the following:

   (1) Expected cost of gain or loss—Based on her new home's exposure to loss from fire, flood, and hurricane damage (among other causes of loss), Mary can expect to suffer losses to both the real property (the building and land) and to any personal property in the house.

   (2) Expenditures on risk management—Mary may choose to install hurricane shutters, hurricane roof straps, and other risk control items to reduce the amount of loss that may occur during a hurricane. Mary will also purchase homeowners insurance on the property.

   (3) Cost of residual uncertainty—Mary now has uncertainty regarding the causes, frequency, and severity of loss to her new property. Although her risk control efforts can mitigate any losses and she has purchased homeowners insurance, Mary will still have some uninsured costs associated with any loss.

Understanding Risk Management; Ethics Canon 1

Direct Your Learning

Educational Objectives

After learning the content of this assignment, you should be able to:

1. Contrast traditional and enterprise risk management.

2. Describe the benefits of risk management and how it reduces the financial consequences of risk for individuals, organizations, and society.

3. Summarize pre-loss and post-loss risk management program goals and the conflicts that can arise as they are implemented.

4. Describe each of the steps in the risk management process.

5. Paraphrase, interpret, and apply the ethical standards set forth in Canon 1—Altruism—and the related Rules and Guidelines of the Code.

6. Define or describe each of the Key Words and Phrases for this assignment.

Study Materials

Required Reading:

- Foundations of Risk Management and Insurance
  - Chapter 2
- Code of Professional Ethics
  - Canon 1 (pages 2.1–2.7, 3.1–3.2)
  - HCS-102 (pages 5.4–5.6)
  - HCS-105 (pages 5.11–5.12)
  - HCS-119 (pages 5.35–5.36)

Study Aids:

- SMART Practice Exam CD-ROM
- SMART Study Aids Review Notes and Flash Cards—Assignment 2

Outline

- **Risk Management**
  - A. Traditional Risk Management
  - B. Enterprise Risk Management by Organizations
    1. Risk Maps
    2. Quadrants of Risk in an Organization
  - C. Traditional Risk Management Contrasted With ERM
- **Risk Management Benefits**
  - A. Reducing the Financial Consequences of Risk
  - B. Benefits to Individuals
  - C. Benefits to Organizations
  - D. Benefits to Society
- **Risk Management Program Goals**
  - A. Pre-Loss Goals
    1. Economy of Operations
    2. Tolerable Uncertainty
    3. Legality
    4. Social Responsibility
  - B. Post-Loss Goals
    1. Survival
    2. Continuity of Operations
    3. Profitability
    4. Earnings Stability
    5. Social Responsibility
    6. Growth
  - C. Conflict Between Goals
- **Risk Management Process**
  - A. Step 1: Identifying Loss Exposures
  - B. Step 2: Analyzing Loss Exposures
  - C. Step 3: Examining the Feasibility of Risk Management Techniques
  - D. Step 4: Selecting the Appropriate Risk Management Techniques
    1. Financial Considerations
    2. Nonfinancial Considerations
  - E. Step 5: Implementing the Selected Risk Management Techniques
  - F. Step 6: Monitoring Results and Revising the Risk Management Program
    1. Establishing Standards of Acceptable Performance
    2. Comparing Actual Results With Standards
    3. Correcting Substandard Performance
    4. Evaluating Standards That Have Been Substantially Exceeded
- **Summary**
- **Canon 1–Altruism (Code)**
  - A. Rule R1.1–Duty to Understand and Abide by All Rules
  - B. Rule R1.2–Actions by Others
  - C. Guidelines
    1. Guideline G-1–The Public Interest
    2. Guideline G-1–Conflicts of Interest
    3. Guideline G-1–Applicable to all CPCUs (and Candidates)
    4. Guideline G-1–Preferential Treatment
  - D. Other Related Code Provisions
  - E. Relevant Hypothetical Case Studies
  - F. Review Questions
- **Hypothetical Case Studies**
  - A. HCS-102
    1. Case HCS-102
    2. Opinion HCS-102
  - B. HCS-105
    1. Case HCS-105
    2. Opinion HCS-105
  - C. HCS-119
    1. Case HCS-119
    2. Opinion HCS-119

Key Words and Phrases

Define or describe each of the words and phrases listed below.

Risk management program (p. 2.3)

Risk management process (p. 2.4)

Pre-loss goals (p. 2.14)

Post-loss goals (p. 2.14)

Review Questions

1. Describe the difference in scope between traditional risk management and enterprise risk management. (pp. 2.4–2.5)

2. Explain how the focus of risk management efforts differs for traditional risk management and enterprise risk management. (pp. 2.4–2.5)

3. List three functions of a risk map in an enterprise risk management (ERM) program. (p. 2.7)

4. Describe the four quadrants of risk an organization uses when implementing an ERM approach. (p. 2.7)

5. Describe how the following factors differ between ERM and traditional risk management approaches. (pp. 2.8–2.9)

   a.　Strategic application

   b.　Risks considered

   c.　Performance metrics

6. Describe the tradeoff between the cost of risk management and the expected cost of loss, and the cost of residual uncertainty. (p. 2.9)

7. Identify the costs used to compute the overall financial consequence of risk for a given asset or activity. (p. 2.11)

8. Identify ways that risk management benefits each of the following entities.

   a. Individuals (p. 2.12)

   b. Organizations (pp. 2.12–2.13)

   c. Society (p. 2.13)

9. Describe four pre-loss operational goals supported by an effective and efficient risk management program. (pp. 2.14–2.16)

10. List six possible post-loss goals for an organization after a significant foreseeable loss has occurred. (p. 2.16)

11. Identify the steps an organization might take to forestall an intolerable shutdown and ensure continuous operations after a loss occurs. (p. 2.17)

12. Identify four events that could trigger the initiation of the risk management process. (p. 2.20)

13. List the six steps in the risk management process. (p. 2.21)

14. Describe four dimensions used to analyze a loss exposure.
    (pp. 2.22–2.23)

15. Describe how an organization uses risk control and risk financing
    techniques to manage loss exposures. (pp. 2.23–2.24)

16. Identify the forecasts an organization might use to analyze the
    costs of a risk management technique. (p. 2.25)

17. List the four steps required to monitor and revise a risk
    management program. (p. 2.26)

18. Don, a CPCU, was an officer of a small insurance company. Another officer of the company, who is not a CPCU, was just convicted of a crime relating to business activities. Based solely on this information, might Don have violated Rule R1.2 of the Code? Explain. (*Code,* pp. 2.3–2.4)

19. In placing the interests of others above his or her own, should a CPCU give preferential treatment to third-party claimants or insureds? Explain. (*Code,* p. 2.7)

20. HCS-105 deals with a situation in which Joe President, CPCU, believed insurance loss costs were not being distributed on an equitable basis. Did Joe's decision violate any of the rules associated with Canon 1? Was Joe's decision contrary to Canon 1? (*Code,* pp. 5.11–5.12)

Application Questions

1. Melissa, the risk manager for Millwright Hockey Supply (MHS) was promoted to chief risk officer when MHS adopted an enterprise risk management approach in January 2006. Describe some of the new risks Melissa must now consider that were not part of her former job duties. (p. 2.8)

2. Using the data below for Lawton Manufacturing, calculate the cost of risk of opening a new manufacturing facility. (p. 2.11)

Risk management department budget	$1.8 million
Retained losses	$16.8 million
Insurance premiums	$26.5 million
Safety system expenses	$5.0 million

3. Provide an example of how each of the following risk management program goals can conflict with the pre-loss goal of economy of operations. (pp. 2.14–2.20)

   a. Tolerable uncertainty

   b. Legality

   c. Social responsibility

4. For each of the following, suggest a standard that a risk management professional might use to gauge performance. (pp. 2.26–2.29)

   a. Product shipments to customers that are damaged in transit

   b. Customer slip-and-fall injuries in a retail shop

   c. Employees injured in warehouse activities

5. Pat, an insurance company underwriter, has just been offered a temporary part-time second job by the Danford Insurance Agency. Danford is completely revamping its automated filing system and needs someone who understands insurance files to assist in this project. Pat, a CPCU candidate, could use the extra money, but she is not sure whether this second job would be ethically appropriate or would violate the Code of Professional Ethics of the American Institute for CPCU. What information in Canon 1 of the Code and the Related Rules and Guidelines might relate to this situation? Explain how this information might be used. (*Code*, pp. 2.1–2.7, 3.1–3.2)

Answers to Assignment 2 Questions

NOTE: These answers are provided to give students a basic understanding of acceptable types of responses. They often are not the only valid answers and are not intended to provide an exhaustive response to the questions.

Review Questions

1. The scope of traditional risk management is on losses generated by hazard risk.

   The scope of enterprise risk management encompasses both hazard and business risks with the intent of maximizing the organization's value.

2. Risk management professionals have traditionally dealt with activities such as monitoring safety programs or processing workers' compensation claims rather than helping achieve organizational gains from exposure to business risk. Enterprise risk management focuses on managing all of the organization's key risks and opportunities with the intent of maximizing the organization's value.

3. A risk map in an Enterprise Risk Management (ERM) program serves the following three functions:
   (1) It depicts risks from all sources to enable comparison of all risks.
   (2) It helps senior management better understand the risks inherent in the organization and to aid them in determining which risks require the most attention.
   (3) It ranks risks based on their relative effect on an organization's key business goals.

4. When implementing an ERM approach, an organization uses the following four quadrants of risk:
   (1) Hazard risk—traditionally managed by risk management professionals.
   (2) Operational risk—pure risks that fall outside the traditional hazard risk category and that could jeopardize service-related or manufacturing-related business functions.
   (3) Financial risk—risks that directly affect an organization's financial position via changes in revenue, expenses, business valuation, or the cost or availability of capital.
   (4) Strategic risk—risks that are fundamental to an organization's existence and business plan because they have a current or future effect on earnings or capital arising from adverse business decisions, improper implementation of decisions, or lack of responsiveness to changes in the industry or changes in demand.

5. Differences between ERM and traditional risk management approaches include the following:
   a. Strategic application
      - In an ERM approach, an executive is placed in charge of risk management to ensure that risk is managed effectively across the organization.
      - Traditional risk management focuses only on hazard risk without examining risks in other functional areas.
   b. Risks considered
      - ERM involves managing all risks affecting an organization's ability to meet its goals, regardless of whether the risks are hazard or business.
      - Traditional risk management normally considers only hazard risks that involve fortuitous losses.
   c. Performance metrics
      - ERM emphasizes results-based performance measurement.
      - Traditional risk management measures success on both an activity and results basis.

6. The tradeoff between the cost of risk management and the expected cost of loss and cost of residual uncertainty is that an organization that spends a relatively large amount on risk management should see smaller expected losses and experience less residual uncertainty than an organization that spends less on risk management.

7. The overall financial consequence of risk for a given asset or activity is broken down into the following costs:
    *   Cost of losses not reimbursed by insurance or other external sources
    *   Cost of insurance premiums
    *   Cost of external sources of funds, such as interest payments to lenders or transaction costs associated with noninsurance indemnity
    *   Cost of measures to prevent or reduce the size of potential losses
    *   Cost of implementing and administering risk management

8. Risk management provides the following benefits to the entities listed:
    a. Individuals—preserves financial resources by reducing an individual's expected losses and reduces anxiety
    b. Organizations—preserves financial resources, provides a sense of confidence that capital is protected against future costs, and reduces the deterrence effect of risk
    c. Society—lowers expected losses and improves allocation of productive resources

9. Four pre-loss operational goals supported by an effective and efficient risk management program are as follows:
    (1) Economy of operations—The organization should not incur substantial costs in exchange for slight benefits.
    (2) Tolerable uncertainty—Keeping manager uncertainty about losses at a tolerable level and providing assurances that losses will be within the bounds of what was anticipated.
    (3) Legality—Satisfying the organization's legal obligations.
    (4) Social responsibility—Acting ethically and fulfilling obligations to the community and society as a whole.

10. Possible post-loss goals after a significant foreseeable loss has occurred include the following six:
    (1) Survival
    (2) Continuity of operations
    (3) Profitability
    (4) Earnings stability
    (5) Social responsibility
    (6) Growth

11. Steps an organization might take to forestall an intolerable shutdown and ensure continuous operations after a loss include the following:
    *   Identify activities whose interruptions cannot be tolerated
    *   Identify the types of events that could interrupt such activities
    *   Determine the standby resources that must be immediately available to counter the effect of those losses
    *   Ensure the availability of the standby resources at even the most unlikely and difficult times

12. The following four events could trigger the initiation of the risk management process:
    (1) A pending insurance renewal
    (2) A serious claim
    (3) A merger or an acquisition
    (4) A new law or regulation

13. The six steps in the risk management process are:
    (1) Identifying loss exposures
    (2) Analyzing loss exposures
    (3) Examining feasibility of risk management techniques
    (4) Selecting the appropriate risk management techniques
    (5) Implementing selected risk management techniques
    (6) Monitoring results and revising the risk management program

14. Four dimensions used to analyze a loss exposure are as follows:
    (1) Loss frequency—number of losses
    (2) Loss severity—amount, in dollars, of a loss for a specific occurrence
    (3) Total dollar loss—total amount of losses for all occurrences in a specified period
    (4) Timing—when losses occur and when loss payments are made

15. Risk control techniques are used to reduce the frequency and severity of loss or make losses more predictable. Risk financing techniques generate funds to finance losses that risk control techniques cannot entirely prevent or reduce.

16. An organization might use the following forecasts to analyze the costs of a risk management technique:
    • A forecast of the dimensions of expected losses
    • A forecast for each feasible combination of risk management techniques, of the effect on the frequency, severity, and timing of these expected losses
    • A forecast of the after-tax costs involved in applying various risk management techniques

17. The four steps required to monitor and revise a risk management program are as follows:
    (1) Establishing standards of acceptable performance
    (2) Comparing actual results with these standards
    (3) Correcting substandard performance or revising standards that prove to be unrealistic
    (4) Evaluating standards that have been substantially exceeded

18. Based solely on the information provided, Don has not violated Rule R1.2. Don must at least sanction or condone another person's wrongful behavior to violate Rule R1.2. Further investigation would be necessary to determine whether Don had done so.

19. No. According to Guideline G1.4, CPCUs should treat both insureds and third-party claimants promptly, equitably, and fairly. Neither party should be given preferential treatment or provided more than he or she is entitled to.

20. Joe's decision did not violate any of the rules associated with Canon 1. Joe President had ethical obligations to competently and consistently discharge his occupational duties and to support efforts to improve the insurance mechanism. These obligations present a special challenge in the

face of Joe's ethical responsibilities toward at least three groups of stakeholders: investors, agents, and insureds. There are probably better solutions to the problem of inadequate auto insurance rates, but they can occur only with the cooperation of legislators and/or regulators. Assuming these opportunities were unsuccessfully explored, Joe apparently made a difficult but defensible decision to withdraw from the state, and he implemented it in an ethical way that violated no Rules. Some may argue that his decision was contrary to Canon 1, serving the public interest. His decision served only a portion of the public, his investors, not the agents or insureds in that state.

Application Questions

1. Melissa is now responsible for all four quadrants of risk that are faced by MHS. In her duties as risk manager, Melissa was responsible for hazard risks such as products liability, workers' compensation, and property loss exposures. Her new job responsibilities include all of her previous hazard risks, in addition to operational, financial, and strategic risks. New risks that Melissa must now address include financial risks, such as currency exchange rate risk, interest rate risk, and investment risks; operational risks, such as product recall and workplace discrimination; and strategic risks, such as intellectual property, union relations and product design.

2. The cost of risk includes the cost of losses not reimbursed, cost of insurance premiums, cost of external sources of funds, cost of risk control measures, and the cost of administering the program. In this example the cost of risk would be as follows:

    $1.8 million + $16.8 million + $26.5 million +$5.0 million = $50.1 million.

3. The risk management program pre-loss goal of economy of operations can conflict with other risk management goals as follows:

    a. Tolerable uncertainty might conflict with the goal of economy of operations because of the cost of risk management efforts necessary to reduce uncertainty to a tolerable level may be excessive.

    b. Legality might conflict with the goal of economy of operations because some required safety standards could require substantial expense to implement.

    c. Social responsibility might conflict with the goal of economy of operations because obligations such as charitable contributions may be expensive.

4. A risk management professional can use the following standards to gauge performance:

    a. Product shipments to customers that are damaged in transit—performance standard: less than 1 percent of all customers file claims for damaged shipments

    b. Customer slip and fall injuries in retail shop—activities standard: hourly inspections of floors for spills or other slippery conditions, use of "Caution wet floor" signs during wet weather conditions.

    c. Employee injuries during warehouse activities—performance standard: Injury frequency rate reduced by 10 percent from previous year.

5. Guideline G1.2 indicates that CPCUs should avoid the appearance of impropriety. This guides Pat to consider whether her working for an insurer full time and for the agency part time would appear improper to her peers, bosses, and clients of the insurer and the agency. Guideline G1.2 also indicates that Pat can ask the Board of Ethical Inquiry for help in solving her dilemma.

Risk Assessment

Direct Your Learning

Educational Objectives

After learning the content of this assignment, you should be able to:

1. Describe the following methods of loss exposure identification:
   - Document analysis
   - Compliance review
   - Personal inspections
   - Expertise within and beyond the organization

2. Explain why data used in risk management decisions need to be relevant, complete, consistent, and organized.

3. Describe the nature of probability with respect to the law of large numbers and theoretical and empirical probability.

4. Interpret the information provided in a simple probability distribution and explain how that information can be used in making basic risk management decisions.

5. Explain how various measures of central tendency and measures of dispersion can be used in analyzing the probabilities associated with risk.

6. Explain how an insurance or a risk management professional can apply normal distributions to analyze loss exposures and project future losses more accurately.

7. Explain how to analyze loss exposures considering the four dimensions of loss and data credibility.

8. Define or describe each of the Key Words and Phrases for this assignment.

Study Materials

Required Reading:

- Foundations of Risk Management and Insurance,
  - Chapter 3

Study Aids:

- SMART Practice Exam CD-ROM
- SMART Study Aids Review Notes and Flash Cards— Assignment 3

Outline

- **Identifying Loss Exposures**
  - A. Document Analysis
    1. Risk Assessment Questionnaires and Checklists
    2. Financial Statements and Underlying Accounting Records
    3. Contracts
    4. Insurance Policies
    5. Organizational Policies and Records
    6. Flowcharts and Organizational Charts
    7. Loss Histories
  - B. Compliance Review
  - C. Personal Inspections
  - C. Expertise Within and Beyond the Organization

- **Data, Probability, and Statistical Analysis**
  - A. Data on Past Losses
    1. Relevant Data
    2. Complete Data
    3. Consistent Data
    4. Organized Data
  - B. Nature of Probability
  - C. Probability Distributions
    1. Theoretical Probability Distributions
    2. Empirical Probability Distributions
    3. Discrete and Continuous Probability Distributions

  - D. Central Tendency
    1. Expected Value
    2. Mean
    3. Median and Cumulative Probabilities
    4. Mode
  - E. Dispersion
    1. Standard Deviation
    2. Coefficient of Variation
  - F. Normal Distribution

- **Analyzing Loss Exposures**
  - A. Loss Frequency
  - B. Loss Severity
    1. Probable Maximum Loss
    2. Maximum Possible Loss
    3. Frequency and Severity Considered Jointly
  - C. Total Dollar Losses
  - D. Timing
  - E. Data Credibility

- **Summary**

Key Words and Phrases

Define or describe each of the words and phrases listed below.

Balance sheet (p. 3.6)

Income statement (p. 3.7)

Statement of cash flows (p. 3.8)

Hold-harmless agreement (p. 3.10)

Indemnification (p. 3.10)

Hazard analysis (p. 3.14)

Theoretical probability (p. 3.18)

Empirical probability (p. 3.18)

Probability analysis (p. 3.18)

Law of large numbers (p. 3.19)

Probability distribution (p. 3.19)

Central tendency (p. 3.25)

Expected value (p. 3.25)

Mean (p. 3.26)

Median (p. 3.27)

Mode (p. 3.30)

Dispersion (p. 3.30)

Standard deviation (p. 3.32)

Coefficient of variation (p. 3.34)

Normal distribution (p. 3.35)

Probable maximum loss (PML) (p. 3.40)

Maximum possible loss (MPL) (p. 3.41)

Review Questions

1. Identify the types of internal and external documents an organization may use to analyze loss exposures. (p. 3.4)

2. Describe advantages and disadvantages of using questionnaires in assessing loss exposures. (pp. 3.5–3.6)

3. Describe how an organization uses the following documents to identify loss exposures.

   a. Financial statements (p. 3.6)

   b. Contracts (pp. 3.9–3.10)

    c.   Insurance policies (pp. 3.10–3.11)

    d.   Organizational policies and records (p. 3.11)

    e.   Flowcharts and organizational charts (pp. 3.11–3.13)

    f.   Loss histories (p. 3.13)

4. Describe how a compliance review may facilitate the identification of loss exposures. (p. 3.13)

5. Identify relevant data an organization may use to assess the following types of loss exposures: (pp. 3.15–3.16)

    a. Property losses

    b. Liability losses

    c. Personnel losses

    d. Net income losses

6. Describe how complete data can aid a risk management professional in loss exposure assessment. (p. 3.16)

7. Identify two factors in past loss data that must be consistent to avoid underestimating or overestimating loss projections. (p. 3.16)

8. Explain the difference between empirical and theoretical probabilities. (p. 3.18)

9. Identify two conditions in which probability analysis is effective for projecting losses. (p. 3.18)

10. List three criteria necessary to accurately forecast future events based on the law of large numbers. (p. 3.19)

11. Identify outcome characteristics common to all (both theoretical and empirical) possibility distributions. (p. 3.20)

12. List two requirements to construct an empirical probability distribution. (p. 3.21)

13. Describe the following two forms of probability distributions and how they are used in analyzing future losses.

    1. Discrete probability distributions (p. 3.23)

    2. Continuous probability distribution (pp. 3.23–3.24)

14. Explain why a risk management or insurance professional considers measures of both central tendency and dispersion when assessing loss exposures. (pp. 3.25; 3.30–3.31)

15. Describe the following common measures of central tendency
    and how a risk management professional uses them in assessing
    loss exposures. (pp. 3.26–3.30)

    a. Mean

    b. Median

    c. Mode

16. Describe the following measures of dispersion and how a risk
    management professional uses them in assessing loss exposures.
    (pp. 3.32–3.35)

    a. Standard deviation

    b. Coefficient of variation

17. Describe a normal distribution and why it is useful to a risk management professional in forecasting loss exposures. (p. 3.35)

18. In a normal distribution, what percentage of outcomes is within two standard deviations above or below the mean? (p. 3.36)

19. Describe how the expected value and the standard deviation of a normal distribution can be helpful in making risk management decisions. (p. 3.37)

20. List four dimensions used in the analysis of a loss exposure. (p. 3.38)

21. Explain how to estimate the probable maximum loss of an occurrence. (pp. 3.40–3.41)

22. List the four categories of loss frequency and the three categories of loss severity used in the Prouty Approach. (p. 3.42)

23. Describe two approaches a risk management professional may use when jointly analyzing the frequency and loss severity of a loss exposure. (p. 3.42)

24. Explain why timing is an important consideration when analyzing loss exposures. (p. 3.45)

Application Questions

1. Using the income statement for Lawton Manufacturing in Exhibit 3-2, *Foundation of Risk Management and Insurance*, calculate the net income loss if a major fire at its manufacturing facility had the following effects on the values reported. (pp. 3.7–3.8)

   a.   Net sales decreased from $1,150,000 to $850,000.

   b.   Cost of goods sold decreased from $850,000 to $570,000.

   c.   S, G & A expenses increased from $271,000 to $275,000.

   d.   Interest expense is unchanged and income tax remains at 40 percent.

2. The risk management professional of ABC Manufacturing has the following data for losses that have occurred during 2006: (pp. 3.15–3.17)

Date	Loss Amount	Cause
1/6/06	$ 500.00	Customer slip and fall
3/17/06	$ 3,500.00	Damage to sales rep auto
3/17/06	$ 800.00	Sales rep injury in auto accident
5/21/06	$ 7,000.00	Assembly line worker back injury
8/11/06	$ 500.00	Office worker back injury

   a.   If the risk management professional for ABC Manufacturing was trying to analyze employee injuries for workers' compensation purposes, what data are relevant?

   b.   Are the data provided complete?

c. Are the data consistent?

d. Organize the employee injury data into an array.

3. The Jones restaurant operation consists of more than thirty restaurants. Based on the past loss experience of Mr. Jones, the estimated probability distribution of the number of fires per year is listed below. (pp. 3.18–3.19)

Number of Fires	Estimated Probability
0	.05
1	.10
2	.22
3	.29
4	.18
5	.10
6	.06
Total	1.00

Based on this information and assuming no changes to Mr. Jones' operation or exposures, what is the probability that the number of fire losses for Mr. Jones next year will be each of the following:

a. More than 1

b. Less than 3

c.   Exactly 2

d.   More than 4

4. Construct an empirical probability distribution from the following
   array of workers' compensation losses. (pp. 3.21–3.23)

Rank	Date	Adjusted Loss Amount
10	12/5	$100
9	08/7	$500
8	01/6	$750
7	02/3	$800
6	02/5	$1,100
5	02/5	$1,500
4	11/8	$1,800
3	07/5	$2,100
2	09/18	$2,800
1	09/4	$10,000

5. The underwriter at Millwright Insurance must choose between two accounts to provide insurance coverage. Both accounts have provided a probability distribution based on past losses. Account A's distribution has a mean of $8,500 and a standard deviation of $17,000. Account B's distribution has a mean of $10,000 and a standard deviation of $18,000. (pp. 3.26–3.27, 3.34–3.35)

   a. Which account has higher expected losses?

   b. Which account has greater variability relative to its mean?

6. Assume that ABC Manufacturing's total losses per year are normally distributed. The average (mean) of the firm's losses is $500,000, and the standard deviation is $40,000. Assuming underlying conditions do not change, what is the probability that its losses next year will be each of the following? (pp. 3.35–3.36)

   a. Between $460,000 and $540,000

   b. Between $500,000 and $540,000

7. Canston Industries has evaluated the following loss exposures using the Prouty Approach. Canston's risk management professional has the following risk financing measures at his disposal: avoidance, purchase of insurance (transfer), or retention (paying losses from cash flow). Which technique should he apply for each loss exposure? (pp. 3.38–3.44)

    a.   Products liability from the sale of explosives (loss frequency—definite; loss severity—severe)

    b.   Employee injury (loss frequency—slight; loss severity—significant)

    c.   Exposure to currency exchange rate risk (loss frequency—moderate; loss severity—slight)

Answers to Assignment 3 Questions

NOTE: These answers are provided to give students a basic understanding of acceptable types of responses. They often are not the only valid answers and are not intended to provide an exhaustive response to the questions.

Review Questions

1. An organization may use the following types of internal and external documents to analyze loss exposures:

    *   Internal documents—financial statements, accounting records, contracts, insurance policies, policy and procedure manuals, flowcharts and organizational charts, and loss histories
    *   External documents—questionnaires, checklists, surveys, Web sites, news releases, and reports from external organizations

2. The advantage of questionnaires in assessing loss exposures is that they capture more descriptive information than checklists about amounts or values exposed to loss. Their disadvantage is that they typically require considerable expense, time, and effort to complete and may still not recognize all loss exposures.

3. An organization can use the following documents to help identify loss exposures:

    a. Financial statements—Balance sheets, income statements, statement of cash flows, and supporting statements help identify major categories of current and past loss exposures and can be used to identify future plans that could lead to new loss exposures. For example, asset entries on a balance sheet indicate property values that could by reduced by loss.

    b. Contracts—Contracts can help identify property and liability loss exposures assumed or transferred by contract and help determine who has assumed responsibility for which loss exposure.

    c. Insurance policies—Policies can reveal many of the organization's insurable loss exposures.

    d. Organizational policies and records—Corporate by-laws, board minutes, employee manuals, procedure manuals, mission statements, and risk management policies may identify existing loss exposures and indicate impending changes that may create new loss exposures.

    e. Flowcharts and organizational charts—Flowcharts show the nature and use of resources involved in an organization's operations and the sequence of and relationships between the operations. They may also reveal bottlenecks where losses could have substantial effects on business operations. An organizational chart helps identify key personnel for whom the organization may have a personnel loss exposure.

    f. Loss histories—An organization's loss history, or that of a comparable organization, can indicate current or future loss exposures.

4. Compliance review determines an organization's compliance with local, state, and federal statutes and regulations and can therefore help the organization minimize or avoid liability loss exposures associated with noncompliance.

5. Relevant data that would be relevant in assessing an organization's loss exposures include the following:

    a. Property losses—data detailing the property's repair or replacement cost at the time it is to be restored

    b. Liability losses—data related to past claims that are substantially the same as the potential future claims being assessed

    c.   Personnel losses—data related to personnel with similar experience and expertise as those being considered as future loss exposures

    d.   Net income losses—data involving similar reductions in revenue and similar additional expenses

6.   Having complete data aids in loss exposure assessment by helping isolate causes of each loss and enabling the risk management professional to make reasonably reliable estimates of the dollar amounts of the future losses.

7.   The following are two factors regarding historical loss data that must be consistent to avoid underestimating or overestimating loss projections:

    (1) Data must be collected on a consistent basis (same accounting methods) for all recorded losses.

    (2) Data must be expressed in constant dollars.

8.   Empirical probabilities, based on actual experience (historical data), are estimates whose accuracy depends on the size and representative nature of the samples being studied. Theoretical probabilities, based on theoretical principles, are constant as long as the physical conditions that generate them remain unchanged.

9.   Probability analysis is effective for projecting losses in organizations that have a substantial volume of data on past losses and that have fairly stable operations.

10.   For accurate forecasts of future events based on the law of large numbers, events must include the following three criteria:

    (1) They must have occurred in the past under substantially identical conditions and have resulted from unchanging, basic causal forces.

    (2) They can be expected to occur in the future under the same, unchanging conditions.

    (3) They have been, and will continue to be, both independent of one another and sufficiently numerous.

11.   Characteristics common to outcomes of both theoretical and empirical probabilities are that the outcomes are mutually exclusive and collectively exhaustive.

12.   The following are two requirements to construct an empirical probability distribution:

    (1) To provide a mutually exclusive, collectively exhaustive list of outcomes, loss categories (bins) must be designated so all losses can be included.

    (2) The distribution must define the probabilities associated with each of the possible categories.

13.   The two forms of probability distributions are described as follows:

    (1) Discrete probability distributions have a finite number of possible outcomes and are typically used to analyze how often something will occur (frequency).

    (2) Continuous probability distributions have an infinite number of possible outcomes and are typically used for severity distributions.

14.   By considering measures of both central tendency and dispersion when assessing loss exposures, a risk management professional can compare the characteristics of those probability distributions. Central tendency indicates the best guess (expected loss) as to what the outcome will be. Dispersion indicates the variation among the values in a distribution and gives an indication of how close to the central tendency outcomes will usually be. Such information could help an insurance professional determine whether to offer insurance coverage to a possible insured.

15. Three common measures of central tendency are as follows:

    a. Mean—the numeric average (the sum of the values in a data set divided by the number of values), often used by a risk management professional as the single best guess to forecast future events.

    b. Median—the value at the midpoint of a sequential data set with an odd number of values, or the mean of the two middle values. A risk management professional might use the median in selecting retention levels or in selecting upper limits of insurance coverage.

    c. Mode—the most frequently occurring value in a distribution, it enables risk management professionals to focus on the outcomes that are the most common.

16. The two common measures of dispersion are used in the following manner to assess loss exposures:

    a. Standard deviation—indicates how widely dispersed the values in a distribution are. It provides a measure of how sure an insurance or risk management professional can be in projecting the frequency or severity of losses.

    b. Coefficient of variation—used to compare two distributions with different means. It could help an underwriter determine to which account to offer coverage or help a risk management professional determine if a particular loss control measure has made losses more or less predictable.

17. A normal distribution is a probability distribution that, when graphed, generates a bell-shaped curve. It is useful to a risk management professional in accurately forecasting the variability around the mean of many physical phenomena.

18. In a normal distribution, 95.44 percent of outcomes are within two standard deviations above or below the mean.

19. The characteristics of the expected value and standard deviation of a normal distribution can help management select an acceptable probability for loss and aid in scheduling maintenance or selecting retention levels on various loss exposures.

20. The following are four dimensions used in the analysis of a loss exposure:

    (1) Loss frequency—number of losses that occur within a specific period

    (2) Loss severity—dollar amount of loss for a specific occurrence

    (3) Total dollar losses—total dollar amount of losses for all occurrences during a specific period

    (4) Timing—when losses occur and when loss payments are made

21. The probable maximum loss of an occurrence is typically estimated to be near the mean of a given loss severity distribution.

22. Four categories of loss frequency used in the Prouty Approach are as follows:

    (1) Almost nil

    (2) Slight

    (3) Moderate

    (4) Definite

    The followng are three categories of loss severity used in the Prouty Approach:

    (1) Slight

    (2) Significant

    (3) Severe

23. Risk management professionals may use the following two approaches when jointly analyzing the frequency and loss severity of a loss exposure:

    (1) Prouty Approach—identifies four categories of loss frequency and three categories of loss severity.

    (2) Total claims distribution—created by combining the frequency and severity distributions.

24. Timing is important to consider when analyzing loss exposures because of the time value of money. Money held in reserve can earn interest until the payment is made. In addition, when a loss is counted affects accounting and tax treatment.

Application Questions

1. Lawton's net income prior to loss was $15,000. The new income statement would be as follows:

Net sales	$ 850,000
Cost of goods sold	(570,000)
Gross profit	280,000
Selling, general, and administrative expenses	(275,000)
Earnings from operations	5,000
Interest expense	(4,000)
Earnings before income taxes	1,000
Income taxes	(400)
Net income	$ 600

Net income before loss	$ 15,000
Net income after loss	600
Net income loss	$ 14,400

2. a. The relevant data are the 3/17 sales rep injury, the 5/21 assembly line worker injury, and the 8/11 office worker injury.

   b. The data are not complete; they do not list the specific cause, time of loss, or treatments used.

   c. Because all the data are 2006 data, they are consistent.

   d. 1) 8/11/06 $500.00
      2) 3/17/06 $800.00
      3) 5/21/06 $7,000.00

3. The probability of Mr. Jones's fire losses are the following:

   a. More than 1—.85 (.22+.29+.18+.10+.06)

   b. Less than 3—.37 (.05+.10+.22)

   c. Exactly 2—.22

   d. More than 4—.16 (.10+.06)

4. There are a number of ways to display a probability distribution. One way is to create a table using bins. This example uses $1,000 bin sizes, but other bin sizes are acceptable.

Bin Size	# of Losses	Percentage of Number of Losses
$0–$1,000	4	40%
$1,001–$2000	3	30%
$2,001–$3,000	2	20%
$3,000 +	1	10%
		100%

5. The underwriter's decision regarding Millwright Insurance accounts A and B considers the following:
   a. Account B has higher expected losses because the mean of past losses for B is $10,000 and only $8,500 for A.
   b. The coefficient of variation is used to determine which account has greater variability relative to its mean.

   $$A = \frac{17,000}{8,500} = 2.$$

   $$B = \frac{18,000}{10,000} = 1.8.$$

   Therefore, A has greater variability.

6. ABC Manufacturing's loss probability will be the following, based on a normal distribution:
   a. Between $460,000 and $540,000—68.26 percent
   b. Between $500,000 and $540,000—34.13 percent

7. Canston's risk management professional should apply the following risk financing measures:
   a. Product liability from the sale of explosives: avoidance
   b. Employee injury: purchase insurance
   c. Exposure to currency exchange rate: retain co-paying losses from cash flow

Narrow the focus of what you need to learn. Remember, the Educational Objectives are the foundation of each of the Institutes' courses, and the exam is based on these Educational Objectives

Risk Control; Ethics Canon 2

Direct Direct Your Learning

Educational Objectives

After learning the content of this assignment, you should be able to:

1. Illustrate the six risk control techniques.

2. Explain how an organization can use risk control techniques and measures to achieve the following risk control goals:

   - Implement effective and efficient risk control measures
   - Comply with legal requirements
   - Promote life safety
   - Ensure business continuity

3. Explain how an insurance or risk management professional evaluates the effects of proposed risk control measures on loss frequency and loss severity.

4. Explain how risk control techniques can be applied to property, liability, personnel, and net income loss exposures.

5. Explain how business continuity management is designed to ensure an organization's survival and continued operations.

6. Paraphrase, interpret, and apply the ethical standards set forth in Canon 2—Continuing Professional Development—and the related Rules and Guidelines of the Code.

7. Define or describe each of the Key Words and Phrases for this assignment.

Required Reading:

- Foundations of Risk Management and Insurance,
  - Chapter 4
- Code of Professional Ethics
  - Canon 2 (pages 2.8–2.17, 3.3–3.6)
  - HCS 104 (pages 5.9–5.10)
  - HCS 108 (page 5.17)
  - HCS 113 (pages 5.24–5.25)

Study Aids:

- SMART Practice Exam CD-ROM
- SMART Study Aids Review Notes and Flash Cards—Assignment 4

Outline

- **Risk Control Techniques**
  - A. Avoidance
  - B. Loss Prevention
  - C. Loss Reduction
  - D. Separation
  - E. Duplication
  - F. Diversification

- **Risk Control Goals**
  - A. Implement Effective and Efficient Risk Control Measures
  - B. Comply With Legal Requirements
  - C. Promote Life Safety
  - D. Ensure Business Continuity

- **Loss Frequency and Loss Severity**

- **Application of Risk Control Techniques**
  - A. Property Loss Exposures
  - B. Liability Loss Exposures
  - C. Personnel Loss Exposures
  - D. Net Income Loss Exposures

- **Business Continuity Management**
  - A. Steps in the Business Continuity Process
  - B. Business Continuity Plan

- **Ethical Considerations**

- **Summary**

- **Canon2–Continuing Professional Development (Code)**
  - A. Rule R2.1–Maintaining Professional Competence
  - B. Guidelines
    1. Guideline G2.1–Ethical Obligation for Continuous Learning
    2. Guideline G2.2–A Matter of Individual Judgment
    3. Guideline G2.3–No Mandatory Recertification
    4. Guideline G2.4–CPD Program
  - C. American Institute Position on Continuous Learning for CPCUs
  - D. Other Related Code Provisions
  - E. Relevant Hypothetical Case Studies
  - F. Review Questions

- **Hypothetical Case Studies**
  - A. HCS-104
    1. Case HCS-104
    2. Opinion HCS-104
  - B. HCS-108
    1. Case HCS-108
    2. Opinion HCS-108
  - C. HCS-113
    1. Case HCS-113
    2. Opinion HCS-113

Key Words and Phrases

Define or describe each of the words and phrases listed below.

Risk control (p. 4.3)

Avoidance (p. 4.4)

Loss prevention (p. 4.5)

Loss reduction (p. 4.7)

Disaster recovery plan (p. 4.8)

Separation (p. 4.9)

Duplication (p. 4.11)

Diversification (p. 4.11)

Life safety (p. 4.16)

Business continuity management (p. 4.23)

Review Questions

1. Explain how proactive and reactive avoidance differ in reducing loss frequency of a loss exposure. (p. 4.4)

2. Describe the purpose of the following loss reduction measures in controlling losses. (pp. 4.8–4.9)

   a.   Pre-loss measures

   b.   Post-loss measures

3. Describe the purpose of a disaster recovery plan. (pp. 4.8–4.9)

4. Identify circumstances in which each of the following techniques would be an effective choice for loss reduction. (pp. 4.9–4.12)

   a.   Separation

b. Duplication

c. Diversification

5. Describe the advantages and disadvantages of using cash flow analysis for the selection of risk control measures. (p. 4.14)

6. List the types of state or federal statutes an organization may need to consider when selecting risk control measures in order to comply with legal requirements. (p. 4.16)

7. Identify possible consequences an organization can face for failure to comply with legal requirements. (p. 4.16)

8. Identify the issues regarding fire, health, and safety a risk management professional should consider when assessing an organization's life-safety loss exposures. (p. 4.16)

9. Identify causes of loss an organization should consider when promoting life safety. (p. 4.16)

10. Explain why a risk management professional should evaluate the effect of a potential risk control measure on both the loss frequency and the loss severity of the organization's loss exposures. (p. 4.17)

11. Describe the possible positive and negative externalities of a risk control measure. (p. 4.18)

12. Identify the factors insurance producers and underwriters commonly consider when examining loss exposures in commercial properties. (p. 4.19)

13. Which risk control techniques are commonly used to control liability loss exposures? (pp. 4.19–4.20)

14. Describe loss prevention and loss reduction measures an organization might use to control work-related injury and illness. (p. 4.22)

15. Explain the purpose of business continuity management. (p. 4.23)

16. Identify potential situations that business continuity management might address to help achieve an organization's goal of survival and continuity of operations after a loss. (p. 4.23)

17. List the six steps in the business continuity process. (p. 4.24)

18. Identify guidelines for design of an effective business continuity plan. (p. 4.25)

19. List the content commonly contained in business continuity plans. (p. 4.25)

20. In your own words, summarize CPCUs' ethical obligations to continuous learning. (*Code*, pp. 2.8–2.9)

21. The American Institute and the CPCU Society jointly sponsor the Continuing Professional Development (CPD) program. What types of activities earn points under the CPD program? (*Code*, pp. 2.11–2.12)

22. HCS-104 involves a situation in which a CPCU who is a broker places business with an insurer that "was rumored to be in financial trouble." (*Code*, pp. 5.9–5.10)

Does the CPCU's act constitute a code violation (Rule R2.1)?

Application Questions

The Cooper Pharmaceutical Company Case. The Cooper Pharmaceutical Company manufactures and distributes both prescription drugs and medicines sold over the counter by pharmacies and other outlets. Cooper has averaged $30 million in revenue and $25 million in expenses over the last five years.

More than half of Cooper's annual expenses are for research and development of new products. With its extensive research facilities, the company has developed and introduced fifty new products over the last decade. Dr. Jackson Ryann, one of Cooper's researchers, is responsible for 75 percent of the new products that Cooper has developed. Cooper has developed and tested many other potential products but has not introduced them because they have proved to be ineffective, dangerous, or both.

Some of Cooper's prescription drugs contain narcotics, which are stored in the factory building pending their use in the products.

About 50 percent of Cooper's revenues are derived from an ulcer remedy. The remedy's formula includes a chemical compound that is manufactured in only one chemical plant in the world. There are other similar ulcer remedies on the market, and management concedes that some of them are equally effective. However, Cooper's product was the first on the market and has acquired a large following among doctors, who usually prescribe it by Cooper's brand name. Management is concerned that any prolonged absence of their ulcer medicine from the market would cause doctors to prescribe another brand, and they might not return to Cooper's brand when it becomes available again.

The testing process for some products is long and complex, sometimes involving several years of testing on dogs, primates, or other relatively long-lived animals, possibly followed by testing on human volunteers. Voluminous records accumulate during such tests and must be retained for many years for use in licensing applications, defense of products liability claims, and future research projects. While Cooper has not been successfully sued for products liability in the last ten years, its risk manager estimates a frequency of one every five years with a MPL of $5–$10 million. However, because a number of Cooper's competitors have paid large products liability claims over the last few years, very few insurers are willing to sell products liability insurance to cover pharmaceuticals.

Cooper stores its research records in fire-resistive filing cabinets in the records room of its research center. The center also houses research laboratories, offices for research personnel, and animals for research. The research center is located in a sprinklered, fire-resistive building adjacent to Cooper's factory. Personnel who handle the animals are thoroughly trained in animal care to ensure the safety of both the animals and employees. Although Cooper has more than 200 employees, its workers' compensation claims have been well below the industry average over the last ten years.

The factory building also is fire resistive and is sprinklered in all areas except the clean room. The clean room, used for manufacturing and packaging processes that require complete sterility, has its own air conditioning system with special filtering equipment to eliminate dust and other potential contaminants and other equipment to maintain the sterile atmosphere. Even very slight contamination of the clean room would require the discontinuation of production for several days until sterility could be reestablished. All workers in the clean room must wear special sterile uniforms and surgical masks.

Both the factory and the research center are five years old. The cost to build the two buildings was over $10 million, which Cooper financed with a thirty-year mortgage on both buildings. The buildings are surrounded by a carefully maintained lawn and are separated from the nearest building by 200 feet. They are located in a medium-sized city with excellent public fire protection and water supply.

1. *Cooper.* Identify the risk control measures used by Cooper for each of the following loss exposures. (pp. 4.19–4.22)

   a. Property loss exposures

   b. Liability loss exposures

   c. Personnel loss exposures

   d. Net income loss exposures

2. *Cooper.* For each of the measures identified in the preceding question, identify the risk control technique the measure exemplifies and which risk control goal the measure supports. (pp. 4.3–4.17)

3. *Cooper.* Describe the effect on the frequency and severity of Cooper's losses that would result from backing up the research files off-site. (pp. 4.11, 4.17–4.18)

4. *Cooper.* Describe some steps that Cooper can take (or has taken) to ensure business continuity (pp. 4.23–4.26)

5. Atwell, Inc., is a school bus company that serves local school districts. Atwell's risk manager, a CPCU, monitors the firm's insurance program only to add or delete vehicles as the fleet changes. Recently, Atwell's board of directors discovered that Atwell management had failed to even consider purchasing an endorsement that would cover any claims resulting from the hijacking of a school bus. Has Atwell's risk manager violated a Rule under the Code of Professional Ethics? Explain.

Answers to Assignment 4 Questions

NOTE: These answers are provided to give students a basic understanding of acceptable types of responses. They often are not the only valid answers and are not intended to provide an exhaustive response to the questions.

Review Questions

1. Proactive avoidance seeks to avoid a loss exposure before it exists, such as by choosing not to engage in an activity. Reactive avoidance seeks to eliminate a loss exposure that already exists, such as by discontinuing an existing activity. Both avoidance methods avoid loss exposures from future activities. Reactive avoidance does not eliminate loss exposures from past activities.

2. a. Pre-loss measures, those applied before a loss occurs, reduce the amount or extent of property damaged and the number of people injured or the extent of injury incurred from a single event.

    b. Post-loss measures, those applied after a loss occurs, focus on emergency procedures, salvage operations, rehabilitation activities, public relations, or legal defenses to halt the spread or to counter the effects of a loss.

3. The purpose of a disaster recovery plan is to ensure that critical resources are available to facilitate an organization's continuity of operations in an emergency. The plan typically includes backup procedures, emergency response, and disaster recovery.

4. The techniques listed would be effective choices for loss reduction in the following situations:

    a. Separation is appropriate if the organization can operate with only a portion of the separated assets or locations left intact.

    b. Duplication is appropriate if an entire asset or activity is so important that the consequence of its loss justifies the expense and time of maintaining a duplicate.

    c. Diversification is more commonly applied to business risks than to hazard risks. Organizations engage in diversification by providing a variety of products and services that are used by a range of customers.

5. An organization's use of cash flow analysis in its selection of risk control measures offers the following advantages:

    - Helps achieve the organization's value-maximization goal by providing a basis of comparison for all value-maximizing decisions.

    - Increases efficiency by reducing unnecessary expenditures on risk control.

    Disadvantages of using cash flow analysis for selection of risk control measures include the following:

    - Weakness of the assumptions that often must be made to conduct the analysis

    - Difficulty of accurately estimating future cash flows

    - Lack of consideration of nonfinancial goals or selection criteria

6. To comply with legal requirements when selecting risk control measures, an organization should consider state or federal statutes regarding fire safety codes, environmental regulations, workers' compensation laws, and disability laws.

7. An organization can face fines, sanctions, or liability for failure to comply with legal requirements.

8. When assessing an organization's fire, health, and safety loss exposures, a risk management professional should consider the characteristics of the people who occupy the building and the types of building occupancies.

9. When promoting life safety, an organization should consider causes of loss such as fire safety, product safety, building collapse, industrial accidents, environmental pollution, and exposure to hazardous activities that may create the possibility of injury or death.

10. A risk management professional should evaluate the effect of a specific potential risk control measure on both loss frequency and loss severity because the measure could reduce loss frequency but increase loss severity, or it could reduce loss severity but increase loss frequency. The risk management professional also must analyze the effect the measure will have on the specified loss exposure and on any other loss exposure.

11. A positive externality exists when a risk control measure implemented for one particular loss exposure reduces the loss frequency or loss severity related to another loss exposure. A negative externality increases loss frequency or loss severity for another loss exposure.

12. When examining loss exposures in commercial properties, insurance producers and underwriters consider construction, occupancy, protection, and environment (COPE).

13. Three risk control techniques are commonly used to control liability losses: avoidance of the activity, loss prevention, and loss reduction.

14. An organization may control work-related injury and illness through loss prevention by using education, training, and safety measures.

    Loss reduction measures for work-related injury and illness include emergency response training and rehabilitation management.

15. The purpose of business continuity management is to identify potential threats to an organization and to provide a methodology for ensuring the organization's continued business operations. Business continuity management is designed to meet the organizational post-loss goals of survival and continuity of operations.

16. Business continuity management can address the following potential situations in order to help achieve an organization's goal of survival and continuity of operations after a loss: interruptions from property losses, information technology (IT) problems, human failures, loss of utility services or infrastructure, reputation losses, and human asset losses.

17. The following are the six steps in the business continuity process:
    (1) Identify the organization's critical functions
    (2) Identify the risks (threats) to the organization's critical functions
    (3) Evaluate the effect of the risks on those critical functions
    (4) Develop a business continuity strategy
    (5) Develop a business continuity plan
    (6) Monitor and revise the business continuity process

18. Guidelines for design of an effective business continuity plan include the following:
    • Design a clear plan that can be quickly read and understood
    • Provide copies of the plan to all relevant parties
    • Provide appropriate training, including periodic rehearsals of crisis procedures.

19. Business continuity plans commonly contain the following content:
    • Strategy the organization will follow to manage the crisis
    • Information about the roles and duties of various individuals in the organization

- Steps that can be taken to prevent any further loss or damage
- Emergency response plan to deal with life and safety issues
- Crisis management plan to deal with communication and reputation issues
- Business recovery and restoration plan to deal with losses to property, processes, or products
- Access to stress management and counseling for affected parties

20. CPCUs must maintain and improve their knowledge and the skills necessary for high levels of competence and performance. Therefore, CPCUs should engage in career-long study that improves their knowledge and skills for all professional roles undertaken.

21. CPCUs can earn points under the CPD program by doing the following:
    - Passing exams in nationally known insurance programs
    - Passing college courses in insurance, risk management, or related business subjects
    - Teaching insurance, risk management, or related business subjects
    - Authoring articles for professional publications
    - Conducting research
    - Serving in CPCU Society positions
    - Serving as graders on exam development committees
    - Attending the CPCU Society annual meeting or other appropriate seminars
    - Meeting state continuing education requirements

22. If the broker was unaware of the insurer's financial difficulties, his placing business with the insurer may raise the question as to whether he had complied with his minimum continuing education obligation under Rule R2.1.

Application Questions

1. The risk control measures Cooper is currently using include the following:
   a. For property loss exposures—using fire resistive construction and sprinklers.
   b. For liability loss exposures—avoiding production of products that have proven to be ineffective, dangerous, or both.
   c. For personnel loss exposures—thorough training of staff handling animals.
   d. For net income loss exposures—in addition to the risk control measures just mentioned, Cooper's diversification of product offerings through research and development of new products reduces the net income exposure related to the to the ulcer remedy.

2. The risk control measures just mentioned are examples of the following techniques and support the following risk control goals:
   a. Fire resistive construction and sprinklers are examples of loss reduction; they would reduce the amount or severity of damage from a fire. They promote the risk control goal of life safety.
   b. Avoiding production of ineffective or dangerous products is an example of avoidance. This measure supports risk control goals of complying with legal requirements for product safety and ensuring business continuity.
   c. Training of personnel to handle animals is an example of both loss prevention and loss reduction. It supports the risk control goal of life safety.
   d. New product development is an example of diversification. It supports the risk control goal to ensure business continuity.

3. Backing up the research files offsite (duplication) will not have an effect on the frequency of loss of the information, but will reduce the severity. A fire (or any other cause of loss) at the research facility may still occur with the same frequency, but the offsite backup of the files will reduce the severity of the loss because copies of the information will be more readily available. It is likely Cooper will suffer some loss of information that has not yet been backed up.

4. One of Cooper's primary business interruption concerns relates to the potential of an interruption of business at the plant that supplies the chemical compound used in the ulcer remedy. Because that plant is the exclusive supplier of that chemical, an interruption in its business could force Cooper to suspend production of the ulcer remedy. One step Cooper could take to ensure its business continuity is to construct a plant to manufacture the necessary chemical compound. Another step would be to stock a supply (six-month or one-year supply) of the compound that would sustain the company's production of the product through any business interruption at the chemical plant.

5. According to one of the Rules of the Code, a CPCU must stay informed on technical matters that are "essential to the maintenance of the CPCU's professional competence...." The facts of this case suggest that Atwell's risk manager has not stayed informed about available insurance coverages or about the status of Atwell's risk management program, both of which are essential to this risk manager's particular role.

Don't spend time on material you have already mastered. The SMART Review Notes are organized by the Educational Objectives found in each course guide assignment and help you track your study.

Risk Financing

Direct Your Learning

Assignment

5

Study Materials

Required Reading:

■ Foundations of Risk Management and Insurance,
  • Chapter 5

Study Aids:

■ SMART Practice Exam CD-ROM

■ SMART Study Aids Review Notes and Flash Cards— Assignment 5

Educational Objectives

After learning the content of this assignment, you should be able to:

1. Explain how individuals or organizations can achieve their overall and risk management goals by fulfilling the following risk financing goals:

   • Pay for losses

   • Manage the cost of risk

   • Manage cash flow variability

   • Maintain an appropriate level of liquidity

   • Comply with legal requirements

2. Describe the following aspects of retention and transfer:

   • Retention funding measures

   • Limitations on risk transfer measures

   • The advantages of both retention and transfer

3. Explain how the following can affect the selection of the appropriate risk financing measure:

   • Ability of a risk financing measure to meet risk financing goals

   • Loss exposure characteristics

   • Characteristics specific to an individual or organization

4. Explain how an organization meets its risk financing goals by using the following risk financing measures:

   • Guaranteed cost insurance   • Pools

   • Self-insurance   • Retrospective rating plans

   • Large deductible plans   • Hold-harmless agreements

   • Captives   • Capital market solutions

   • Finite risk plans

5. Explain how risk financing measures are applied to the four types of loss exposures.

6. Define or describe each of the Key Words and Phrases for this assignment.

Outline

- **Overview of Risk Financing**

- **Risk Financing Goals**
  - A. Pay for Losses
  - B. Manage the Cost of Risk
  - C. Manage Cash Flow Variability
  - D. Maintain an Appropriate Level of Liquidity
  - E. Comply With Legal Requirements

- **Retention and Transfer**
  - A. Retention
    1. Retention Funding Measures
    2. Advantages of Retention
  - B. Transfer
    1. Limitations on Risk Transfer Measures
    2. Advantages of Transfer

- **Selecting Appropriate Risk Financing Measures**
  - A. Ability of Retention and Transfer to Meet Risk Financing Goals
    1. Loss Exposure Characteristics Affecting the Selection of Appropriate Risk Financing Measures
    2. Individual- or Organization-Specific Characteristics Affecting the Selection of Appropriate Risk Financing Measures

- **Risk Financing Measures**
  - A. Guaranteed Cost Insurance

  - B. Self-Insurance
  - C. Large Deductible Plans
  - D. Captive Insurers
    1. Operation of a Captive
    2. Special Types of Group Captives
    3. Ability of a Captive to Meet Risk Financing Goals
    4. Finite Risk Insurance Plans
  - E. Pools
  - F. Retrospective Rating Plans
  - G. Hold-Harmless Agreements
  - H. Capital Market Solutions
    1. Securitization
    2. Hedging
    3. Contingent Capital Arrangements
    4. Ability of Capital Market Solutions to Meet Risk Financing Goals
  - I. Combinations of Risk Financing Measures

- **Application of Risk Financing Measures**
  - A. Property Loss Exposures
  - B. Liability Loss Exposures
  - C. Personnel Loss Exposures
  - D. Net Income Loss Exposures

- **Summary**

Key Words and Phrases

Define or describe each of the words and phrases listed below.

Risk financing (p. 5.3)

Retention (p. 5.3)

Transfer (p. 5.3)

Insurance (p. 5.4)

Alternative risk transfer (ART) (p. 5.4)

Primary layer (p. 5.22)

Excess layer (p. 5.22)

Excess coverage (p. 5.22)

Umbrella policy (p. 5.22)

Buffer layer (p. 5.22)

Self-insurance (p. 5.24)

Large deductible plan (p. 5.25)

Captive insurer, or captive (p. 5.26)

Risk retention group (p. 5.28)

Rent-a-captive (p. 5.28)

Protected cell company (PCC) (p. 5.29)

Finite risk insurance plan (p. 5.30)

Pool (p. 5.32)

Retrospective rating plan (p. 5.32)

Loss limit (p. 5.34)

Capital market (p. 5.37)

Securitization (p. 5.37)

Insurance securitization (p. 5.37)

Hedging (p. 5.39)

Derivative (p. 5.40)

Contingent capital arrangement (p. 5.41)

Review Questions

1. Describe the expenses that comprise an organization's cost of risk regardless of whether losses are retained or transferred. (p. 5.7)

2. Identify the factors that affect an organization's maximum cash flow variability level. (p. 5.8)

3. Describe internal and external methods an organization might use to increase cash liquidity. (p. 5.9)

4. Describe the four planned retention funding techniques available to an organization. (p. 5.12)

5. Identify two limitations on the risk transfer measures available to individuals and organizations. (pp. 5.14–5.15)

6. Identify the advantages of each of the following risk financing techniques: (pp. 5.13–5.15)

    a.   Retention

    b.   Transfer

7. Describe the respective abilities of using retention and transfer to meet an organization's risk financing goals. (p. 5.17)

8. Identify the loss exposure characteristics that help an organization determine which loss exposures to retain and which to transfer. (pp. 5.18–5.19)

9. Explain how the following individual- or organization-specific characteristics affect retention levels. (pp. 5.20–5.21)

   a. Risk tolerance

   b. Financial condition

   c. Core operations

d.   Ability to diversify

e.   Ability to control losses

f.   Ability to administer the retention plan

10. Explain the difference between a self-insurance plan and a large deductible plan. (p. 5.25)

11. Identify decisions regarding the following that an organization should consider when establishing a captive:

a.   Captive operation (pp. 5.27–5.28)

b.   Domicile selection (p. 5.28)

12. Describe three special types of group captives. (pp. 5.28–5.29)

13. Describe how organizations typically benefit from using the following risk financing plans: (pp. 5.32–5.33)

    a. Pools

    b. Retrospective rating plans

14. Describe the advantages and disadvantages of using hedging as a risk financing measure. (pp. 5.40–5.41)

15. Identify the two types of tangible property loss exposures and the commonly used risk financing measures used with each. (p. 5.43)

16. Describe the kinds of measures an organization might implement to manage personnel loss exposures. (p. 5.44)

17. Describe methods an organization might use to manage net income losses. (p. 5.43)

Application Questions

The Cooper Pharmaceutical Company Case. The Cooper Pharmaceutical Company manufactures and distributes both prescription drugs and medicines sold over the counter by pharmacies and other outlets. Cooper has averaged $30 million in revenue and $25 million in expenses over the last five years.

More than half of Cooper's annual expenses are for research and development of new products. With its extensive research facilities, the company has developed and introduced fifty new products over the last decade. Dr. Jackson Ryann, one of Cooper's researchers, is responsible for 75 percent of the new products that Cooper has developed. Cooper has developed and tested many other potential products but has not introduced them because they have proved to be ineffective, dangerous, or both.

Some of Cooper's prescription drugs contain narcotics, which are stored in the factory building pending their use in the products.

About 50 percent of Cooper's revenues are derived from an ulcer remedy. The remedy's formula includes a chemical compound that is manufactured in only one chemical plant in the world. There are other similar ulcer remedies on the market, and management concedes that some of them are equally effective. However, Cooper's product was the first on the market and has acquired a large following among doctors, who usually prescribe it by Cooper's brand name. Management is concerned that any prolonged absence of their ulcer medicine from the market would cause doctors to prescribe another brand, and they might not return to Cooper's brand when it becomes available again.

The testing process for some products is long and complex, sometimes involving several years of testing on dogs, primates, or other relatively long-lived animals, possibly followed by testing on human volunteers. Voluminous records accumulate during such tests and must be retained for many years for use in licensing applications, defense of products liability claims, and future research projects. While Cooper has not been successfully sued for products liability in the last ten years, its risk manager estimates a frequency of one every five years with a MPL of $5–$10 million. However, because a number of Cooper's competitors have paid large products liability claims over the last few years, very few insurers are willing to sell products liability insurance to cover pharmaceuticals.

Cooper stores its research records in fire-resistive filing cabinets in the records room of its research center. The center also houses research laboratories, offices for research personnel, and animals for research. The research center is located in a sprinklered, fire-resistive building adjacent to Cooper's factory. Personnel who handle the animals are thoroughly trained in animal care to ensure the safety of both the animals and employees. Although Cooper has more than 200 employees, its workers' compensation claims have been well below the industry average over the last ten years.

The factory building also is fire resistive and is sprinklered in all areas except the clean room. The clean room, used for manufacturing and packaging processes that require complete sterility, has its own air conditioning system with special filtering equipment to eliminate dust and other potential contaminants and other equipment to maintain the sterile atmosphere. Even very slight contamination of the clean room would require the discontinuation of production for several days until sterility could be reestablished. All workers in the clean room must wear special sterile uniforms and surgical masks.

Both the factory and the research center are five years old. The cost to build the two buildings was over $10 million, which Cooper financed with a thirty-year mortgage on both buildings. The buildings are surrounded by a carefully maintained lawn and are separated from the nearest building by 200 feet. They are located in a medium-sized city with excellent public fire protection and water supply.

1. *Cooper.* What risk financing measures could Cooper use for each of the following types of loss exposures: (pp. 5.42–5.45)

    a.   Property loss exposures

    b.   Liability loss exposures

    c.   Personnel loss exposures

    d.   Net income loss exposures

2. *Cooper.* For each of the risk financing measures suggested in the preceding question, explain which risk financing technique it is an example of and which risk financing goal it supports. (pp. 5.3–5.9)

3. *Cooper.* Suppose Cooper is considering forming a captive to insure its product liability loss exposures.

    a.   What characteristics of the product liability loss exposures would influence the decision?

b. What characteristics of Cooper as an organization would influence the decision? (pp. 5.18–5.19, 5.26–5.29)

4. *Cooper*. Cooper has the financial and psychological ability to handle a $1 million aggregate retention each year on its general liability loss exposures. Cooper wants to take a more active role in settling and defending routine third-party general liability claims. Moreover, Cooper believes it has all the necessary expertise on its own staff to handle its loss control activities. Which would be more appropriate for Cooper—a self-insurance plan with excess liability insurance or a large deductible plan? Explain. (pp. 5.24–5.26)

Answers to Assignment 5 Questions

NOTE: These answers are provided to give students a basic understanding of acceptable types of responses. They often are not the only valid answers and are not intended to provide an exhaustive response to the questions.

Review Questions

1. The following expenses comprise an organization's cost of risk regardless of whether losses are retained or transferred:
   - Administrative expenses—include the cost of internal administration and the cost of purchased services.
   - Risk control expenses—incurred to reduce loss frequency, reduce the severity of losses, or increase the predictability of future losses.
   - Risk financing expenses—incurred to manage the risk financing measures used to meet risk financing goals.

2. An organization's maximum cash flow variability level depends on the organization's size, its financial strength, management's degree of risk tolerance, and the degree to which the organization's stakeholders are willing to accept risk.

3. An organization might use the following methods to increase cash liquidity:
   - Internal method—selling assets or retaining cash flow
   - External method—borrowing, issuing a debt instrument, or issuing stock

4. The four planned retention funding techniques available to an organization are as follows:
   (1) Current expensing of losses—an approach that relies on current cash flows to cover the cost of losses
   (2) Using an unfunded reserve—an accounting entry recognizing the organization's potential liability to pay for a loss, but not specifying the assets that are to pay for a potential loss
   (3) Using a funded reserve—a reserve supported with cash, securities, or other liquid assets allocated to meet the obligations that the reserve represents
   (4) Borrowing funds—an approach that indirectly uses an organization's own resources to pay for losses and in time uses its own earnings to repay the loan.

5. The following are two limitations on the risk transfer measures available to individuals and organizations:
   (1) Risk transfer measures are not typically pure transfers but are some combination of retention and transfer. The individual or organization pays at least some portion of the loss.
   (2) The ultimate responsibility for paying for the loss remains with the individual or organization. If the other party (such as an insurer) cannot or will not pay for a loss, the loss must be absorbed by the individual or organization.

6. a. Advantages of using retention as a risk financing technique include cost savings, control of the claim process, timing of cash flows, and incentives for risk control.
   b. Advantages of using transfer as a risk financing technique include reducing exposure to large losses, reducing cash flow variability, providing ancillary services, and avoiding adverse employee and public relations.

7. Using retention to meet risk financing goals can be the most economical risk financing measure, depending on how the organization structures and manages its retention. Using transfer to meet risk financing goals typically offers the organization the greatest certainty regarding its ability to pay losses and the greatest cash flow certainty and is also useful in preventing liquidity problems.

8. Frequency and severity are two loss exposure characteristics that help an organization determine which loss exposures to retain and which to transfer. For most loss exposures, risk financing through retention is appropriate. For low frequency, high severity loss exposures, risk transfer measures are appropriate.

9. Individual- or organization-specific factors affect retention levels in the following ways:
    a. Risk tolerance—Generally, the higher an individual's organization's willingness to accept risk, the higher the likelihood that more risk will be retained.
    b. Financial condition—The more financially secure an organization is, the more loss exposures it can retain without causing liquidity or cash flow variability problems.
    c. Core operations—An organization is better able to retain loss exposures directly related to its core operations.
    d. Ability to diversify—If an organization can diversify its loss exposures, it can offset losses that occur and can more accurately forecast future losses.
    e. Ability to control losses—The more risk control an organization can undertake, the more loss exposures it can typically retain.
    f. Ability to administer the retention plan—Organizations that can fulfill the greater administrative requirements of retention can use retention more efficiently.

10. The difference between a self-insurance plan and a large deductible plan is the following:
    *   Self insurance—The insured is responsible for adjusting and paying its own losses up to the attachment point of the excess coverage insurance.
    *   Large deductible plan—The insurer adjusts and pays all claims. The insurer then seeks reimbursement from the insured for claims that fall below the deductible level.

11. When establishing a captive, an organization should consider the following issues:
    a. Captive operation—types of loss exposures the captive will cover, domicile, and whether business outside of the parent's business will be accepted
    b. Domicile selection—initial capital requirements, taxes, and annual fees; reputation and regulatory environment; premium and investment restrictions; and support of infrastructure in terms of accountants, bankers, lawyers, captive managers, and other services within the domicile

12. Three special types of group captives are as follows:
    (1) Risk retention group (RRG)—A group captive formed under the requirements of the liability Risk Retention Act of 1986 to insure the parent organization.
    (2) Rent-a-captive—An arrangement under which an organization rents capital from a captive to which it pays premiums and receives reimbursement for its losses.
    (3) Protected cell company (PCC)—A corporate entity separated into cells so that each participating company owns an entire cell but only a portion of the overall company. Because statute requires the PCC to be separated into cells, each member is assured that other members and third parties cannot access its assets in the event that any of those other members become insolvent. This protection is not necessarily provided by a rent-a-captive.

13. Organizations benefit from using risk financing plans, as follows:

    a. Pools can reduce an organization's cost of risk and keep the uncertainty of the cost associated with its retained losses at a tolerable level. They are often used by organizations that are too small to use a captive insurer.

    b. Retrospective rating plans can provide financial stability if the loss limit and maximum premium are set at the proper levels. If a retrospective rating plan covers more than one type of loss exposure, the insured benefits from the stability provided through diversification by retaining losses from different types of loss exposures under a single plan.

14. Using hedging as a risk financing measure has the following advantages and disadvantages:

    • Advantages—Hedging against possible net income losses from price changes can reduce an organization's business risk loss exposures and reduce its dependence on traditional financial and insurance markets for its risk transfer needs.

    • Disadvantage—Hedging can destabilize an organization's general risk financing plan and its entire financial structure if earnings or surpluses are seriously jeopardized by speculative investments in hedging instruments.

15. Two types of tangible property loss exposures include the following:

    • Real property loss exposures—Losses tend to be low frequency, high severity losses that are typically transferred rather than retained. Common risk financing measures include guaranteed cost insurance, captives, pools, and large deductible plans.

    • Personal property loss exposures—Losses tend to high frequency and low severity that are often better managed with retention measures. In addition to retention, transfer measures such as self-insurance, guaranteed cost insurance, and captives are commonly used for personal property loss exposures.

16. Few risk transfer measures are available to finance personnel loss exposures; therefore an organization might better manage personnel loss exposures through risk control.

17. An organization might use the following methods to manage net income losses:

    • Use risk financing measures that finance property, liability, or personnel loss exposures, which indirectly finance net income loss exposures as well

    • Use business income insurance to provide coverage for net income losses generated by hazard risk

    • Use capital market solutions to offset net income losses caused by a specific trigger

    • Use derivatives for net income losses generated by speculative risks

Application Questions

1. Cooper could use the following risk financing measures:

    a. Property loss exposures—Cooper may purchase guaranteed cost insurance for the buildings and personal property.

    b. Liability loss exposures—Products liability loss exposures could be transferred through a pool or guaranteed cost insurance (although it may be expensive or unavailable), or such exposures could be retained with a risk retention group or captive.

    c. Personnel loss exposures—Cooper would probably retain most of the personnel loss exposures, but may choose to purchase life insurance for Dr. Jackson Ryann, a key employee.

d.   Net income loss exposures—Cooper could purchase guaranteed cost insurance (business income policies) to protect against certain causes of loss. Hedging may be used if Cooper is exposed to certain financial risks, such as commodity prices, interest rate risk, or currency exchange risks, but none of those facts are stated in the case.

2. The risk financing measures identified in the preceding question are examples of the following techniques and support the following risk financing goals:

a.   Guaranteed cost insurance is a risk transfer measure that supports the risk financing goals of paying for losses, managing cash flow variability, maintaining appropriate level of liquidity, and complying with legal requirements (mortgage requirements).

b.   The risk retention group and captive examples are retention measures that support the risk financing goals of managing the cost of risk. If structured properly, they may also support paying for losses, managing cash flow variability, and complying with legal requirements.

c.   Most personnel loss exposures must be retained, a technique that supports the risk financing goal of managing the cost of risk.

d.   Guaranteed cost insurance is a risk transfer measure that supports the risk financing goals of paying for losses, managing cash flow variability, and maintaining appropriate level of liquidity.

3. Cooper may be influenced by the following characteristics when deciding to form a captive to insure its products liability loss exposures:

a.   The loss exposure characteristics that are relevant include the frequency and severity of potential losses. Cooper's products liability loss exposures are low frequency, high severity events that typically should be transferred. However, as noted in the case, insurance may not be available because of large losses by other insureds. Therefore, retention through a captive may be necessary.

b.   The relevant characteristics of Cooper as an organization are its risk tolerance, financial condition, core operations, ability to diversify, ability to control losses, and ability to administer the plan. The most important characteristics that may indicate a captive is possible are that Cooper is in good financial condition, products liability is directly related to Cooper's core operations, and Cooper has the ability to control losses through research and development. What is unknown is Cooper's risk tolerance and ability to administer the plan.

4. A self-insurance plan with excess liability insurance above the $1 million retention would meet Cooper's needs better than a large deductible plan. The self-insurance plan would allow Cooper to achieve its goal of administering its own claims within the self-insured retention. A large deductible plan would leave claim administration with the insurer.

Financial Services and Insurance Markets; Ethics Canon 3

Direct Your Learning

Assignment

6

Educational Objectives

After learning the content of this assignment, you should be able to:

1. Compare each type of consumer based on the following: insurance needs, knowledge of the market, market access methods, negotiating ability, and choice of risk financing alternatives.

2. Explain how producers provide consumers with access to insurers.

3. Describe the role of banks in the distribution of insurance products and services.

4. Explain how admitted insurers, nonadmitted insurers, residual markets, and government programs meet the insurance needs of customers.

5. Explain how insurers use reinsurance and financial markets as risk financing techniques.

6. Explain the role in insurance markets of third-party administrators (TPAs), special investigative units (SIUs), inspectors, consultants, and regulators.

7. Explain how each of the following influences competition in insurance markets: number and size of competing insurers, substitutes for insurance, knowledge of the market, and size and growth of overall market.

8. Paraphrase, interpret, and apply the ethical standards set forth in Canon 3—Legal Conduct—and the related Rules and Guidelines of the Code.

9. Define or describe each of the Key Words and Phrases for this assignment.

Study Materials

Required Reading:

- Foundations of Risk Management and Insurance,
  - Chapter 6
- Code of Professional Ethics
  - Canon 3 (pages 2.18-2.26, 3.7-3.8)
  - HCS 115 (page 5.28)
  - HCS 118 (page 5.34)
  - HCS 122 (pages 5.39-5.40)

Study Aids:

- SMART Practice Exam CD-ROM
- SMART Study Aids Review Notes and Flash Cards—Assignment 6

Outline

- **Insurance Markets Overview**
  - A. Consumer Profile
    1. Individuals
    2. Small Businesses
    3. Middle Markets
    4. National Accounts
  - B. Producers
    1. Agents
    2. Brokers
    3. Banks
    4. Excess and Surplus Lines Intermediaries
  - C. Insurers
    1. Admitted and Nonadmitted Insurers
    2. Residual Markets
    3. Government Programs
  - D. Reinsurance
    1. Reinsurance Intermediaries
    2. Reinsurers
  - E. Financial Markets

- **Roles of Third Parties**
  - A. Third-Party Administrators (TPAs)
  - B. Special Investigative Units (SIUs)
  - C. Inspectors
  - D. Consultants
  - E. Regulators

- **Insurance Markets and Competition**
  - A. Number and Size of Competing Insurers
  - B. Substitutes for Insurance
  - C. Knowledge of the Market
  - D. Size and Growth of the Overall Insurance Market

- **Summary**

- **Canon 3–Legal Conduct (Code)**
  - A. Rule R3.1–Dishonesty, Deceit, Fraud
    1. Guideline G3.1–Misrepresentation or Concealment
  - B. Rule R3.2–Financial Gain, Personal Benefit
  - C. Rule R3.3–Violation of Law or Regulation; Conviction of a Felony
    1. Guideline G3.2–Unfair Competition
    2. Guideline G3.3–Inappropriate Compensation
    3. Guideline G3.4–Awareness of Applicable Laws and Regulations
  - D. Other Related Code Provisions
  - E. Relevant Hypothetical Case Studies
  - F. Review Questions

- **Hypothetical Case Studies**
  - A. HCS-115
    1. Case HCS-115
    2. Opinion HCS-115
  - B. HCS-118
    1. Case HCS-118
    2. Opinion HCS-118
  - C. HCS-122
    1. Case HCS-122
    2. Opinion HCS-122

Key Words and Phrases

Define or describe each of the words and phrases listed below.

Nonadmitted insurer (p. 6.13)

Admitted insurer (p. 6.13)

Residual market (p. 6.15)

Reinsurance (p. 6.17)

Ceding commission (p. 6.17)

Retrocession (p. 6.17)

Financial market (p. 6.18)

Securities (p. 6.18)

Money market (p. 6.18)

Primary market (p. 6.19)

Secondary market (p. 6.19)

Third-party administrator (TPA) (p. 6.20)

Special investigative unit (SIU) (p. 6.20)

Review Questions

1. Identify five characteristics, in addition to size, that distinguish types of insurance customers and influence their demand for insurance products and services. (p. 6.5)

2. Describe how insurance needs differ for the following types of consumers. (pp. 6.6–6.8)

   a.   Individuals

   b.   Small businesses

c.   Middle markets

d.   National accounts

3. List typical ways insurers might distinguish between commercial accounts of differing size (small business, middle markets, and national accounts). (p. 6.6)

4. Give one reason that a large organization might benefit from using captives for insurance coverage. (p. 6.8)

5. Describe the three types of brokers categorized according to the scope of their operations. (p. 6.11)

6. Explain how banks have become involved in insurance markets. (p. 6.12)

7. Identify reasons that banks have become involved in the distribution of insurance products. (p. 6.12)

8. Describe circumstances in which a producer might place business with a nonadmitted insurer. (pp. 6.13–6.14)

9. Describe the following types of insurers with whom a producer might place insurance business. (pp. 6.13–6.16)

   a. Admitted insurer

   b. Nonadmitted insurer

c. Residual market

d. Government program

10. Describe ways individuals and organizations can obtain coverage
    if they are not able to do so through the admitted market. (p. 6.15)

11. Identify types of loss exposures commonly insured through
    residual markets. (p. 6.16)

12. Identify the services that may be provided by a reinsurance
    intermediary. (p. 6.17)

13. Identify financial markets used by insurers and reinsurers to share both risk and reward with investors. (pp. 6.18–6.19)

14. Explain how a corporation might benefit from primary and secondary financial market mechanisms. (p. 6.19)

15. Explain how insurers and reinsurers can function as both issuers and investors in financial markets. (p. 6.19)

16. Identify the types of services provided by third parties that allow insurance markets to operate more efficiently and effectively. (p. 6.19)

17. Identify the administrative services a third-party administrator (TPA) may provide. (p. 6.20)

18. List the ways the following third parties can help prevent fraudulent insurance-related activity. (p. 6.20)

    a. Special investigative units (SIUs)

    b. National Insurance Crime Bureau (NICB)

19. Identify types of inspectors that may be employed by an insurer. (pp. 6.20–6.21)

20. Identify the three product classifications of insurers in the insurance market. (p. 6.21)

21. Identify the factors affecting insurer competition. (p. 6.23)

22. Identify the factors affecting the number of insurance market competitors. (pp. 6.24–6.25)

23. According to Guideline G3.1 of the Code of Professional Ethics, what kinds of acts and omissions are among those considered dishonest, deceitful, or fraudulent, in violation of Rule R3.1? (*Code*, pp. 2.19–2.20)

24. According to Guideline G3.2, what anticompetitive activities are specifically not considered a violation of the Code? (*Code*, pp. 2.22–2.23)

25. HCS-122 involves a conflict-of-interest situation involving CPCU Agent, who apparently intended to perform a public service. CPCU Agent's actions possibly could have violated Rule R3.1 or R3.2. How could the conflict of interest in this situation have been avoided? (*Code*, pp. 5.39–5.40)

Application Questions

Jackson Manufacturing Case. Cara Ryann is the risk manager for Jackson Manufacturing, a large auto parts manufacturer. Jackson Manufacturing has three plants, all located in Michigan, with more than 5,000 employees and annual revenues of $100 million. Cara has been approached by a small local independent insurance agent, Cooper Smith, who is seeking to be the broker for all of Jackson Manufacturing's insurance transactions. Cooper's agency is in its second year of operation. Most of its clients purchase auto and homeowners' insurance through the agency. (pp. 6.4–6.15)

1. *Jackson.* What characteristics of Jackson Manufacturing and Cooper Smith may make it difficult for Cooper Smith to competently represent Jackson Manufacturing in insurance transactions?

2. *Jackson.* Cara Ryann has selected Cooper Smith's agency to be Jackson Manufacturing's broker of record for insurance transactions. One major loss exposure that Cara has had trouble insuring in the past is environmental liability because Jackson uses some highly toxic chemicals in its production process. In fact, Cara has just received notice of an environmental liability claim for $50 million resulting from an industrial accident last year. What options does Cooper have in trying to insure this loss exposure?

3. Eileen Jones is the CEO of Carnston Bank and Trust (CB&T). She has been paying close attention to how her local banking competitors have expanded their operations into insurance products and services. Eileen is interested in expanding CB&T's operations in this area and has identified the following three potential opportunities:

   (1) Acquire a large local agency/brokerage

   (2) Acquire a small local insurer that specializes in medical malpractice insurance

   (3) Develop CB&T's own insurance agency/brokerage (which is time consuming and expensive)

   Which opportunity provides CB&T with the quickest entry into insurance markets that would allow CB&T to compete with the other local banks offering insurance products and services? (pp. 6.12–6.13)

4. One of the reasons Eileen is interested in insurance products and services is an analysis that was done by a bank employee that predicts double digit growth rates in property-casualty insurance for the foreseeable future. Explain whether the analysis that was done at CB&T is accurate or not. (pp. 6.26–6.27)

5. Listed below are some abbreviated statements of fact. For each statement listed, explain whether the individual has violated any Rules of the Code of Professional Ethics. Assume each individual is bound by the Code and that proper complaints have been filed. State any other reasonable assumptions.

   a. A claim representative is highly competent, but she is known to have received (and not paid the fines for) thirty-five parking tickets in the past two years.

   b. An insurance company employee assists in falsifying the financial condition of his company because his boss ordered him to do so.

   c. A CPCU candidate cheats on a CPCU national exam.

   d. An insurance broker, to save a large account, helps her client understate the amount of a prior loss.

6. Milford Peterson, a business owner, contacted independent insurance agent Sue Brown, CPCU, to purchase insurance on his fleet of commercial vehicles. The following events occurred on the dates shown:

May 1: Sue quoted a premium, Milford signed an application, and Sue accepted a down payment, giving Milford a written thirty-day binder with Colossal Casualty Insurance Group.

May 10: One of Milford's trucks struck and damaged a parked car. Sue accepted a claim report and issued an agency draft to the owner of the parked car, based on a damage estimate provided by the car owner.

May 25: Sue received and acknowledged notice that Colossal Casualty had rejected Milford's application. Sue did not notify Milford that his application had been rejected.

May 29: Milford received from Sue a written thirty-day extension on the binder and an additional bill, which he promptly paid to Sue.

June 13: One of Milford's trucks seriously injured a pedestrian, and Milford reported the claim directly to Colossal Casualty.

Describe which Rules of the Code of Professional Ethics of the American Institute for CPCU Sue may have violated in her handling of this situation.

Reduce the number of Key Words and Phrases that you must review. SMART Flash Cards contain the Key Words and Phrases and their definitions, allowing you to set aside those cards that you have mastered.

Answers to Assignment 6 Questions

NOTE: These answers are provided to give students a basic understanding of acceptable types of responses. They often are not the only valid answers and are not intended to provide an exhaustive response to the questions.

Review Questions

1. The following are five characteristics, in addition to size, that distinguish types of insurance customers and influence their demand for insurance products and services:

   (1) Insurance needs

   (2) Knowledge of the insurance markets

   (3) Methods of assessing the insurance market

   (4) Negotiating ability

   (5) Access to alternative risk financing measures

2. Individuals and organizations have both real property and personal property insurance needs as well as liability insurance needs. However, their loss exposures vary widely in value and use. The following are typical property and liability needs of the insurance market consumers:

   a. Insurance needs of individuals are the least complex and include real property (homes); personal property, such as furniture, electronics, and automobiles; and liability arising out of their personal actions and ownership and use of property.

   b. Insurance needs of small businesses are somewhat complex and can be covered by a limited number of commercial insurance policies, such as a businessowners policy, a workers' compensation policy, and commercial auto policies.

   c. Insurance needs of middle markets are more complex and vary according to the products or services they provide. Those needs also include property, liability, and workers' compensation exposures.

   d. Insurance needs of national accounts are highly complex. These organizations are likely to combine commercial insurance coverages with sophisticated retention plans and captive insurers.

3. Insurers may consider one of more of the following in order to distinguish between commercial accounts of differing size:

   - Level of premium revenue
   - Commissions generated by the client
   - Number of employees
   - Organization's revenue or income

4. Large organizations may benefit from using captives for insurance coverage because captives provide them with additional flexibility to bypass the standard commercial insurance market and access reinsurance markets directly.

5. Three types of brokers categorized based on the scope of their operations are the following:

   (1) Local—operate in small geographic areas, targeting individuals, small businesses, and middle markets.

   (2) Regional—operate in multi-state regions, targeting middle markets, national account organizations, and larger small business accounts.

(3) National—operate nationally, sometimes internationally, and cater to the risk management needs of middle markets and national account organizations.

6. Banks' preferred mode of entry into the insurance industry has been by acquiring independent agents and brokers rather than becoming insurers. Banks appear to have more interest in distributing insurance products than underwriting them.

7. Banks have become involved in the distribution of insurance products for the following reasons:
    • Growing and diversifying the sources of revenues
    • Increasing product offerings to current customers
    • Cross-selling banking and insurance products and services

8. A producer might place business with a nonadmitted insurer if the loss exposures are unique, unusual, or hard-to-place coverages, such as for a customer who requires high limits of insurance or a customer who has had significant recent losses. The producer must first make a reasonable effort to place the coverage with an admitted insurer.

9. A producer may place insurance business with the following types of insurers:
    a. Admitted insurer—licensed by a state insurance department to do business in the insured's home state.
    b. Non-admitted insurer—not licensed by a state insurance department to do business in the insured's home state.
    c. Residual market—provides insurance through a shared risk mechanism to those who cannot obtain coverage in the admitted market.
    d. Government program—provides coverage that private insurers are unwilling or unable to provide.

10. Individuals and organizations can obtain coverage through the nonadmitted market or through residual markets if they are not able to do so through the admitted market.

11. Types of loss exposures commonly insured through residual markets include homeowners, commercial property, auto, and workers' compensation exposures.

12. Services that may be provided by a reinsurance intermediary include coverage and premium negotiation, claim adjusting, accounting, and underwriting advice.

13. Money markets, which trade short-term securities, and capital markets, which trade long-term securities, are financial markets used by insurers and reinsurers to share risk and reward with investors.

14. Primary markets enable corporations to raise additional cash by selling new shares of stock or by borrowing and issuing new bonds to investors. Secondary market mechanisms enable investors to buy and sell previously issued securities. The liquidity of these markets means that buyers and sellers know they can resell their securities whenever desired.

15. Insurers and reinsurers function as investors because they provide capital for both short-term and long-term investments. Insurers and reinsurers are issuers because they are active in financial markets; some are publicly-traded organizations that have issued stock on financial markets to investors to raise funds for operations. Insurers have also securitized natural hazard risk through the use of catastrophe bonds issued on the capital markets.

16. Third parties' services that allow insurance markets to operate more efficiently and effectively include administrative services, investigative services, inspections, consulting services, and regulatory oversight.

17. A third-party administrator (TPA) may provide the following administrative services:
    - Marketing
    - Underwriting
    - Loss control
    - Claim handling
    - Regulatory compliance
    - Legal assistance

18. Third parties help prevent insurance fraud in the following ways:
    a. Special investigative units (SIUs) investigate suspect claims, train insurer personnel to detect fraud, work with local attorneys and law enforcement to prosecute fraud, and promote public awareness of fraud.
    b. The National Insurance Crime Bureau (NICB) assists insurers and law enforcement agencies in the identification, detection, and prosecution of insurance criminals.

19. An insurer may employ the following type of inspectors:
    - Safety inspector to ensure that insureds are meeting policy requirements
    - Engineer to determine a property's condition and likelihood of suffering a loss
    - Property inspector to determine value and condition before issuing a property insurance policy
    - Property inspector in a hazard-prone area

20. The three product classifications of insurers are property-casualty insurers, life-health insurers, and multi-line insurers.

21. The factors affecting insurer competition include the number and size of competing insurers, the existence of insurance substitutes, the buyers' knowledge of the market, and the size and growth of the overall insurance market.

22. The factors affecting the number of insurance market competitors include the following:
    - Ease with which competitors can enter the market
    - Size of the organizations in that industry
    - Geographic region

23. Guideline G3.1 describes the following acts and omissions as dishonest, deceitful, or fraudulent and in violation of Rule R3.1: concealment or misrepresentation of any fact or information that is material to the suitability, efficacy, scope, or limitations of an insurance policy or surety bond or to the financial condition or quality of service of an insurer or a reinsurer.

24. Activities related to competition that are not considered in violation of the Code include participation in a legally enforceable covenant not to compete, in a rating bureau, or in a similar activity sanctioned or required by law.

25. By fully disclosing his interest in the club's insurance business and refraining from influencing other directors in their choice of insurance, Agent may be able to abide by his duties to the club and under the Rules of the Code. Specifically, he could have avoided a conflict of interest by taking both of the following steps:
    - Fully disclosing to the club's board the amount of commission and other compensation he or his firm stands to receive for placing the club's coverage
    - Disqualifying himself from voting on or influencing the decision-making process of the club in any manner that has a bearing on his or his firm's business interest.

Application Questions

1. Jackson Manufacturing is a large organization with complicated insurance needs. As the risk manager, Cara should have a thorough knowledge of insurance markets and probably needs a large broker. Cooper's agency is small, and most of its clients purchase personal lines insurance coverages. Therefore, Cooper is probably not practiced at servicing the needs of large national accounts. Cooper's agency probably does not offer the full range of services that Jackson Manufacturing requires, nor is Cooper familiar enough with the commercial lines markets to provide Cara with the market information necessary to negotiate competitive insurance terms.

2. If Cooper cannot find adequate coverage in the admitted market, he could contact an excess and surplus lines broker to attempt to obtain environmental liability coverage for Jackson Manufacturing in the nonadmitted market.

3. Acquiring a large local agency/brokerage would provide CB&T with the quickest entry into the insurance market and the greatest ability to distribute a broad range of insurance products and services. Most of Eileen's competitors have opted to acquire independent agents and brokers as the preferred mode of entry into distributing insurance products and services. Starting an agency/brokerage from scratch is time-consuming and expensive, and acquiring a medical malpractice insurer will not provide CB&T with the ability to distribute a broad range of insurance products and services.

4. The analysis performed by CB&T appears to be flawed. The property-casualty insurance market in the U.S. is a mature market that has seen declining growth over the past few decades. The reasons for this decline include saturation of the market, declines in population growth, and the growth of alternative risk financing tools.

5. a. The claim representative's failure to pay multiple parking ticket fines does not appear to violate any rules of the Code. Although she has broken the law, the violations are not related to her professional activities.

    b. The employee's falsifying information violates the following Code rules:
    -   R3.1; the action is fraudulent, deceitful, and dishonest.
    -   R3.2; the CPCU has allowed the pursuit of financial gain (keeping his job) to interfere with his sound professional judgment.
    -   R3.3; the behavior is against the law.

    c. Cheating on the CPCU nation exam violates Rule R3.1. In the conduct of professional activities (taking the exam), the candidate committed a dishonest and deceitful act.

    d. The broker's behavior violates Rule R3.1. Helping a client understate the amount of a prior loss is fraudulent. It also violates Rule R3.2 because the broker allowed the pursuit of financial gain to interfere with sound professional judgment.

6. Sue received and acknowledged notice that Milford's application was rejected but did not notify Milford. Sue then sent Milford a thirty-day extension on the binder and an additional bill. Her behavior violates the following rules:
    -   R3.1. CPCUs shall not engage in any act or omission of a dishonest, deceitful, or fraudulent nature.
    -   R3.2. CPCUs should not allow the pursuit of financial gain to interfere with sound professional judgment and skills.

Insurance Mechanism

Direct Your Learning

Assignment

7

Study Materials

Required Reading:

■ Foundations of Risk Management and Insurance
  • Chapter 7

Study Aids:

■ SMART Practice Exam CD-ROM

■ SMART Study Aids Review Notes and Flash Cards—Assignment 7

Educational Objectives

After learning the content of this assignment, you should be able to:

1. Explain how insurance benefits individuals, organizations, and society.

2. Describe the core and supporting functions performed by insurers.

3. Explain the dynamics of supply and demand in establishing product prices and the factors that affect the supply and demand for insurance.

4. Describe the following economic issues related to insurance pricing:
   • Adverse selection
   • Moral and morale hazard
   • Actuarial compared with social equity
   • Timing

5. Describe the main sources of revenues and expenses for insurers.

6. Explain how the profitability of insurers is measured.

7. Explain how pooling reduces risk in society.

8. Compare pooling and insurance.

9. Define or describe each of the Key Words and Phrases for this assignment.

Outline

- **Benefits of Insurance**

- **Functional View of Insurance**
  - A. Marketing
  - B. Underwriting
  - C. Claims
  - D. Supporting Functions

- **Economic View of Insurance**
  - A. Insurance Supply
    1. Capacity to Assume New Business
    2. Investment Opportunities
    3. Production Costs
    4. Regulatory Environment
  - B. Insurance Demand
    1. Insurance Mandates and Regulation
    2. Risk Tolerance
    3. Financial Status
    4. Real Services Rendered
    5. Tax Incentives
  - C. Economic Issues Related to Insurance Pricing
    1. Adverse Selection
    2. Moral and Morale Hazard
    3. Actuarial Equity Compared With Social Equity
    4. Timing

- **Financial View of Insurance**
  - A. Insurer Financial Statements
  - B. Revenue
    1. Premiums
    2. Investments
  - C. Expenses
  - D. Profitability
    1. Net Underwriting Gain or Loss
    2. Overall Gain or Loss from Operations

- **Social View of Insurance**
  - A. Pooling
  - B. Pooling and Risk Reduction
  - C. Insurance Compared With Pooling

- **Summary**

Key Words and Phrases

Define or describe each of the words and phrases listed below.

Underwriting (p. 7.7)

Insolvency risk (p. 7.14)

Written premiums (p. 7.14)

Policyholders' surplus (p. 7.14)

Premium-to-surplus ratio (p. 7.14)

Loss reserve (p. 7.26)

Unearned premium reserve (p. 7.27)

Earned premiums (p. 7.29)

Unearned premiums (p. 7.29)

Paid losses (p. 7.30)

Incurred losses (p. 7.30)

Loss adjustment expenses (LAE) (p. 7.30)

Net underwriting gain or loss (p. 7.32)

Overall gain or loss from operations (p. 7.32)

Review Questions

1. List the ways insurance benefits individuals, organizations, and society. (pp. 7.3–7.5)

2. Explain how an organization can achieve risk financing goals through the use of insurance. (pp. 7.3–7.4)

3. List risk sharing mechanisms an insurer may use to promote risk control. (p. 7.4)

4. Identify three core functions and three supporting functions performed by an insurer. (pp. 7.6–7.9)

5. Identify the components likely to be included in a successful marketing program. (p. 7.6)

6. Explain the role of information systems in the daily operation of insurers. (p. 7.9)

7. Identify the factors that determine the supply of insurance. (p. 7.13)

8. Describe two variables that affect an insurer's claim-paying ability (and therefore its capacity to assume new business) and the measurement method used for each. (p. 7.14)

9. Describe how the following measures indicate an insurer's capacity to assume new business. (p. 7.14)

    a.   Policyholders' surplus

    b.   Premium-to-surplus ratio

10. Describe two main types of state regulatory constraints that affect the supply of insurance. (p. 7.16)

11. List the factors that affect the demand for insurance. (p. 7.17)

12. List three examples of insurance that is commonly required by mandate or statute, resulting in an increased demand for insurance. (pp. 7.18–7.19)

13. Identify factors that affect an individual's risk tolerance. (p. 7.19)

14. Describe how an insurer can increase the demand for its insurance products. (p. 7.20)

15. Describe the pricing goal of an insurance transaction and how to determine when that goal is accomplished. (p. 7.21)

16. Describe four key issues that affect the proper functioning of insurance market pricing. (pp. 7.21–7.26)

17. Identify two social equity concepts that apply to insurance pricing. (pp. 7.24–7.25)

18. Identify the two major sources of revenue for individual insurers. (p. 7.29)

19. Describe the following types of premium and the accounting treatment of each. (p. 7.29)

    a. Written premiums

    b. Earned premiums

    c. Unearned premiums

20. Describe the six largest expenses for an insurer. (pp. 7.30–7.31)

21. Describe how insurer profitability is estimated. (p. 7.31)

22. Describe the following three specific ratios used to measure an insurer's underwriting performance. (p. 7.32)

    a. Loss ratio

    b. Expense ratio

    c. Trade basis combined ratio

23. Explain why it is important to analyze several years of an insurer's operations to obtain an accurate measure of profitability. (p. 7.33)

24. Describe the traits of an independent, or uncorrelated, loss exposure. (p. 7.34)

25. Describe the likelihood of extreme outcomes when using a pooling arrangement. (p. 7.36)

26. Describe the effect of pooling on the frequency of loss, severity of loss, and the probability distribution of losses. (p. 7.36)

27. Identify the two key differences between pooling and insurance. (pp. 7.37–7.38)

28. Identify the sources of additional financial resources an insurer owns in the event of a loss. (p. 7.38)

Application Questions

1. The terrorist attacks of September 11, 2001, Hurricanes Rita and Katrina, and subsequent events have all had a substantial effect on the economics of the insurance business. (pp. 7.9–7.26)

   a. What do higher prices tell us about the supply of insurance?

   b. How, if at all, has public attitude toward risk affected the demand for insurance?

   c. What effect does the combination of a decrease in supply and an increase in demand have on the market equilibrium for insurance?

2. Kathleen, the chief actuary at Sommer Insurance Company, has determined that eye color is a predictor of the frequency of auto accidents. By analyzing thousands of auto accidents, Kathleen has discovered that individuals with light eye color (green or blue) are twice as likely to have an auto accident as individuals with a dark eye color (brown). She wants to use this information in setting Sommer's auto insurance rates. Describe any social equity issues a regulator may raise if Sommer does decide to charge individuals with light-colored eyes higher auto rates. (p. 7.25)

3. In 2006, Sommer Insurance had the following results:

Written premiums:	$1,200,000
Earned premiums:	$800,000
Incurred losses:	$650,000
Underwriting expenses:	$225,000
Investment income:	$195,000

Calculate (a) Sommer's net underwriting gain or loss and (b) its overall gain or loss from operations. (p. 7.32)

4. The Atwell Bus Corporation is a publicly held corporation providing school bus transportation to public and private schools in Midland County. Atwell owns 200 school buses, garaged in three different cities within the county. Its major competitors are two larger bus companies that operate in the same general area. School districts and private schools generally award contracts to the lowest bidder from among the bus companies, but they also consider overall performance and level of service in their evaluations. (pp. 7.34–7.37)

   a. Give one example in each of the following categories of a loss exposure faced by Atwell:

      (1) Correlated

      (2) Uncorrelated

   b. Suppose Atwell were to enter into a formal arrangement with the Green Bus Company, a similar company that operates in another state, to pool the losses suffered by both companies. How would this arrangement affect Atwell's risks with respect to each of the loss exposures you identified in a., above? Explain.

   c. Suppose, instead, Atwell were to participate in a formal pool with fifteen other school bus companies. How, if at all, would this arrangement change your answer to b., above? Explain.

Answers to Assignment 7 Questions

NOTE: These answers are provided to give students a basic understanding of acceptable types of responses. They often are not the only valid answers and are not intended to provide an exhaustive response to the questions.

Review Questions

1. Insurance benefits individuals, organizations, and society in the following ways:
    - Indemnifies individuals and organizations for covered losses
    - Enables individuals and organizations to manage cash flow uncertainty
    - Enables individuals and organizations to meet legal requirements
    - Promotes risk control
    - Frees up insured's financial resources for other expenditures or investments
    - Supports insured's credit
    - Helps reduces social burden

2. Insurance helps an organization achieve risk financing goals in the following ways:
    - Indemnifies for covered losses—Insurance indemnifies the insured, subject to applicable deductibles and policy limits, for losses of covered loss exposures resulting from covered causes of loss.
    - Manages cash flow uncertainty—Insurance helps limit the financial affect on the insured's cash flow to any deductible payments and any loss amounts that exceed the policy limits.
    - Meets legal requirements—Insurance is often used or required to satisfy statutory requirements and contractual requirements that arise from business relationships.

3. The following risk sharing mechanisms promote risk control:
    - Deductibles
    - Premium credit incentives
    - Contractual requirements

4. Three core functions performed by an insurer are marketing, underwriting, and claims. The supporting functions performed by an insurer include investments, loss control, premium auditing, reinsurance, actuarial activities, and information systems.

5. A successful marketing program is likely to include the following components:
    - Market research to determine potential buyer's needs
    - Advertising and public relations programs to inform potential buyers about the insurer's products
    - Training programs to equip the insurer's employees and producers to meet the public's needs
    - Production goals and strategies tailored to the insurer's target audience
    - Effective motivation and management of the producer network

6. Information systems are important to insurers because of the vast amount of data associated with insurance operations. The data are used to conduct daily operations, manage marketing efforts, underwrite policies, track investments, and pay claims.

7. The following factors determine the supply of insurance:
    - Capacity to assume new business
    - Investment opportunities
    - Production costs
    - Regulatory environment

8. The following two variables affect an insurer's claim-paying ability:
    (1) The number and size of the policies sold (the liabilities), measured by the insurer's total written premiums
    (2) The funds available to pay for the promises made under those policies (its assets), measured by assets that can be liquidated to pay for claims

9. These measures indicate an insurer's capacity to assume new business and its ability to pay claims that are greater than expected in the following ways:
    a. Policyholders' surplus is the difference between an insurer's assets and its liabilities and is a measure of how much capital the insurer has to pay claims.
    b. Premium-to-surplus ratio indicates an insurer's financial strength by relating net written premium to policyholders' surplus.

10. Two types of state regulatory constraints that affect the supply of insurance are the following:
    (1) Business practices regulation, such as licensing, policy language, minimum financial requirements, and participation in residual markets
    (2) Price regulation, which limits prices by regulating rate increases and the underwriting factors used in setting premiums

11. The following factors affect the demand for insurance:
    - Insurance mandates and regulation
    - Risk tolerance
    - Financial status
    - Real services rendered
    - Tax incentives

12. The following types of insurance are commonly required by mandate or statute, resulting in an increased demand for insurance:
    - States require auto insurance
    - States require employers to provide workers' compensation benefits
    - Mortgage lenders require insurance to protect their interest in the property
    - Creditors may require insurance for loan collateral
    - Business contracts may require liability insurance

13. An individual's level of risk tolerance may change with age, with economic or social conditions, or as a result of a significant loss event, such as a hurricane.

14. To increase the demand for its insurance products, an insurer might do the following:
    - Offer services valued by the consumer, such as fast claim service, loss control services, or a personable sales force
    - Introduce new insurance products, such as extended warranty products for autos, warranties for home buyers, and insurance against financial losses resulting from identity theft

15. The pricing goal of an insurance transaction is to collect premiums that in the aggregate are adequate to generate an operating profit. The goal is accomplished when the insurance premium for each policy is set at a level that reflects the loss exposure the policy covers, with allowances for expenses, profits, contingencies, and an adjustment for investment income.

16. The following four key issues can affect the proper functioning of insurance market pricing:

    (1) Adverse selection—Consumers with the greatest probability of loss are those most likely to purchase insurance.

    (2) Moral and morale hazard—Loss costs are assumed by the insurer, and therefore the insureds are less careful.

    (3) Actuarial compared with social equity—Legislators and the public have identified certain insurance-rate variables that are socially unacceptable and may not be reflected in rating plans.

    (4) Timing—A delay can occur between the date of occurrence, the date the loss is discovered, and the date the loss is paid. The longer the time before the amount is paid, the harder it is for the insurer to forecast the size of payment.

17. The following are two social equity concepts that apply to insurance pricing:

    (1) Insurers should relate the amount each person should pay for insurance to that person's ability to pay rather than to his or her loss exposure or expense factor.

    (2) Insurers should not increase an insured's premium because of criteria that are beyond that individual's control.

18. The following are two major sources of revenue for individual insurers:

    (1) Premiums—payments by insureds to purchase insurance

    (2) Investments—interest, dividends, capital gains, and other earnings on funds held by the insurer

19. The following are types of premium characterized by an insurer:

    a. Written premiums—Total premiums on all policies written (put into effect) for a particular period. Written premiums are made up of earned premiums and unearned premium.

    b. Earned premiums—The portion of written premiums that corresponds to coverage that has already been provided. It is characterized by an insurer as revenue.

    c. Unearned premiums—The portion of written premiums that corresponds to coverage that has not yet been provided. It is characterized by an insurer as a liability.

20. The following are the six largest expenses for an insurer:

    (1) Losses, which can be up to 80 percent of all expenses. Insurers establish loss reserves for amounts estimated to settle claims that have occurred but have not yet been paid.

    (2) Loss adjustment expenses, incurred to investigate, defend, and settle claims.

    (3) Acquisition expenses, incurred when selling a policy to a new customer including marketing, advertising, and underwriting expenses.

    (4) General expenses, including overhead, and expenses incurred by departments, such as human resources, accounting, legal, research, product development, customer service, and building maintenance.

    (5) Taxes and fees, including income tax, premium taxes, licenses, and funds for participation in state insurance programs.

    (6) Investment expenses, incurred to pay for professional investment managers to oversee the insurer's investment programs.

21. Insurer profitability is estimated by examining either underwriting performance (underwriting gain or loss) or overall operating performance (gain or loss from operations).

22. The following three specific ratios are used to measure an insurer's underwriting performance:

   a. Loss ratio—compares an insurer's incurred losses to its earned premiums for a specific period.

   b. Expense ratio—compares an insurer's underwriting expenses to its written premium for a specific period.

   c. Trade basis combined ratio—combines the loss ratio and expense ratio to compare inflows and outflows from insurance underwriting.

23. It is important to analyze several years of an insurer's operations to obtain an accurate measure of profitability because any company might have a single bad year that is offset by a pattern of profitability over a longer period.

24. A loss exposure is considered independent, or uncorrelated, when a loss at one loss exposure has no effect on the probability of a loss at another loss exposure.

25. As the number of participants in the pool grows, extreme outcomes become less likely at the pool level.

26. Pooling does not change the frequency or severity of an individual loss exposure, but it does change the probability distribution of the loss because the sources of the loss exposures and the resources to pay for losses have been combined. The result is that the uncertainty around the expected value has decreased.

27. The following are two key differences between pooling and insurance:

   (1) Pooling is a risk sharing mechanism, whereas insurance is a risk transfer mechanism.

   (2) The insurer introduces additional financial resources that enable the insurer to provide a stronger guarantee that sufficient funds will be available in the event of a loss, further reducing risk.

28. An insurer owns additional financial resources in the event of a loss from the following sources:

   - Initial capital from investors
   - Retained earnings

Application Questions

1. The terrorist attacks of September 11, 2001, Hurricanes Rita and Katrina, and subsequent events have resulted in the following:

   a. High prices indicate that there has been a decrease in the supply of insurance. This decrease in supply may be because less reinsurance is available and because some insurers have left the market.

   b. These types of high profile events often increase the public's awareness of risk. Therefore, individuals tend to become more risk averse and increase their demand for insurance.

   c. As a result of lower supply and higher demand, the market equilibrium would result in a lower quantity of insurance and a higher price.

2. The second concept in social equity is that an insurer should not increase an insured's premium because of criteria that are beyond that individual's control. Because people do not have control over their eye color (it is genetically determined), some regulators may be reluctant to allow rates based on it as a rating variable.

3. a. Net underwriting gain or loss = Earned premiums – (Incurred losses + Underwriting expenses)

$$= \$800,000 - (\$650,000 + \$225,000)$$

$$= 800,000 - 875,000$$

Net underwriting loss = ($75,000).

b. Overall gain or loss from operations = Net underwriting gain or loss + Investment gain or loss

$$= (\$75,000) + \$195,000$$

Overall gain from operations = $120,000.

4. a. (1) An example of a correlated loss exposure is a bus breakdown caused by a defective design in Atwell's buses.

(2) An example of an uncorrelated loss exposure is a serious bus accident resulting in multiple deaths.

b. The arrangement with Green would have the following effects on Atwell's loss exposures:

(1) The correlated loss exposure—Assuming both Atwell's and Green's fleets included buses with the same defect (perfectly positively correlated loss), the risks would be unchanged. If losses are not perfectly positively correlated, some risk could be reduced through pooling, although the magnitude is less than with uncorrelated losses.

(2) The uncorrelated loss exposure—Although the number of serious accidents for which Atwell would be required to share resources with Green would increase, Atwell's share of the losses would become more predictable, reducing Atwell's risks.

c. A pool with fifteen other school bus companies would further reduce Atwell's risks involving uncorrelated loss exposures.

Insurable Risks; Ethics Canon 4

Direct Your Learning

Educational Objectives

After learning the content of this assignment, you should be able to:

1. Explain why each of the six characteristics of an ideally insurable loss exposure is important to the insurance mechanism.

2. Explain how the six characteristics of an ideally insurable loss exposure apply to commercial insurance loss exposures.

3. Explain how the six characteristics of an ideally insurable loss exposure apply to personal insurance loss exposures.

4. Explain how state and federal governments are involved in the insurance market and the rationale for, and level of, their involvement.

5. Paraphrase, interpret, and apply the ethical standards set forth in Canon 4—Diligent Performance—and the related Rules and Guidelines of the Code.

6. Define or describe each of the Key Words and Phrases for this assignment.

Study Materials

Required Reading:

- Foundations of Risk Management and Insurance
  - Chapter 8
- Code of Professional Ethics
  - Canon 4 (pages 3.9–3.11, 2.27–2.35)
  - HCS 103 (pages 5.7–5.8)
  - HCS 112 (pages 5.22–5.23)
  - HCS 116 (pages 5.29–5.30)

Study Aids:

- SMART Practice Exam CD-ROM
- SMART Study Aids Review Notes and Flash Cards— Assignment 8

Outline

- **Characteristics of an Ideally Insurable Loss Exposure**
  - A. Pure Risk
  - B. Fortuitous
  - C. Definite and Measurable
  - D. Large Number of Similar Exposure Units
  - E. Independent and Not Catastrophic
  - F. Economically Feasible Premium

- **Commercial Loss Exposures**
  - A. Property
    1. Fire Cause of Loss
    2. Windstorm Cause of Loss
    3. Flood Cause of Loss
  - B. Liability
    1. Premises and Operations Liability
    2. Products Liability
  - C. Personnel
    1. Death Cause of Loss
    2. Retirement Cause of Loss
  - D. Net Income
    1. Net Income Loss Associated With Property Losses
    2. Net Income Loss Associated With Liability Losses

- **Personal Loss Exposures**
  - A. Property
  - B. Liability
  - C. Net Income
  - D. Life, Health, and Retirement
    1. Life Loss Exposures
    2. Health Loss Exposures
    3. Retirement Cause of Loss

- **Government Programs**
  - A. Rationale for Government Involvement
    1. Fill Unmet Needs
    2. Compel Insurance Purchase
    3. Obtain Efficiency and Provide Convenience
    4. Achieve Collateral Social Purpose
  - B. Level of Government Involvement
  - C. Federal Compared With State Programs

- **Summary**

- **Canon 4–Diligent Performance (Code)**
  - A. Rule R4.1–Performing Occupational Duties
    1. Guideline G4.1–Employment, Contractual, and Civil Disputes Involving Diligent Performance
  - B. Rule R4.2–Improving the Insurance Mechanism
    1. Improving the Insurance Mechanism; G4.2 and Related Guidelines
  - C. Other Related Code Provisions
  - D. Relevant Hypothetical Case Studies
  - E. Review Question

- **Hypothetical Case Studies**
  - A. HCS-103
    1. Case HCS-103
    2. Opinion HCS-103
  - B. HCS-112
    1. Case HCS-112
    2. Opinion HCS-112
  - C. HCS-116
    1. Case HCS-116
    2. Opinion HCS-116

Key Phrase

Define or describe the phrase listed below.

Fortuitous loss (p. 8.6)

Review Questions

1. Identify the six characteristics of an ideally insurable loss exposure. (p. 8.4)

2. Explain why insurance is designed to cover pure, not speculative, risk. (p. 8.5)

3. Identify the factors an insurer must be able to determine for a loss exposure to be definite in time, cause, and location. (p. 8.6)

4. Describe the types of losses an insurer might consider uninsurable because the premium charged would not be economically feasible. (p. 8.10)

5. Describe two common sources of liability risk faced by many commercial organizations. (pp. 8.17–8.18)

6. Compare the insurability of personnel losses caused by an employee's death and those caused by an employee's retirement. (pp. 8.19–8.20)

7. Identify property loss factors used in determining the degree of insurability of personal residences for fire, windstorm, and flood causes of loss. (p. 8.22)

8. Identify common sources of liability risk faced by individuals. (p. 8.23)

9. Identify the bases on which government insurance programs vary. (p. 8.27)

10. List three categories of government insurance programs.
    (p. 8.27)

11. Identify the major difference between the objectives of private
    market insurance and government provided insurance. (p. 8.27)

12. Identify reasons for government involvement in insurance.
    (p. 8.28)

13. Identify three levels of governmental participation in governmental
    insurance programs. (p. 8.30)

14. What is the relationship between continuous learning and
    competent performance? (*Code*, p. 2.28)

15. What is the most appropriate remedy for employer-employee disputes? (*Code*, p. 2.28)

16. The Board of Ethical Inquiry (BEI) will hear ethics complaints involving Rule R4.1 only under certain circumstances. What circumstances are specified in Guideline G4.1? (*Code*, p. 2.28)

17. How might a CPCU violate Rule R4.2? (*Code*, pp. 2.33–2.34)

18. HCS-112 presents a situation involving a risk manager, a CPCU, who refuses to accept competitive bids for his employer's insurance coverages. (*Code*, pp. 5.29–5.30)

    a. Does the failure to hear competitive bids constitute a violation of Rule R4.1?

    b. If a complaint was filed with the BEI, would it hear the case?

Application Questions

The Shore Point Mall Case. Shore Point Mall is a mall of sixtiy retail stores located along the Outer Banks of North Carolina's coastal shoreline. Outer Banks Insurance Company, a small local property insurer that insures more than 40 percent of properties in the Outer Banks area, is considering selling a commercial property policy to Shore Point Mall that includes coverage for windstorm damage.

1. *Shore Point Mall.* Determine whether Shore Point Mall exhibits all six characteristics of an ideally insurable loss exposure for windstorm damage. (pp. 8.14–8.15)

2. *Shore Point Mall.* Outer Banks Insurance Company is also considering selling personal auto insurance policies at a discounted rate to all mall employees. Determine whether the employees of Shore Point Mall exhibit all six characteristics of an ideally insurable loss exposure. (pp. 8.22–8.25)

3. The Pennsylvania state insurance commissioner is concerned that the state's workers' compensation insurance market is not competitive. Only a few insurers are selling workers' compensation in Pennsylvania, and rates are high relative to many other comparable states. Describe some of the considerations the insurance commissioner should take into account before recommending that the state become involved in providing workers' compensation insurance to employers in Pennsylvania. (pp. 8.27–8.31)

4. According to Rule R4.2, CPCUs and CPCU candidates should support efforts to improve the insurance mechanism. Give one example to illustrate how a CPCU or a CPCU candidate working in each of the following functions could help improve the insurance mechanism. (*Code*, pp. 2.30–2.32)

    a.   Marketing

    b.   Underwriting

    c.   Claims

5. An agent is found professionally negligent in an errors and omissions lawsuit and is required to pay the plaintiff $500,000 in damages. Explain whether the individual has violated any Rules of the Code of Professional Ethics. Assume the agent is bound by the Code and that proper complaints have been filed. State any other reasonable assumptions. (*Code*, pp. 2.27–2.31)

6. Which specific provisions in the Code of Professional Ethics
   of the American Institute for CPCU refer to CPCUs' obligations
   to assist in improving insurance contracts? (*Code*, p. 2.30)

Consult the registration booklet that accompanied this course guide for
complete information regarding exam dates and fees. Plan to register with
the Institutes well in advance of your exam. If you have any questions, or need
updated registration information, contact the Institutes (see page iv).

Answers to Assignment 8 Questions

NOTE: These answers are provided to give students a basic understanding of acceptable types of responses. They often are not the only valid answers and are not intended to provide an exhaustive response to the questions.

Review Questions

1. The six characteristics of an ideally insurable loss exposure are as follows:

    (1) Pure risk

    (2) Fortuitous losses

    (3) Definite and measurable

    (4) Large number of similar exposure units

    (5) Independent and not catastrophic

    (6) Affordable

2. Insurance is designed to cover pure, not speculative, risk because the purpose of insurance is to indemnify the insured for a loss, not to enable the insured to profit from the loss. If the loss exposure has a possibility of gain, the insurance premium the insurer would have to charge would offset the potential gain.

3. An insurer must be able to determine the following to consider a loss exposure definite in time, cause, and location:

    - The event that led up to the loss
    - When that event or series of events occurred
    - Where that event occurred

4. Losses an insurer might consider uninsurable because the premium charged would not be economically feasible are those involving only low-severity losses and those involving a high frequency of loss.

5. Among sources of liability risk faced by many commercial organizations are the following two:

    - Premises and operations liability—liability because of bodily injury or property damage caused by an accident on owned or rented premises or away from the premises if it arises out of the ongoing operations
    - Products liability—liability because of bodily injury or property damage resulting from defective or inherently dangerous products

6. Personnel losses caused by an employee's death generally exhibit the six characteristics of an ideally insurable loss exposure. Such a loss exposure involves pure risk that is fortuitous, independent, and not catastrophic and that is usually economically feasible to insure.

    Personnel losses caused by an employee's retirement do not meet the six characteristics of an ideally insurable loss exposure because retirement is usually planned (not a fortuitous loss) and because the loss may not be economically feasible to insure.

7. In determining the degree of insurability of residences for fire, windstorm, and flood causes of loss, insurers identify buildings with higher-than-normal hazards, guard against arson-for-profit, avoid excessive concentration of loss exposures, ensure adequate diversification of exposures, and carefully establish the insurable value of the property subject to loss.

8. Individuals face the following common sources of liability risk:
   - Real property ownership (premises) liability loss exposures
   - Personal property ownership liability loss exposures
   - Liability loss exposures arising from their behavior toward others

9. Government insurance programs vary on the bases of the following:
   - Purpose or rationale
   - Level of governmental involvement
   - Whether the program is run at the federal or state level

10. The following are three categories of government insurance programs:
    (1) Property-casualty insurance plans
    (2) Social insurance plans
    (3) Financial security plans

11. Private market insurance objectives differ from government provided insurance objectives in that private insurance seeks to provide actuarial equity, and government provided insurance programs aim to provide social equity.

12. Government involvement in insurance occurs for the following reasons:
    - To fulfill insurance needs unmet by private insurers
    - To compel people to buy a particular type of insurance
    - To obtain greater efficiency and/or provide convenience to insurance buyers
    - To achieve collateral social purposes

13. Governmental participation in governmental insurance programs includes the following three roles:
    (1) Exclusive insurer
    (2) Partner with private insurers
    (3) Competitor to private insurers

14. The relationship between continuous learning and competent performance is that continuous learning is a prerequisite to competent performance.

15. Employer-employee disputes are best resolved through the procedures established for this purpose within the organization or through civil legal action. The Code of Ethics in not a remedy for employer-employee disputes.

16. The BEI will hear an ethics complaint concerning alleged violations of Rule R4.1 only after all other remedies have been exhausted and either a proven violation has caused unjust harm to another and brings substantial discredit on the CPCU designation or it would be in the public interest to take disciplinary action.

17. A CPCU could violate Rule R4.2 by supporting changes in the insurance mechanism that would come at the expense of the public or by putting personal interests ahead of public interests.

18. Regarding the risk manager in HCS-112,
    a. From the facts presented in the case, it is difficult to determine if the risk manager has violated Rule R4.1. By renewing with the same insurer, he may be acting in his employer's best interest or he may be failing to fulfill his occupational duties by not hearing competitive bids.
    b. The BEI would hear the case only after all other remedies have been exhausted. In this case, it would be up to the employer to take appropriate actions first. If the employer takes no action, the BEI would not hear the case.

Application Questions

1. Shore Point Mall does meet the first three characteristics for windstorm damage. Windstorm is a pure risk, fortuitous, and definite and measurable. Because the mall is a retail mall, it probably does meet the fourth characteristic of being a large number of similar exposure units. However, from Outer Banks Insurance Company's perspective, the windstorm cause of loss is probably not independent and not catastrophic. Outer Banks Insurance has insured a large percentage of the local market, and a major hurricane would affect a large percentage of its insureds. This may make it difficult for Outer Banks Insurance to charge a feasible premium and still maintain its claim-paying ability.

2. The mall employees' auto insurance exposures meet the first four characteristics: pure risk, fortuitious, definite and measurable, and among large number of similar exposure units. The exposures may not be independent because the employees will be parking their autos in the mall parking lot during work hours. Therefore, a single event, such as vandalism, could affect many of the insureds at the same time. However, the severity of such damage would likely be a less than for potential losses resulting from the mall's windstorm exposure. Therefore, premiums could still be economically feasible.

3. The Pennsylvania insurance commissioner should consider why the state needs to be involved in the workers' compensation insurance market. It appears that the rationale is to fill insurance needs unmet by private insurers (provide insurance at an affordable rate) or to obtain greater efficiency in the market (increase competition)—the two major reasons the state should be involved. The commissioner needs to determine how the state would be involved—as the exclusive insurer, a partner with private insurers, or as a competitor to private insurers.

4. A CPCU or CPCU candidate could help improve the insurance mechanism in the following ways:
    a. Marketing—perform market research to determine the needs of potential buyers
    b. Underwriting—encourage product innovation and develop marketable policy forms and rating plans
    c. Claims—train claim representatives to achieve fair settlements in accordance with the applicable insurance policy provisions

5. The agent's situation violates Rule R4.1 because the CPCU did not competently discharge his duties as an agent. However, under Guideline G4.1, it is unlikely that the BEI would take action. Other remedies, such as a lawsuit, appear to be adequate. The agent did no discredit to the CPCU designation itself nor is there any public interest at stake, according to the short statement of facts. Additional information might change this answer.

6. Rule R4.2 requires CPCUs to support efforts to effect improvements in contract design that will both inure to the benefit of the public and improve the overall efficiency of insurance. Guideline G4.3 states that CPCUs should assist in improving the language, suitability, adaptability, and general efficacy of insurance contracts and surety bonds.

Legal Environment of Insurance; Ethics Canon 5

Direct Your Learning

Educational Objectives

After learning the content of this assignment, you should be able to:

1. Describe the common-law system.

2. Contrast civil and criminal law.

3. Explain how liability is determined and remedied under tort law.

4. Explain the ways in which contract law influences the insurance industry.

5. Given a case, determine whether the elements of a contract are present.

6. Explain how void, voidable, and canceled contracts are unenforceable.

7. Explain how fraud, concealment or misrepresentation, mistake, duress, or undue influence affect the genuineness of assent and insurance contract enforcement.

8. Describe the common agency relationships in the insurance industry.

9. Paraphrase, interpret, and apply the ethical standards set forth in Canon 5—Maintaining and Raising Professional Standards—and the related Rules and Guidelines of the Code.

10. Define or describe each of the Key Words and Phrases for this assignment.

Study Materials

Required Reading:

■ Foundations of Risk Management and Insurance
  • Chapter 9
■ Code of Professional Ethics
  • Canon 5 (pages 2.36–2.40, 3.12–3.13)
  • HCS-108 (page 5.17)
  • HCS-111 (page 5.21)
  • HCS-114 (pages 5.26–5.27)

Study Aids:

■ SMART Practice Exam CD-ROM
■ SMART Study Aids Review Notes and Flash Cards—Assignment 9

Outline

■ **Legal Foundations**

    A. Common Law

    B. Criminal and Civil Law

■ **Tort Law**

    A. Negligence

    B. Intentional Torts

       1. Strict Liability

    C. Remedies

■ **Contract Law**

    A. Elements of an Enforceable Contract

       1. Agreement

       2. Capacity to Contract

       3. Consideration

       4. Legal Purpose

    B. Oral and Temporary Contracts

    C. Contract Enforcement

       1. Void, Voidable, and Canceled Contracts

       2. Genuine Assent

■ **Agency Law**

■ **Summary**

■ **Canon 5–Maintaining and Raising Professional Standards (Code)**

    A. Rule R5.1–Bring Qualified People Into the Business

    B. Rule R5.2–Assist Others in Pursuing CPCU and Other Studies

    C. Rule R5.3–Support Measures to Foster Competence and Ethical Conduct

    D. Rule R5.4–Support Regulatory Investigations

    E. Guidelines

       1. Guideline G5.1–Setting an Example

       2. Guideline G5.2–Encouraging Others' Professional Development

    F. Other Related Code Provisions

    G. Relevant Hypothetical Case Studies

    H. Review Question

■ **Hypothetical Case Studies**

    A. HCS-108

       1. Case HCS-108

       2. Opinion HCS-108

    B. HCS-111

       1. Case HCS-111

       2. Opinion HCS-111

    C. HCS-114

       1. Case HCS-114

       2. Opinion HCS-114

Key Words and Phrases

Define or describe each of the words and phrases listed below.

Civil-law system (p. 9.3)

Common-law system (p. 9.3)

Doctrine of *stare decisis* (p. 9.3)

Criminal law (p. 9.4)

Civil law (p. 9.4)

Tort (p. 9.6)

Tortfeasor (p. 9.6)

Negligence (p. 9.7)

Proximate cause (p. 9.8)

Intentional tort (p. 9.8)

Strict liability, or absolute liability (p. 9.9)

Compensatory damages (p. 9.10)

Special damages (p. 9.10)

General damages (p. 9.10)

Punitive, or exemplary damages (p. 9.10)

Injunction (p. 9.11)

Contract (p. 9.11)

Promisor (p. 9.11)

Promisee (p. 9.11)

Privity of contract (p. 9.12)

Breach of contract (p. 9.12)

Consideration (p. 9.14)

Flat cancellation (p. 9.15)

Binder (p. 9.17)

Void contract (p. 9.19)

Voidable contract (p. 9.19)

Canceled contract (p. 9.19)

Genuine assent (p. 9.20)

Fraud (p. 9.20)

Material fact (p. 9.20)

Duress (p. 9.22)

Undue influence (p. 9.22)

Agency (p. 9.23)

Review Questions

1. Explain the difference between civil-law systems and common-law systems (p. 9.3)

2. Describe how a court resolves a case when using the doctrine of *stare decisis*. (p. 9.3)

3. Describe the analysis of prior cases a court uses to resolve a case in common law using the doctrine of *stare decisis*. (p. 9.4)

4. Identify the types of legal matters for which the following laws are applied. (p. 9.4)

   a. Criminal law

   b. Civil law

5. Contrast the burden of proof requirements for criminal and civil law. (p. 9.4)

6. Identify the aspects of the insurance industry that are influenced by the following types of civil law. (p. 9.6)

   a.   Tort law

   b.   Contract law

   c.   Agency law

7. List three broad tort classifications that result in legal liability. (p. 9.6)

8. Identify the four essential elements of negligence required for a plaintiff to bring a liability lawsuit based on negligence. (p. 9.7)

9. Describe the criterion used by courts to evaluate the duty of care conduct of a defendant. (p. 9.7)

10. Identify two situations in which strict liability can be imposed by tort law. (p. 9.9)

11. Explain the type of tort action remedy provided by the following. (pp. 9.10–9.11)

    a.   Compensatory damages

    b.   Special damages

c. General damages

d. Punitive damages

e. Injunction

12. Identify the four elements essential to the formation of any
    enforceable contract. (p. 9.12)

13. Identify each of the following factors in establishing an
    enforceable contract. (p. 9.12)

    a. Requirements for a valid offer to exist

    b. Alternatives for the response to an offer

14. Describe the consideration each party pays when forming an insurance contract. (p. 9.14)

15. Describe the circumstances in which the courts might refuse to enforce an otherwise valid insurance contract on grounds that it is against the public interest. (p. 9.15)

16. Explain why a void contract is not legally enforceable or binding. (p. 9.19)

17. Identify how and when a legally enforceable contract may be canceled. (p. 9.19)

18. Identify circumstances in which an insurance contract might be unenforceable on grounds that genuine assent is lacking. (p. 9.20)

19. Identify the six elements courts consider when evaluating allegations of fraud. (p. 9.20)

20. Explain how concealment and misrepresentation might affect genuine assent in an insurance contract. (p. 9.20)

21. Describe how an agent's actual and apparent authority is established. (pp. 9.23–9.24)

22. Identify the obligations of the following parties in an agency relationship. (p. 9.24)

    a.   Agent's fiduciary duty to principal (producer to insurer)

    b.   Principal's duty to agent (insurer to producer)

23. Describe the questions the court must answer to establish the existence of an agency contract in the following types of cases. (p. 9.24)

    a.   Insurance contract cases

    b.   Tort cases between an insurer and its employees

24. In what four general ways can a CPCU assist in maintaining and raising professional standards in the insurance business? (*Code*, p. 2.36)

25. HCS-108 involves John Johnson, a longtime CPCU. Because Johnson was not bound by the Code of Professional Ethics, the Board of Ethical Inquiry (BEI) could take no disciplinary action against him even though he did violate Rule R5.2 of the Code. (*Code*, p. 5.17)

    a.   What did Johnson do—or not do—that violated Rule R5.2?

    b.   Assuming he were subject to the Code, what disciplinary action(s) would the BEI most likely consider in Johnson's case?

Application Questions

1. Martin Blasting Company was hired to remove a large rock that was preventing a builder from pouring the foundation of a new office building. Martin Blasting used dynamite to break the large rock into smaller pieces that could be removed from the job site. Two neighboring buildings were damaged by the blast, and three workers in those two buildings suffered injuries. (pp. 9.6–9.11)

   a. Explain whether Martin Blasting can be held liable.

   b. If Martin Blasting is held liable, describe the types of damages it may have to pay.

2. Anthony wants to purchase auto insurance on his new minivan. He enters Jenn Insurance Agency and tells Jenn that he would like to purchase auto insurance. Explain whether each of the following constitutes an offer and/or acceptance of an enforceable insurance contract. (pp. 9.11–9.23)

   a. Anthony completes an insurance application for Millwright Auto Insurance Company.

   b. Millwright Auto issues a policy.

c. Anthony tells Jenn that he likes the quote that Millwright Auto has provided and pays Jenn the premium.

3. Jim has noticed that his neighbor often falls asleep with candles burning in the living room and kitchen. Jim approaches Jenn Insurance Agency in an attempt to purchase homeowners insurance coverage on his neighbor's house. Jim thinks he has the opportunity to make a profit because, he believes, "it is only a matter of time before my neighbor's house catches fire." Jenn sells Jim a homeowners' insurance policy on the neighbor's house because she did not notice that the address Jim supplied on the application was not his address, but his neighbor's. Jim pays the premium and leaves with a copy of the insurance policy issued by Millwright Homeowners Insurance Company. Determine whether Jim's recently purchased insurance policy has all of the elements of a contract. (pp. 9.12–9.16)

4. Amanda is the loan officer for Surewell Bank and Trust (SB&T), a local bank that primarily provides mortgage loans to homeowners. Amanda was instructed by her boss to try to get mortgage borrowers to purchase their homeowners insurance from Millwright Homeowners Insurance Company, a local insurer for which SB&T distributes homeowners and auto insurance policies. Amanda has been telling applicants that they have a much better chance of getting the loan approved if they purchase homeowners insurance from Millwright Homeowners Insurance Company through her. Describe the influence Amanda's actions may have on genuine assent. (pp. 9.20–9.23)

5. Describe two specific ways a CPCU candidate can accomplish each of the following. (*Code*, pp. 2.36–2.40, 3.12–3.13)

   a.   Help attract qualified individuals into the insurance business

   b.   Encourage other people in insurance to aspire to the highest levels of professional competence and achievement

   c.   Encourage and assist other students of insurance

   d.   Set an example of professional behavior that serves as an inspirational model for others

Answers to Assignment 9 Questions

NOTE: These answers are provided to give students a basic understanding of acceptable types of responses. They often are not the only valid answers and are not intended to provide an exhaustive response to the questions.

Review Questions

1. Civil-law systems are based on a comprehensive code of written laws that apply to all legal questions. Common-law systems do not rely on written laws to answer all legal questions, but rely on prior case rulings, or precedents.

2. Courts resolve cases using the doctrine of *stare decisis* by following earlier court decisions when the same issues arise.

3. A court performs the following analysis of prior cases when resolving a case in common law using the doctrine of *stare decisis*:

   • Seeks similar cases in its own state

   • Seeks similar cases in other states

   • Analyzes rulings in reasonably similar cases

   • Determines distinctions and similarities in the current case and prior cases

   • If situations are unprecedented, the judge consults all applicable law in an attempt to arrive at a fair decision

4. Civil and criminal law apply to the following types of legal matters:

   a. Criminal law—defines offenses; regulates the investigating, charging, and trying of accused offenders; and establishes punishments for convicted offenders.

   b. Civil law—applies to all legal matters that are not crimes and that do not involve private rights.

5. The burden of proof requirement for criminal law requires the prosecution to establish guilt beyond a reasonable doubt. In civil-law cases, the injured party is required to establish a case by a preponderance of evidence.

6. The insurance industry is influenced by the following types of civil law:

   a. Tort law—affects the determination of legal liability under liability insurance policies.

   b. Contract law—affects the interpretation of insurance policies.

   c. Agency law—determines the relationship between insurers and their producers.

7. Three tort classifications of legal liability are (1) negligence, (2) intentional torts, and (3) strict liability torts.

8. A plaintiff can bring a liability lawsuit for negligence if the following four essential elements for negligence are met:

   (1) The defendant owed a legal liability of care to the plaintiff.

   (2) The defendant breached the duty of care owed to the plaintiff.

   (3) The defendant's breach of duty was the proximate cause of the plaintiff's injury or damage.

   (4) The plaintiff suffered actual injury or damage.

9. Courts evaluate the duty of care conduct of a defendant by applying the reasonably prudent person test. The fact-finder determines whether the defendant behaved in a way that a reasonable person of ordinary prudence would behave under similar circumstances.

10. The following are two situations in which strict liability can be imposed by tort law:

(1) Ultrahazardous activities—inherently dangerous activities that might result in harming another, including using dangerous substances, engaging in dangerous activities, keeping wild animals in captivity, or keeping domesticated animals known to be abnormally dangerous

(2) Sale of dangerously defective products—sale of products that are defective and unreasonably dangerous to the person or property of users or consumers

11. Applicable tort remedies are as follows:

a. Compensatory damages—payment awarded to indemnify a victim for actual harm. The amount represents monetary losses actually sustained plus any additional monetary losses inferred from the facts and circumstances of the case.

b. Special damages—compensatory damages for actual losses the plaintiff claims resulted from the defendant's wrongful act, such as medical expenses, damage to property, and damage resulting from loss of use of the damaged property.

c. General damages—compensatory damages that do not have an economic value and are presumed to follow from the type of wrong claimed by the plaintiff, such as pain and suffering, mental anguish, bereavement, and loss of consortium.

d. Punitive damages—payments awarded, over and above what is awarded as compensatory damages, to punish a defendant for a reckless, malicious, or deceitful act or to deter similar conduct.

e. Injunction—a court-ordered equitable remedy requiring a party to act or refrain from acting.

12. The following four elements are essential to the formation of an enforceable contract:

(1) Agreement

(2) Capacity to contract

(3) Consideration

(4) Legal purpose

13. The following factors are required to establish an enforceable contract:

a. Requirements for a valid offer to exist—intent to contract, definite terms, and communication to offeree

b. Alternatives for the response to an offer—accept the offer, reject the offer, or make a counter-offer

14. When forming an insurance contract, the insurer's consideration is its promise to make payment on the occurrence of an insured event. The insured's consideration is payment of the premium or the promise to pay the premium.

15. Courts may refuse to enforce an otherwise valid insurance contract if any the following circumstances are true about the contract:

• It tends to harm the public.

• It is illegal.

• It tends to increase crime or encourage violations of the law.

16. A void contract is not legally enforceable or binding, because it lacks one or more elements of an enforceable contract.

17. A legally enforceable contract may be canceled after it is acknowledged as a legally valid contract and then terminated according to its own contractual terms.

18. An insurance contract may be unenforceable on grounds that genuine assent is lacking as a result of the following circumstances:
    - Fraud
    - Concealment or misrepresentation
    - Mistake
    - Duress
    - Undue influence

19. The courts consider the following six elements when evaluating allegations of fraud:
    (1) A false representation
    (2) Of a material fact
    (3) Knowingly made
    (4) With intent to deceive
    (5) On which the other party has placed justifiable reliance
    (6) To his or her detriment

20. Genuine assent in an insurance contract can be affected by the following:
    - Concealment—An insured's failure to disclose the answers to specific questions in the insurance application may give the insurer adequate grounds for denying any obligation to make payment under the policy.
    - Misrepresentation—Incorrect answers in the application regarding information that would affect the insurer's decision to provide or maintain insurance or to settle a claim.

21. An agent's actual authority is established through a formal written contract. An agent's apparent authority is established in situations in which it is reasonable for the customer to assume that an agency relationship exists.

22. The following are obligations in an agency relationship:
    a. Agent's fiduciary duty to principal (producer to insurer)
       - Loyalty and accounting
       - Obedience
       - Reasonable care
       - Information
    b. Principal's duty to agent (insurer to producer)
       - Agreed-upon period of employment
       - Duty of compensation
       - Duty of reimbursement
       - Duty of indemnity

23. Courts answer the following questions to establish the existence of an agency contract:
    a. Insurance contract cases—Courts must answer questions about the existence of the agency contract, the extent of the agent's authority, and the fulfillment of agency obligations.
    b. Tort cases between an insurer and its employees—Courts must answer questions about whether any employment relationship existed and whether the tort in question was committed within the scope of that employment.

24. A CPCU can assist in maintaining and raising professional standards in the insurance business by doing the following:

    - Bringing qualified people into the business
    - Assisting others in pursuing CPCU and other studies
    - Supporting measures to foster competence and ethical conduct
    - Supporting regulatory investigations

25. Regarding HCS-108

    a. Johnson violated Rule R5.2 by discouraging fellow employees from pursuing CPCU studies.

    b. If Johnson were subject to the Code, disciplinary action(s) the BEI would most likely consider would be admonition, reprimand, or public censure.

Application Questions

1. a. Martin Blasting can likely be found liable under strict liability because blasting is usually considered an inherently dangerous activity.

    b. Martin Blasting would be liable for compensatory damages for the bodily injury and property damage inflicted by the blasting. A court may award punitive damages when a defendant's actions were reckless, malicious, or deceitful; however, the facts of this case do not indicate that Martin's actions exhibited any of those qualities.

2. The status of an offer/acceptance is as follows:

    a. Anthony completes an insurance application—Completing an insurance application constitutes an offer.

    b. Millwright Auto issues a policy—Issuing a policy constitutes an acceptance.

    c. Anthony tells Jenn that the insurer's price quote is acceptable and pays the premium—Paying a premium constitutes an acceptance.

3. Whereas it appears that Jim and Millwright Homeowners have an agreement, the capacity to contract, and consideration, the contract does not appear to have a legal purpose. Jim does not have an insurable interest in the property he is attempting to insure. Insurance contracts lacking an insurable interest are not enforceable because they present moral hazards and are against the public's best interests.

4. Amanda is exerting economic pressure on loan applicants to persuade them to purchase homeowners insurance through her bank. In general, economic pressure does not constitute duress or undue influence; therefore, her actions should have no affect on genuine assent.

5. A CPCU candidate can perform the following tasks to accomplish goals:

    a. To help attract qualified individuals into the insurance business:

       - Discuss the benefits of working in the insurance industry with students in a college business or insurance class
       - Support the formation and maintenance of a scholarship fund through the local CPCU chapter

    b. To encourage other people in insurance to aspire to the highest levels of professional competence and achievement:

       - Provide positive feedback to coworkers and staff about their job performance
       - Set a good example

c.   To encourage and assist other students of risk management or insurance:
   - Mentor a coworker who is studying
   - Teach a course
d.   To set an example of professional behavior that serves as an inspirational model for others:
   - Perform professional duties competently
   - Speak before attendees at a CPCU educational meeting or program

The Insurance Policy; Ethics Canon 6

Direct Your Learning

Assignment

10

Study Materials

Required Reading:

■ Foundations of Risk Management and Insurance
  • Chapter 10
■ Code of Professional Ethics
  • Canon 6 (pages 2.41–2.47, 3.14-3.15)
  • HCS-110 (page 5.20)
  • HCS-111 (page 5.21)
  • HCS-117 (pages 5.31–5.33)

Study Aids:

■ SMART Practice Exam CD-ROM
■ SMART Study Aids Review Notes and Flash Cards— Assignment 10

Educational Objectives

After learning the content of this assignment, you should be able to:

1. Describe the following distinguishing characteristics of insurance policies:
   • Indemnity
   • Utmost good faith
   • Fortuitous losses
   • Contract of adhesion
   • Exchange of unequal amounts
   • Conditional
   • Nontransferable

2. Explain why some insurance policies do not have the distinguishing characteristics common to most insurance contracts.

3. Explain the role of the courts in resolving coverage disputes:
   • Compare questions of liability and questions of coverage.
   • Compare questions of law and questions of fact.

4. Describe waiver and estoppel.

5. Describe an insurer's alternatives in coverage disputes regarding property claims and liability claims.

6. Describe the damages and other penalties that may be assessed against an insurer in a coverage dispute.

7. Paraphrase, interpret, and apply the ethical standards set forth in Canon 6—Professional Relationships—and the related Rules and Guidelines of the Code.

8. Define or describe each of the Key Words and Phrases for this assignment.

Outline

Key Words and Phrases

Define or describe each of the words and phrases listed below.

Principle of indemnity (p. 10.4)

Contract of indemnity (p. 10.4)

Collateral source rule (p. 10.6)

Utmost good faith (p. 10.6)

Contract of adhesion (p. 10.9)

Reasonable expectations doctrine (p. 10.10)

Conditional contract (p. 10.13)

Declaratory judgment action (p. 10.16)

Waiver (p. 10.17)

Estoppel (p. 10.17)

Reservation of rights letter (p. 10.19)

Nonwaiver agreement (p. 10.20)

Review Questions

1. List the distinguishing characteristics of an insurance policy. (p. 10.4)

2. Identify reasons that an insurance policy might not fully indemnify an insured after a covered loss. (p. 10.5)

3. Explain the distinction between a contract of indemnity and a valued policy. (p. 10.5)

4. Identify two policy characteristics that help an insurer reduce or avoid moral hazards associated with indemnification. (p. 10.5)

5. Identify two reasons an insurance policy might be vulnerable to misrepresentation or opportunism and how the concept of utmost good faith helps prevent occurrences of such abuses. (p. 10.6)

6. Explain why insurance is not intended for losses that are not fortuitous losses. (p. 10.8)

7. Identify factors courts consider when determining whether to classify an insured as a sophisticated insured. (p. 10.10)

8. Explain how an insurer makes certain that the tangible consideration offered by the insured in an insurance contract is equitable. (p. 10.12)

9. Explain why insurance policies are conditional contracts. (p. 10.13)

10. Identify possible causes of coverage disputes between insurers and insureds. (p. 10.15)

11. Describe insurance-related issues that may be resolved through the courts. (pp. 10.15–1.17)

12. Describe issues that might be resolved by a declaratory judgment action. (p. 10.16)

13. Describe circumstances in insurance that might give rise to waiver and/or estoppel. (p. 10.17)

14. Describe the sequence of events from which estoppel generally arises in insurance. (p. 10.17)

15. Describe how waiver and estoppel differ regarding the intention to relinquish rights. (pp. 10.17–10.18)

16. List an insurer's alternatives when an insured files a claim (property or liability). (pp. 10.19–10.21)

17. Identify the two purposes of a reservation of rights letter in a claim investigation. (p. 10.19)

18. Describe the extent of a liability insurer's duty to defend the insured. (p. 10.21)

19. List the benefits of an insurer's sound legal defense. (p. 10.22)

20. Identify the additional payments an insurer may be required to pay if the insurer has mishandled a claim. (p. 10.22)

21. Describe types of insurer behavior that may provide a basis for a bad-faith claim, possibly resulting in the imposition of punitive damages. (p. 10.24)

22. What sorts of legal limitations on the scope of their professional duties should CPCUs be aware of? (*Code*, p. 2.41)

23. Under what circumstances may a CPCU disclose confidential or privileged information? (*Code*, pp. 2.41–2.42)

24. In HCS-110, what actions did Ann Underwriter take that were considered a violation of Rule R6.1, which requires CPCUs to keep informed of legal limitations? (*Code*, p. 5.20)

25. HCS-111 involves a case in which an insurance company representative discloses information to the company underwriting department but not to regulatory authorities. Would the information disclosure to the underwriting department constitute a violation of Rule R6.2? (*Code*, p. 5.21)

Application Questions

1. Tony was bragging to his new neighbors about how little he paid for his auto insurance for his sixteen-year-old son, who has been ticketed for speeding three times in the last two months. When one neighbor asked how he was able to buy insurance for such a low premium, Tony replied that he told the insurer that his son is twenty-five years old and has a perfect driving record. The neighbor asked Tony if he thought that what he was doing was wrong. Tony responded, "No, I've been paying premiums for twenty years without a claim. I'm just getting a discount they owe me anyway." Which of the distinguishing characteristics of insurance policies is Tony's policy missing? (pp.10.4–10.14)

2. Millwright Art Museum (MAM) paid $5 million at a June 2005 auction for the only known painting by Cassandra Cole, a famous nineteenth century sculptor. MAM insured the painting under a valued policy for $5.1 million with Art Insurance Company, which renewed the policy in June 2006. On August 1, more than fifty paintings by Cole were discovered in a storage area at a European museum. On September 4, 2006, a fire destroyed the wing of the MAM where the Cole painting was on display. The market value of the original Cole painting at the time of the loss was only $1 million. Should Art Insurance pay the full $5.1 million valued policy? Would that payment violate the principle of indemnity? (pp. 10.4–10.6)

The Mark's Motorcycle Case. Mark was riding his motorcycle on the shoulder of the road to pass traffic that was at a standstill during rush hour. As Mark approached Bill's car, Bill opened his driver-side door directly into Mark's path. Mark suffered a broken arm and back injuries as a result of the collision with Bill's door. Bill contends that he was opening the door to see why traffic was stopped. Mark contends that Bill intended to injure him with the door. Bill's auto policy contains an exclusion for intentional acts.

3. *Mark's Motorcycle*. What questions of liability, coverage, law, or fact may a court be asked to interpret based on Mark and Bill's accident? (pp. 10.14–10.19)

4. *Mark's Motorcycle*. The court decides that Bill is liable for Mark's injuries but rules that Bill did not intentionally open the door to injure Mark. Nevertheless, Bill's auto insurer denies the claim based on the intentional acts exclusion. Bill sues his auto insurer. What types of damages might Bill be eligible for? (pp. 10.22–10.24)

5. *Mark's Motorcycle*. Bill's insurance agent, a CPCU, was overheard at a cocktail party telling a group of friends the story of Mark and Bill's accident. The agent used Bill's real name and facts about the case in relaying the story to his friends. Does the agent's story constitute a violation of Rule R6.2 regarding confidential information? (*Code*, pp. 2.41–2.47, 3.14–3.15)

Answers to Assignment 10 Questions

NOTE: These answers are provided to give students a basic understanding of acceptable types of responses. They often are not the only valid answers and are not intended to provide an exhaustive response to the questions.

Review Questions

1. The following are the seven distinguishing characteristics of an insurance policy:
   - Indemnity
   - Utmost good faith
   - Fortuitous losses
   - Contract of adhesion
   - Exchange of unequal amounts
   - Conditional
   - Nontransferable

2. An insurance policy might not fully indemnify an insured after a covered loss because most insurance policies contain a dollar limit, a deductible, or other provisions or limitations on the amount to be paid.

3. A contract of indemnity compensates the insured only for the value of the loss. In a valued insurance policy, the insurer agrees to pay a preestablished dollar amount in the event of an insured total loss, which may overindemnify or underindemnify the insured.

4. In order to reduce or avoid moral hazards associated with indemnification, an insurance policy should not do the following:
   - Overindemnify the insured
   - Indemnify insureds more than once per loss

5. An insurance policy may be vulnerable to misrepresentation or opportunism for the following two reasons:
   (1) One party to a contract has information the other party does not (information asymmetry).
   (2) The costly verification of information may lead an insurer to fail to verify information provided by the insured.

   These situations could affect underwriting decisions and lead to adverse selection. The concept of utmost good faith obligates all parties to act with complete honesty and to disclose all relevant facts and therefore helps prevent these situations.

6. Insurance is not intended for losses that are not fortuitous because if an insured knows of a loss in advance and the insurer does not, the insured has an information advantage over the insurer. This situation promotes adverse selection, thereby increasing the losses in the pool the insurer insures.

7. The factors a court may consider to determine whether an insured is a sophisticated insured include the following:
   - Size of the insured organization
   - Size of the organization's risk management department
   - Use of an insurance broker or legal counsel with expertise in insurance policies
   - Relative bargaining power of the insured in relation to the insurer

8. An insurer makes sure that the tangible consideration exchanged by the insured for an insurance contract is equitable by charging a premium that is directly proportional to the insured's expected losses on an actuarially sound basis.

9. Insurance policies are conditional contracts because the insurer is obligated to pay for losses incurred by the insured only if the insured has fulfilled all of the policy conditions.

10. Causes of coverage disputes between insurers and insureds include the following:
    - Disagreements over facts of the case
    - Interpretation of the insurance policy
    - Actions or inactions of the insurer or insured
    - Application of waiver and estoppel

11. Courts resolve the following four types of insurance-related issues:
    (1) Questions of liability—Courts can determine whether the insured is legally obligated to pay damages to a third party.
    (2) Questions of coverage—Courts can interpret an insurance policy to determine whether the insurer is obligated to pay the claim.
    (3) Questions of law—Courts can determine how the laws apply to the facts at hand.
    (4) Questions of fact—Courts can hear the evidence and determine the facts.

12. A declaratory judgment action resolves questions of coverage, such as whether there has been an "occurrence," whether a given exclusion applies, or whether the insurer has an obligation to defend the insured against a specific set of allegations.

13. Waiver and estoppel may arise in insurance when an insured sues for payment of damages under a policy and the insurer denies the claim based on a defense such as fraud, misrepresentation, concealment, mistake, or breach of a condition.

14. In insurance law, estoppel generally arises from the following sequence of events:
    (1) The insurer falsely represents a material fact.
    (2) The insured assumes a reasonable reliance on the representation.
    (3) The insured suffers resulting injury or detriment.

15. In insurance law, a waiver is an intentional relinquishment of rights. In estoppel there is no intentional relinquishment of rights.

16. An insurer's alternatives when an insured files a claim include the following:
    - Deny the claim with appropriate justification (justified refusal)
    - Investigate the claim under a reservation of rights letter, nonwaiver agreement, or both
    - Investigate, defend, and/or pay the claim without any reservation

17. The following are two purposes of a reservation of rights letter in a claim investigation:
    (1) To protect the insurer's right to deny coverage later, if warranted, without facing the accusation that its earlier actions waived that right
    (2) To inform the insured that a coverage problem might exist and give the insured an opportunity to protect the insured's interests

18. A liability insurer's duty to defend the insured is broader than its duty to pay damages. The insurer must defend the insured whenever the plaintiff alleges damages that could conceivably be covered by the policy, even if a lawsuit appears to be groundless, false, or fraudulent.

19. A sound legal defense can benefit an insurer in the following ways:
    - A strong defense may result in a judgment favoring the insured in which no damages are paid.
    - A legal decision in the insured's favor may establish case law that discourages similar claims.
    - A strong defense signals plaintiffs' attorneys and would-be claimants that the insurer will vigorously defend similar claims rather than pay them.
    - Evidence introduced through a sound defense can reduce the amount of damages payable.

20. An insurer may be required to pay the following additional payments if a claim has been mishandled:
    - Compensatory damages for breach of contract
    - Fines or penalties assesses by regulatory authorities for violations of unfair claims settlement practices acts
    - Punitive damages for bad faith

21. An insurer's improper behaviors that might provide a basis for a bad-faith claim and possibly result in the imposition of punitive damages for bad faith include the following:
    - Wrongful denial of a claim
    - Delay of a claim investigation or payment
    - Improper investigation of a claim
    - Misrepresentation of material facts

22. CPCUs should beware of what constitutes the unauthorized practice of law or other professions. For example, they should not engage in the practice of law unless they are licensed attorneys and should not give advice about securities transactions unless they hold a securities license.

23. CPCUs should disclose confidential or privileged information only when required by law or only to a person who must have the information in order to discharge legitimate occupational or professional duties.

24. Underwriting practices predicated on the ethnic origin of the applicant would generally be considered unlawful discrimination under applicable state and federal statutes and regulations. By automatically classing as below average the applicants of one ethnic group who live in a rundown section of the city, Ann Underwriter would illustrate that she is ignorant of these legal limitations on her activities as an underwriter. She would not only have violated the Rule that requires her to keep informed but would also have violated Rule R6.1 by exceeding her legal limitations.

25. Regarding HCS-111, the CPCU had not breached any Rule of the Code unless he had a legal duty to report his findings to OSHA. He did not violate Rule R6.2 because the disclosure to the underwriting department was "made to a person who necessarily must have the information in order to discharge legitimate occupational or professional duties," a disclosure is specifically permitted.

Application Questions

1. Tony's policy fails to exhibit utmost good faith. Utmost good faith requires that a person applying for insurance make a full and fair disclosure of the risk presented by the loss exposures to be insured.

2. Valued policies can violate the principle of indemnity by underinsuring or overinsuring a particular loss exposure. In this case, Art Insurance would still pay the full $5.1 million because the policy was in force at the time of the loss and the painting was destroyed in the fire. The payment would violate the principle of indemnity.

3. Courts can be called on to answer questions of liability, coverage, law, or fact. In this case, the courts could be asked to determine the facts—whether Bill intentionally opened his door to cause the accident. The courts could also answer the question of who is liable for the accident—Mark by driving illegally on the shoulder of the road or Bill by opening his door. Finally, the courts may be asked to determine whether the exclusion for intentional acts in Bill's auto policy applies to this situation.

4. If Bill's insurer denies the claim even though the courts have ruled that Bill's actions were not intentional, Bill could be entitled to compensatory damages if he can show that he suffered a financial loss, such as the money he had to pay Mark for his injuries, as a result of the claim denial. Bill may also be able to collect punitive damages if he could prove bad faith on the part of his insurer. Bill would not collect any penalties under any unfair claims settlement practices act, because those penalties are generally paid to the state, not to the claimant.

5. Bill's agent, a CPCU, may have violated Rule R6.2 regarding confidential information. The agent had collected the information he shared at the cocktail party for business purposes (claim settlement), and he shared it with others who did not have a need for the information. It is unclear whether the information should be considered confidential. Whereas the information does not relate to Bill's health or income, it does have a direct bearing on his reputation and may therefore be sufficient to be considered confidential.

Actively capture information by using the open space in the SMART Review Notes to write out key concepts. Putting information into your own words is an effective way to push that information into your memory.

Insurance Policy Analysis; Ethics Canon 7

Direct Your Learning

Educational Objectives

After learning the content of this assignment, you should be able to:

1. Explain how the physical construction of an insurance policy influences policy analysis.

2. Given an insurance coverage case, explain how common policy provisions affect the coverage provided and the actions taken by the insured or insurer.

   • Describe the contents and purpose of the six common policy provisions of a property-casualty insurance policy.

   • Explain the six reasons that policies contain exclusions.

3. Differentiate between pre-loss and post-loss policy analysis.

4. Paraphrase, interpret, and apply the ethical standards set forth in Canon 7—Public Education—and the related Rules and Guidelines of the Code.

5. Define or describe each of the Key Words and Phrases for this assignment.

Study Materials

Required Reading:

■ Foundations of Risk Management and Insurance
   • Chapter 11

■ Code of Professional Ethics
   • Canon 7 (pages 2.48–2.52, 3.16–3.17)
   • HCS-106 (pages 5.13–5.14)
   • HCS-107 (pages 5.15–5.16)
   • HCS-109 (pages 5.18–5.19)

Study Aids:

■ SMART Practice Exam CD-ROM

■ SMART Study Aids Review Notes and Flash Cards—Assignment 11

Outline

- **Physical Construction of Insurance Policies**
  - A. Self-Contained and Modular Policies
  - B. Preprinted Forms
    1. Standard Forms
    2. Nonstandard Forms
  - C. Manuscript Forms
  - D. Related Documents
- **Common Policy Provisions**
  - A. Declarations
  - B. Definitions
  - C. Insuring Agreements
    1. Scope of Insuring Agreements
    2. Insuring Agreements for Extended, Additional, Supplemental Coverages
    3. Other Provisions Functioning as Insuring Agreements
  - D. Conditions
  - E. Exclusions
    1. Eliminate Coverage for Uninsurable Loss Exposures
    2. Assist in Managing Moral and Morale Hazards
    3. Reduce Likelihood of Coverage Duplications
    4. Eliminate Coverages Not Needed by the Typical Insured
    5. Eliminate Coverages Requiring Special Treatment
    6. Assist in Keeping Premiums Reasonable
  - F. Miscellaneous Provisions
- **Policy Analysis**
  - A. Pre-Loss Policy Analysis
  - B. Post-Loss Policy Analysis
    1. DICE Review
    2. Determining Amounts Payable

- **Canon 7–Public Education**
  - A. Rule R7.1–Support Efforts to Provide Information
  - B. Rule R7.2–Provide Accurate Information
    1. Guideline G7.4–Deceptive Advertising or Business Practice
  - C. Other Guidelines
    1. Guideline G7.1–All CPCUs Should Improve Public Understanding
    2. Guidelines G7.2 and G7.3–Remain Current in Areas of Change
    3. Guideline G7.5–Limitations of Insurance
    4. Guideline G7.6–Objective Public Information
  - D. Related Code Provisions
  - E. Relevant Hypothetical Case Studies
  - F. Review Questions
- **Summary**
- **Hypothetical Case Studies**
  - A. HCS-106
    1. Case HCS-106
    2. Opinion HCS-106
  - B. HCS-107
    1. Case HCS-107
    2. Opinion HCS-107
  - C. HCS-109
    1. Case HCS-109
    2. Opinion HCS-109

Key Words and Phrases

Define or describe each of the words and phrases listed below.

Monoline policy (p. 11.3)

Package policy (p. 11.3)

Coverage part (p. 11.3)

Self-contained policy (p. 11.4)

Modular policy (p. 11.4)

Manuscript form (p. 11.9)

Insuring agreement (p. 11.16)

Policy condition (p. 11.23)

Review Questions

1. Identify the advantages of the modular approach to policy construction. (p. 11.5)

2. Explain why insurance professionals might find policy analysis more difficult with multiple self-contained policies than with a single modular policy. (p. 11.5)

3. Differentiate between pre-printed and manuscript forms. (pp. 11.8–11.10)

4. Identify the types of related documents that might become part of and alter an insurance policy by being attached or referenced within the policy. (pp. 11.10–11.12)

5. List two general policy interpretation rules applied when an endorsement conflicts with the policy to which it is attached. (p. 11.11)

6. Describe the six common policy provisions contained in an insurance policy. (pp. 11.13–11.29)

7. Describe two broad categories of insuring agreements that clarify the scope of the insurer's obligations. (p. 11.20)

8. Explain the distinction between coverage provided by named-perils and that provided by special-form property insurance. (p. 11.20)

9. List the six purposes of exclusions in an insurance policy. (p. 11.24)

10. Identify loss exposures typically excluded from a policy because they are considered uninsurable. (p. 11.25)

11. Explain how policy exclusions assist in reducing moral and morale loss exposures. (p. 11.26)

12. Explain the importance of conducting pre-loss policy analysis for each of the following entities. (p. 11.30)

    a.   Insurer

    b.   Insured

13. Identify the skills required to conduct a pre-loss policy analysis. (p. 11.31)

14. Identify sources of information an insured uses to develop scenarios for pre-loss policy analysis. (p. 11.31)

15. Describe how an insurance professional uses the DICE method in post-loss policy analysis. (pp. 11.32–11.33)

16. Many CPCUs are not in leadership positions within the insurance business. How can they improve the public understanding of insurance and risk management? (*Code*, pp. 2.48–2.49)

17. To avoid violating Rule R7.2 – Provide Accurate Information, what types of activities should a CPCU avoid? (*Code*, pp. 2.48–2.49)

18. HCS-106 involves Polly Browne, a CPCU who advertises health insurance for "anyone, regardless of age or health." How was her conduct evaluated in light of Rule R7.2? (*Code*, pp. 5.13–5.14)

Application Questions

1. Eileen, the owner of a high-rise office complex in New York City, has been negotiating with a consortium of insurers to design a property insurance program to provide enough coverage for her multi-billion dollar property. Eileen was not satisfied with the wording of the flood exclusion on the standard form the insurers wanted to use, so she negotiated the wording of the exclusion with the insurers. While the policy was in force, Eileen's property was damaged when a water tower on the roof of the building ruptured and poured millions of gallons of water through the building. Eileen's insurer denied the claim based on the wording of the flood exclusion. Eileen's broker told her not to worry because in court cases involving the standard flood exclusion, the courts have "always found for the insured" in similar situations. Is Eileen's broker correct in telling Eileen not to worry? Will the courts side with her? Why or why not? (pp.11.3–11.10)

2. On January 1, 2006, Pennsylvania changed its workers' compensation (WC) laws to provide WC benefits for individuals injured on their commute to or from work. An employee of PSB Manufacturing was injured on his way to work on February 15, 2006, and filed a WC claim. PSB's WC insurer denied the claim, stating that, because its policy was issued in October of 2005, it does not cover changes to laws that occur during the policy period. PSB's WC insurer is using the NCCI's Workers' Compensation and Employers' Liability Insurance Policy Form (WC 00 00 00 A) with the relevant provision shown below. Was PSB's WC insurer justified in denying the claim? Why or why not? (pp. 11.10–11.12)

WORKERS' COMPENSATION INSURANCE

B. We Will Pay

We will pay promptly when due the benefits required of you by the workers' compensation law.

GENERAL SECTION

C. Workers' Compensation Law

Workers' Compensation Law means the workers or workmen's compensation law and occupational disease law of each state or territory named in Item 3. A. of the Information Page. It includes any amendments to that law which are in effect during the policy period. It does not include any federal workers or workmen's compensation law, any federal occupational disease law or the provisions of any law that provide non-occupational disability benefits.

Source: Workers' Compensation and Employers' Liability Policy
WC 00 00 00 A, Copyright 1991, National Council on Compensation
Insurance. All rights reserved.

3. John's car was broken into while he was at a baseball game. His driver side window was broken and his golf clubs, radar detector, and laptop computer were stolen from the trunk. John filed a claim with his auto insurer. The insurer paid for the damage to the car, but told John that the theft of his personal property was excluded from coverage. The claim adjuster told John to file a claim for the stolen property with his homeowners insurer. Why would John's auto insurer exclude this type of claim? (pp. 11.26–11.27)

4. In what specific ways can a CPCU candidate or CPCU accomplish each of the following? (*Code*, pp. 2.48–2.52, 3.16–3.17)

   a. Assist in keeping the public informed of insurance-related legislation that might favorably or adversely affect the public

   b. Communicate objective and factual information about insurance to the public

   c. Stress the importance of loss prevention and loss reduction

5. A state legislature recently considered a bill that would repeal its no-fault auto insurance law and support the equitable distribution of loss costs. Luis Sanchez, CPCU, strongly believed that this law should not be repealed, and he urged other CPCUs to lobby against the bill. Another member of the local CPCU chapter questioned whether it was appropriate under the Code of Professional Ethics for CPCUs to take a position on political issues. (*Code*, p. 3.17)

a.   Was it appropriate for Luis Sanchez to lobby against this bill?

b.   Was it appropriate for Luis Sanchez to urge other CPCUs to lobby against this bill?

Answers to Assignment 11 Questions

NOTE: These answers are provided to give students a basic understanding of acceptable types of responses. They often are not the only valid answers and are not intended to provide an exhaustive response to the questions.

Review Questions

1. The advantages of using the modular approach to policy construction include the following:
   - Carefully designed and coordinated provisions in the various forms minimize the possibility of gaps and overlaps.
   - Consistent terminology, definitions, and policy language make coverage interpretation easier for the insured.
   - Fewer forms are required to meet a wide range of needs.
   - Underwriting is simplified because much of the basic information that must be analyzed applies to all lines of insurance.
   - Adverse selection problems can be reduced.
   - Insurers often give a package discount when several coverages are included in the same policy.

2. Insurance professionals might find policy analysis more difficult with multiple self-contained policies than with a single modular policy for the following reasons:
   - Self-contained policies often include multiple copies of related forms and endorsements, use inconsistent terminology, and have more gaps and overlaps in coverage.
   - Modular policies offer a better framework for policy analysis.

3. Most insurance policies are assembled from one or more preprinted forms, which are designed to be used by many insureds. The forms themselves are not altered or customized for each insured. Manuscript forms are unique forms developed through negotiation between the insurer and insured. Pre-printed standard forms are the easiest forms to evaluate during policy analysis because they are widely used and more consistently interpreted by the courts and because insurance professionals generally have more experience working with these forms. Manuscript forms are the most difficult forms to interpret because they often contain unique wording and can vary widely in their interpretation.

4. The following documents may become part of an insurance policy by being attached or referenced within the policy:
   - Completed application—In some jurisdictions, statutes require that any written application be made part of the policy for certain types of insurance.
   - Endorsements—Endorsements are added to modify a basic policy form. Policies in several lines of business have "standard" endorsements that are included in most of the policies written in that line.
   - Insurer's bylaws—With certain types of policies, such as those with mutual or reciprocal insurers, the insurer's bylaws regarding rights and duties are specified in the policy.
   - Relevant statutes—With certain types of insurance, such as workers' compensation and auto no-fault insurance, the relevant statutes are incorporated into the policy by reference.
   - Insurer's rating manual—Some policies incorporate the insurer's rating manual by referring to it in the policy language.
   - Miscellaneous documents—Some frequently incorporated documents include premium notes, inspection reports, and specification sheets or operating manuals relating to safety equipment or procedures.

5. The following two policy interpretation rules apply when an endorsement contradicts the policy to which it is attached:

   (1) An endorsement takes precedence over any conflicting terms in the policy.

   (2) A handwritten endorsement supersedes a computer-printed or typewritten one.

6. The following six policy provisions are commonly contained in an insurance policy:

   (1) Declarations—contain information regarding who or what is covered, and where and when coverage applies.

   (2) Definitions—define terms used throughout the entire policy or form.

   (3) Insuring agreements—state for each line of insurance offered in the policy that the insurer will, under certain circumstances, make a payment or provide a service.

   (4) Conditions—qualify an otherwise enforceable promise of the insurer. Examples are the insured's obligation to pay premiums, report losses promptly, provide appropriate documentation for losses, cooperate with the insurer in any legal proceedings, and refrain from jeopardizing an insurer's rights to recover from responsible third parties.

   (5) Exclusions—state what the insurer does not intend to cover, thereby limiting coverage and clarifying the coverages granted by the insurer.

   (6) Miscellaneous provisions—deal with the relationship between the insured and the insurer or help to establish working procedures for implementing the policy.

7. Two broad categories of insuring agreements that clarify the scope of the insurer's obligations are as follows:

   (1) Comprehensive, all-purpose insuring agreements, which provide extremely broad, unrestricted coverage that applies to virtually all causes of loss or all situations. The coverage is clarified and narrowed by exclusions, definitions, and other policy provisions.

   (2) Limited or single-purpose insuring agreements, which restrict coverage to certain causes of loss or to certain situations. Exclusions, definitions, and other policy provisions serve to clarify and narrow coverage, but may also broaden the coverage.

8. Coverage provided by named-perils and special-form property insurance differ as follows:

   • A named-perils policy restricts coverage to the perils (causes of loss) identified in the policy.

   • A special-form policy provides protection against perils that the form does not specifically exclude.

9. The following are six purposes of exclusions:

   (1) Eliminate coverage for uninsurable loss exposures

   (2) Assist in managing moral and morale hazards

   (3) Reduce likelihood of coverage duplications

   (4) Eliminate coverages not needed by the typical insured

   (5) Eliminate coverages requiring special treatment

   (6) Assist in keeping premiums reasonable

10. The following loss exposures are typically excluded from a policy because they are considered uninsurable:

   • War

   • Intentional acts of the insured

   • Earthquake

- Flood damage to fixed-location property
- Normal wear and tear
- Inherent vice

11. Policy exclusions assist in reducing moral hazard incentives by eliminating coverage for intentional harmful results. Some exclusions assist in managing morale hazards by making insureds themselves bear the losses that result from their own carelessness.

12. It is important for both the insurer and the insured to conduct pre-loss policy analysis for the following reasons:

    a. Insurer—to be better able to answer the insured's questions regarding coverage before any claims are filed and to ensure that the insurance policies being sold are the appropriate policies for the insured's loss exposures

    b. Insured—to ensure that the insurance policy being purchased is appropriate for their loss exposures

13. The following skills are required to conduct an accurate pre-loss policy analysis:

    - Understanding the alternative ways in which insurance policies customarily describe coverage in addressing loss exposures
    - Identifying and evaluating insurance policy provisions that depart from the customary approach
    - Understanding the loss exposure or loss exposures to which the policy applies

14. An insured uses the following sources of information to develop scenarios for pre-loss policy analysis:

    - Past loss experience—Insureds examine past losses and analyze the current insurance policy to ensure that it will provide coverage if any of the past losses were to occur again in the future.
    - Friends, neighbors, co-workers, and family members—Particularly for insureds who have never suffered a loss before, such people can provide information about losses and the claim process.
    - Insurance producers or customer service representatives consulted in the insurance transaction—Insureds may seek information from insured's representatives, who may have specialized knowledge of loss exposures, an understanding of the alternative ways coverage is described, and an awareness of policy provisions that may depart from the customary wording.

15. An insurance professional uses the DICE method to create a decision tree to determine whether the insurance policy provides coverage. The DICE method represents four sections of a property-casualty policy: declarations, insuring agreement, conditions, and exclusions.

16. Many CPCUs, such as producers and claim representatives, deal directly with members of the public. These CPCUs can improve the public understanding of insurance and risk management by explaining insurance policies and transactions as clearly and completely as possible. CPCUs can also support CPCU Society chapter activities, such as speaker bureaus, that improve public understanding of insurance.

17. A CPCU should not engage in deceptive advertising or business practices that could mislead the public or contribute to widespread misunderstanding or misuse of insurance.

18. Rule R7.2 and Guideline G7.4 specifically instruct against engaging in deceptive advertising practices. In the opinion of the BEI, the advertising practices of the insurer would constitute deceptive advertising; therefore, Ms. Browne violated Rule R7.2.

Application Questions

1. Eileen should be worried. Her broker's comment that "courts always side with the insured" applies to the standard flood exclusion, which is an example of a contract of adhesion. However, Eileen negotiated the wording of the flood exclusion, which makes this policy a manuscript policy. Manuscript policies, because the insured participated in determining the wording of the policy, are not generally considered contracts of adhesion. Therefore, the court's interpretation of the standard flood exclusion may not be relevant to Eileen's case. The courts may or may not side with Eileen in answering the question of coverage in this manuscript policy.

2. The NCCI coverage form states that the policy includes any amendments to the law that are in effect during the coverage period. Therefore, PSB's WC insurer would not be justified in denying this claim.

3. The auto insurance policy excludes theft of personal property to avoid duplications in coverage. Theft of personal property is covered by most homeowners and renters policies; therefore, there is no need for this coverage in an auto policy.

4. A CPCU candidate or CPCU may engage in the following activities:

    a. To assist in keeping the public informed of insurance-related legislation: CPCUs could offer to write a weekly column for the local newspaper to inform the public of insurance-related legislation that might favorably or adversely affect the public.

    b. To communicate objective and factual information about insurance to the public: CPCUs could speak at civic events, providing objective and factual information about insurance to the public.

    c. To stress the importance of loss prevention and loss reduction: CPCUs could discuss the benefits of loss prevention and loss reduction with clients who believe they have full coverage and emphasize that insurance does not cover all loss exposures.

5. The Code applies as follows to Luis's political actions regarding the state legislation to repeal the no-fault auto insurance law:

    a. CPCUs are not prohibited from taking a position on proposed legislation and lobbying for that position. However, Luis must be scrupulously careful not to appear to act for either the American Institute for CPCU or the CPCU Society.

    b. It is entirely appropriate for Luis to encourage other CPCUs to share his political position, but each must act as an individual, not as a representative of either the American Institute or the CPCU Society.

Policy Analysis: Declarations and Insuring Agreement; Ethics Canon 8

Direct Your Learning

Educational Objectives

After learning the content of this assignment, you should be able to:

1. Given a case involving a property or liability insurance policy, analyze each of the following to determine whether coverage exists:

    *   Insured parties, including insured parties identified by name, insured parties identified by relationship, additional insured parties, multiple insured parties, and parties not insured

    *   Insurable interest

    *   Premiums

    *   Policy period and coverage territory provisions

    *   Insured events and cause of loss

2. Paraphrase, interpret, and apply the ethical standards set forth in Canon 8—Integrity of the CPCU Designation—and the related Rules and Guidelines of the Code.

3. Define or describe each of the Key Words and Phrases for this assignment.

Study Materials

Required Reading:

*   ■ Foundations of Risk Management and Insurance
    *   Chapter 12
*   ■ Code of Professional Ethics
    *   Canon 8 (pages 2.53–2.60, 3.18–3.20)
    *   HCS-120 (page 5.37)
    *   HCS-121 (page 5.38)

Study Aids:

*   ■ SMART Practice Exam CD-ROM
*   ■ SMART Study Aids Review Notes and Flash Cards—Assignment 12

Outline

■ **Declarations**

A. Insured Parties

1. Insured Parties Identified by Name

2. Insured Parties Identified by Relationship

3. Additional Insureds

4. Multiple Insured Parties and Separation of Interests

5. Parties Not Insured

B. Insurable Interest

1. Reasons for Insurable Interest Requirement

2. Basis of Insurable Interest

3. Multiple Parties With Insurable Interests

C. Premiums

D. Policy Period

E. Coverage Territory Provisions

■ **Insuring Agreement**

A. Insured Events in Property Insurance Policies

1. Covered Property

2. Covered Cause of Loss

3. Covered Consequences

4. Covered Location

5. Covered Period

B. Insured Events in Liability Insurance Policies

1. Covered Activity

2. Alleged Legal Responsibility to Pay Covered Damages

3. Covered Consequences

4. Covered Location

5. Covered Period

■ **Summary**

■ **Canon 8–Integrity of the CPCU Designation**

A. Rule R8.1–Use of the CPCU Designation and Key

1. Guideline G8.1–Authorized Uses of the CPCU Key and Designation

2. 1998 Advisory Opinion–Internet Use and Telephone Listings

B. Rule R8.2–Overstating CPCU

1. Guideline G8.2–Misrepresentation

C. Rule R8.3–Comparison With Non-CPCUs

D. Rule R8.4–Acting as a Representative of the American Institute

E. Other Related Code Provisions

F. Relevant Hypothetical Case Studies

G. Review Questions

■ **Hypothetical Case Studies**

A. HCS-120

1. Case HCS-120

2. Opinion HCS-120

B. HCS-121

1. Case HCS-121

2. Opinion HCS-121

Key Words and Phrases

Define or describe each of the words and phrases listed below.

Insured party (p. 12.6)

Named insured (p. 12.6)

Insurable interest (p. 12.6)

Loss payee (p. 12.7)

Loss payable clause (p. 12.7)

Mortgagee (p. 12.8)

Mortgage clause (p. 12.8)

Separation of interests provision (p. 12.11)

Bailee (p. 12.12)

No benefit to bailee provision (p. 12.12)

Assignment (p. 12.13)

Assignment provision (p. 12.13)

Factual expectancy (p. 12.17)

Joint tenancy (p. 12.18)

Tenancy by the entirety (p. 12.18)

Tenancy in common (p. 12.18)

Tenancy in partnership (p. 12.19)

Policy period (p. 12.19)

Policy schedule (p. 12.23)

Ensuing loss (p. 12.24)

Supplementary payments (p. 12.30)

Occurrence-basis coverage (p. 12.32)

Claims-made coverage (p. 12.32)

Retroactive date (p. 12.32)

Review Questions

1. Explain why it is important for an insurance professional to review the entire policy when performing the post-loss policy analysis. (p. 12.3)

2. What information is typically found in the declarations section (on the declarations page)? (p. 12.4)

3. Identify an important distinction between "you" and "an insured" in a typical insurance policy. (p. 12.6)

4. List the types of insured parties for whom an insurance policy might provide rights. (p. 12.7)

5. Identify actions designated to the first named insured in most insurance policies. (p. 12.7)

6. Describe how the rights under a policy of a mortgagee differ from those of a typical loss payee. (pp. 12.8–12.9)

7. Identify parties that may qualify for status as an insured on the bases of the following relationships. (p. 12.10)

   a.   Members of a class

   b.   Legal substitutes for the named insured

8. Explain how the qualifications for insurable interest differs in life insurance and property-casualty insurance policies. (p. 12.14)

9. Identify three reasons insurance policies have an insurable interest requirement. (p. 12.15)

10. Describe how insurable interest might arise from the following bases. (pp. 12.16–12.17))

   a. Ownership in property

   b. Contractual obligations

   c. Exposure to legal liability

   d. Factual expectations

   e. Representation of another party

11. Describe how the extent of insurable interest regarding property
    varies in each of the following types of joint ownership.
    (pp. 12.18–12.19)

   a. Joint tenancy

   b. Tenancy by the entirety

   c. Tenancy in common

   d. Tenancy in partnership

12. Identify the elements required in each of the following types of insurance for an event to meet the requirements of an insured event. (p. 12.22)

   a. Property insurance

   b. Liability insurance

13. Describe the coverage approaches and burden of proof requirements for basic, broad, and special form coverage. (p. 12.24)

14. Describe categories of covered consequences under the following types of policies. (p. 12.25–12.28)

   a. Property insurance policy

   b. Liability insurance policy

15. Identify the two locations relevant to a covered liability event. (p. 12.31)

16. Explain the difference in coverage triggers for occurrence-based and claims-made coverage. (p. 12.32)

17. Could a CPCU be sanctioned under the Code for using the CPCU key or the letters "CPCU" in a way not permitted by the Guidelines and Advisory Opinions under Canon 8? Explain. (*Code*, p. 2.54)

18. How may the CPCU key and designation appropriately be used? (*Code* pp. 2.54–2.56)

19. What specific violation of the Code of Professional Ethics was involved in each of the following case studies?

    a. HCS-120 (*Code*, p. 5.37)

b. HCS-121 (*Code*, p. 5.38)

Application Questions

1. Using the ISO HO-3 declarations page and the policy form in Appendix A, answer the following questions.

a. Who is (are) the named insured(s) on the HO-3 policy?
    (pp. 12.4–12.7)

b. Do the Smiths have a mortgage on the home being insured?
    (pp. 12.7–12.9)

c. Is the Smiths' eleven-year-old son a named insured?
    An insured? (pp. 12.9–12.14)

d. If the Smiths still owed $100,000 on the mortgage, what is
    the mortgagee's insurable interest in the property? What is
    the Smiths' insurable interest? (pp. 12.14–12.19)

e.   If a fire (a covered peril) occurred at the Smiths' house on April 29, 2005, does the HO-3 policy shown provide coverage? If the fire occurred April 29, 2006? (pp. 12.19–12.21)

f.   Is the detached garage at the residence considered covered property? (pp. 12.22–12.24; HO-3 policy, p. 3)

g.   Is the land the residence is constructed on considered covered property? (pp. 12.22–12.24; HO-3 policy, p. 3)

h.   In what location(s) is the Smiths' personal property covered? (pp. 12.22–12.24; HO-3 policy, p. 3)

i.   Is the HO-3 policy coverage for Coverages A and B on a "named-perils" basis or an "all-risks" basis? Explain. Which basis is Coverage C? (pp. 12.24–12.25; HO-3 policy, p. 8)

j. If the Smiths' eleven-year-old son is found liable for accidentally breaking a neighbor's window, would the HO-3 policy provide coverage? (pp. 12.27–12.28; HO-3 policy, p. 16)

2. Explain whether each of the following individuals has violated any Rules of the Code of Professional Ethics. Assume each individual is bound by the Code and that proper complaints have been filed. State any other reasonable assumptions. (*Code*, pp. 2.53–2.56)

a. Tom Smith, a CPCU, buys a personalized license plate reading, "IMACPCU."

b. Betty T. Agent, CPCU, owns a firm named "Betty T. Agent, CPCU, & Associates."

Answers to Assignment 12 Questions

NOTE: These answers are provided to give students a basic understanding of acceptable types of responses. They often are not the only valid answers and are not intended to provide an exhaustive response to the questions.

Review Questions

1. It is important for an insurance professional to review the entire policy when performing the post-loss policy analysis for the following reasons:
   - Not all of the provisions related to a specific section of a policy appear in the section they address.
   - Each property and liability insurance policy has a different structure.
   - Variations occur among provisions of a specific type across property-casualty insurance policies.
   - The absence of a common policy provision can have a significant effect on policy analysis.

2. The declarations contain unique information provided by and about the insured as well as the following:
   - Numbers and edition dates of all attached coverage forms and endorsements
   - Name of the insured(s) and names of persons or organizations whose additional interests are covered
   - Premium
   - Policy inception and expiration dates
   - Coverage territory
   - Physical address and description of the covered property or operations
   - Dollar amounts of applicable policy limits and deductibles

3. An important distinction between "you" and "an insured" in a typical insurance policy is that "an insured" can include more parties than "you", as follows:
   - "You" means the named insured shown in the declarations and any other person or organization qualifying as a named insured or meeting the definition of "you" under the policy.
   - "An insured" means not only the named insured but also any other person or organization that qualifies as an "insured" under the policy.

4. An insurance policy might provide rights for the following types of insured parties:
   - Insured parties identified by name
   - Insured parties identified by relationship
   - Additional insureds
   - Multiple insured parties

5. The following tasks are designated for the first named insured in most insurance policies:
   - Pay premium
   - Cancel policy
   - Receive notice of cancellation
   - Make policy changes with the insurer's consent
   - Receive claim and occurrence data from the insurer
   - Receive returned premiums

6. A mortgagee's rights under a policy are somewhat stronger than those of a typical loss payee because the standard mortgage clause is viewed as a separate policy between the insurer and the mortgagee. The mortgagee's rights under the policy cannot be impaired by an act of omission of the insured.

7. Parties with the following relationships with the named insured may qualify for status as an insured:
   a. Members of a classes
      • Spouse
      • Family members
      • Household residents
      • Employees
      • Officers and directors
      • Other classes stated in the policy based on personal or business relationships
   b. Legal substitutes for the named insured, who do not qualify as separate insureds but are acceptable legal substitutes for the named insured. They can collect only for the named insured's covered losses, not for their own. The following are examples of legal substitutes:
      • Legal representatives
      • Personal representatives
      • Heirs and assignees

8. Requiring that the insured have an insurable interest ensures that the insured is actually exposed to potential loss. In life insurance policies, insurable interest must be present at the time the policy is purchased. In property-casualty insurance policies, insurable interest must be present at the time of the loss.

9. Insurance policies have an insurable interest requirement for the following three reasons:
   (1) It supports the principle of indemnity.
   (2) It prevents the use of insurance as a wagering mechanism.
   (3) It reduces the moral hazard incentive that insurance may create for the insured.

10. Insurable interest might arise from the following bases:
   a. Ownership interest in property—The extent of legal ownership determines the extent of insurable interest in the property.
   b. Contractual obligations—Insurable interest through contractual obligations can relate to contractual rights regarding either persons or property.
   c. Exposure to legal liability—Insurable interest is based on potential legal liability or arising from a financial interest in property.
   d. Factual expectancy—A party experiences economic advantage if an insured event does not occur or economic harm if the event does occur.
   e. Representation of another party—The party derives its interest from its relationship with the party whom it represents.

11. The extent of insurable interest varies with each of the following types of joint ownership:
   a. Joint tenancy—Ownership transfers to a surviving joint tenant upon the death of the other; therefore each party has an insurable interest equal to the full property value.
   b. Tenancy by the entirety—Similar to joint tenancy; each spouse has an insurable interest to the full extent of the property value.

c. Tenancy in common—Each party's insurable interest is limited to that owner's share of the property.

d. Tenancy in partnership—Both the partnership entity and the individual partners have an insurable interest in property used by the partnership.

12. The elements required for an event to meet the requirements of an insured event include the following:

a. Property insurance
   • Covered property
   • Covered cause of loss
   • Covered consequences
   • Covered location
   • Covered period

b. Liability insurance
   • Covered activity
   • Alleged legal responsibility to pay covered damages
   • Covered consequences
   • Covered location
   • Covered period

13. The coverage approach and burden of proof requirements are the same for basic-form and broad-form. They specifically name the perils that are insured against. To enforce coverage, the insured has the burden of proof to show that a covered peril was the proximate cause of covered loss consequences. The special-form provides broad coverage and names certain hazards and causes of loss that are excluded. The insurer must be able to prove that the loss resulted from a peril or hazard that the policy excludes.

14. The following are categories of covered consequences:

a. Property insurance policy
   • Reduction in value—reduction in property value because of damage by a covered loss (direct loss)
   • Increased cost to replace or repair—replacement cost coverage to replace the property if it is damaged (direct loss)
   • Loss of revenue—loss of income resulting from property damage (indirect loss)
   • Extra expense—extra expenses incurred by a business or family when damaged or destroyed property is not useable (indirect loss)

b. Liability insurance policy
   • Damages for which the insured is legally liable to a third party
   • Defense costs incurred to defend against a third-party claim for covered bodily injury or property damage brought against the insured, even when the claim seems to be false or fraudulent.

15. The two locations relevant to a covered liability event are (1) the location of the incident and (2) the location of the lawsuit brought by a claimant against an insured.

16. Coverage in an occurrence-based policy is triggered by the actual happening of bodily injury or property damage during the policy period. Coverage in a claims-made policy is triggered by a claim alleging bodily injury or property damage that is made during the policy period, as long as the covered event occurs after the retroactive date.

17. Yes, a CPCU could be sanctioned under the Code for using the CPCU key or the letters "CPCU" in a way not permitted by the Guidelines and Advisory Opinions under Canon 8. The relevant Guidelines are referred to in Rule R8.1, and a violation of these Guidelines would be a Rule violation. This is the only case in which Guidelines become part of a Rule and are therefore enforceable.

18. The use of the CPCU key and designation must be dignified and professional. The specific uses of the CPCU authorized by the Code are after the holder's name on:

    • Business cards

    • Stationery

    • Office advertising

    • Signed articles

    • Business and professional listings

    • Telephone listings

    Other proposed uses should be submitted to the American Institute's ethics counsel for prior approval.

19. The specific violations of the Code of Professional Ethics in the designated HCSs are as follows:

    a. HCS-120—Smith's use of the CPCU letters on a pen (an object) clearly violates Guideline G8.1 incorporated by Rule R8.1.

    b. HCS-121—The ad copy violates Guideline G8.1 incorporated by Rule R8.1 because the undignified and unprofessional ad compromises the dignity of the CPCU designation.

Application Questions

1. a. From the declarations page, the named insureds are Peter and Jennifer Smith.

   b. State Local Mortgage Assn. is listed as the first mortgagee in the declarations; therefore the Smiths have a mortgage on the property insured.

   c. The Smiths' eleven-year-old son is not a named insured but is an insured by virtue of being a family member.

   d. State Local Mortgage Assn.'s insurable interest in the property is the balance of the mortgage, $100,000. The Smiths' insurable interest is the full value of the property, which, assuming it is fully insured, would be $200,000.

   e. According to the declarations page, the policy period does not begin until April 30, 2005. Therefore, a fire that starts on April 29, 2005, would not be covered. A fire that starts on April 29, 2006, would be covered.

   f. HO-3 policy, Coverage B – Other Structures provides coverage for: "…other structures on the 'residence premises' set apart from the dwelling by clear space. This includes structures connected to the dwelling by only fence, utility line, or similar connection." Therefore, the detached garage would be considered covered property.

   g. Both Coverage A and Coverage B exclude land. Coverage A states, "We do not cover land, including land on which the dwelling is located." Therefore, the Smith's land would not be considered covered property.

h. The Smiths' property is covered anywhere in the world under Coverage C – Personal Property, which states, "We cover personal property owned or used by an 'insured' while it is anywhere in the world."

i. Coverages A and B, are on an "all risks" basis: "We insure against risk of direct physical loss to property described in Coverages A and B. We do not insure, however, for loss:…" This is then followed by a list of losses not covered. Coverage C (page 10), however, is on a "named-perils" basis: "We insure for direct physical loss to the property described in Coverage C caused by any of the following perils…." This is followed by the list of perils that personal property is covered against.

j. Yes, HO-3, Section II – Liability Coverages provides coverage of the broken window with the following language: "If a claim is made or a suit is brought against an 'insured' for damages because of 'bodily injury' or 'property damage' caused by an 'occurrence' to which this coverage applies we will…." Because the Smiths' son is an insured and the act of accidentally breaking the window is not specifically excluded, the property damage would be covered.

2. According to the Code of Professional Ethics,

a. A personalized license plate reading "IMACPCU" violates R8.1 (and G8.1.a.3). CPCUs are not allowed to affix the initials CPCU to objects.

b. A firm named "Betty T. Agent, CPCU, & Associates" violates R8.1 (and G8.1.a.3). CPCUs are not allowed to include the initials CPCU in firm names.

Plan to register with the Institutes well in advance of your exam. Please consult the registration booklet that accompanied this course guide for complete information regarding exam dates and fees.

Policy Analysis: Conditions and Exclusions; Ethics Canon 9

Direct Your Learning

Educational Objectives

After learning the content of this assignment, you should be able to:

1. Given a case, analyze each of the following to determine whether coverage exists:

   - Concealment, misrepresentation, or fraud provisions
   - Coverage maintenance provisions
   - Insured's duties in event of loss provisions
   - Insurer's duties in event of loss provisions
   - Property insurance exclusions
   - Liability insurance exclusions

2. Paraphrase, interpret, and apply the ethical standards set forth in Canon 9—Integrity of the Code—and the related Rules and Guidelines of the Code.

3. Define or describe each of the Key Words and Phrases for this assignment.

Study Materials

Required Reading:

■ Foundations of Risk Management and Insurance
  - Chapter 13

■ "Reporting Ethics Violations," Course Guide Reading 13-1

■ Code of Professional Ethics
  - Canon 9 (pages 2.61–2.66, 3.21)
  - HCS-101 (pages 5.2–5.3)
  - HCS-104 (pages 5.9–5.10)

Study Aids:

■ SMART Practice Exam CD-ROM

■ SMART Study Aids Review Notes and Flash Cards—Assignment 13

Outline

- **Conditions**
  - A. Concealment, Misrepresentation, or Fraud Provisions
  - B. Coverage Maintenance Provisions
    1. Cancellation Provisions
    2. Policy Modification Provisions
    3. Examination of Books and Records Provision
    4. Inspections and Surveys Provision
    5. Increase in Hazard Provisions
  - C. Insured's Duties in the Event of Loss
    1. Report Losses Promptly to the Insurer
    2. Cooperate With the Insurer
  - D. Insurer's Duties in the Event of Loss
    1. Property Insurance Policies
    2. Liability Insurance Policies

- **Exclusions**
  - A. Property Insurance Exclusions
    1. Ordinance or Law Exclusion
    2. Earth Movement
    3. War
    4. Governmental Action
  - B. Liability Insurance Exclusions
    1. Expected or Intended Injury
    2. Pollution
    3. Exclusion of Certified Acts of Terrorism

- **Summary**

- **Reporting Ethics Violations (Course Guide Reading 13-1)**

- **Canon 9–Integrity of the Code**
  - A. Rule R9.1–Supporting Candidates Who Meet Ethical Standards
    1. Guideline G9.1–Maintaining Standards
  - B. Rule R9.2–Reporting Violations
    1. Guideline G9.2–Reporting Adverse Information
    2. Guideline G9.3–Committee Service
  - C. Rule R9.3–Reporting Unauthorized Use of the Designation
  - D. Other Related Code Provisions
  - E. Relevant Hypothetical Case Studies
  - F. Review Questions

- **Hypothetical Case Studies**
  - A. HCS-101
    1. Case HCS-101
    2. Opinion HCS-101
  - B. HCS-104
    1. Case HCS-104
    2. Opinion HCS-104

Reading 13-1

Reporting Ethics Violations

This reading is adapted from an actual e-mail exchange between the American Institute's ethics counsel and a CPCU candidate. The messages have been altered to obscure the person's identity. However, they reinforce part of this assignment's discussion regarding the reporting of a complaint and illustrate some practical matters involved in filing an ethics complaint.

——Original Message——

From: greg@isp.net

Sent: February 18, 20XX

To: ethicscounsel

Subject: Ethics

Dear Sir:

I know a CPCU in my office who, in my opinion, has violated several of the canons of the code of ethics. How does one go about reporting these alleged infractions, and is there a way to do it anonymously? I am currently a CPCU candidate.

——Reply——

From: ethicscounsel

Sent: February 18, 20XX

To: greg@isp.net

Subject: RE: Ethics

Dear "Greg,"

The response to a violation of the Code of Professional Ethics of the American Institute for CPCU lies in disciplinary action by the Board of Ethical Inquiry (BEI) that ensues from a formal complaint.

Let me respond first to your anonymity concerns. At this point you are obviously anonymous to me, and if you wish we can continue a brief exploratory discussion by e-mail or telephone without the need to reveal your identity.

Should you decide to file a formal complaint against one or more CPCUs, the Disciplinary Rules, Procedures, and Penalties of the Code of Professional Ethics of the American Institute (IV. Procedures, A. Complaints, paragraph (1)) provide that "All complaints alleging a violation of the *Code of Professional Ethics* shall be submitted in writing to [ethics counsel - that's me] and signed by the complainant. Since disciplinary action requires a proven violation of one or more Rules of the Code, it is most helpful if a formal complaint identifies the Rule(s) you believe have been violated. You may be assured that I and the Board of Ethical Inquiry are accustomed to handling confidential matters with due sensitivity to both the complainant and the subject of the complaint.

Paragraph (2) provides that "a copy of the complaint shall be furnished by Counsel to the person or persons against whom the complaint is lodged." It is only fair that a person accused of some misdeed know the basis of the accusation. If the CPCUs in question have been convicted of a crime, disciplined by regulatory authorities, or otherwise subjected to disciplinary action in some form that is on the public record, it might not be necessary to divulge your identity to pursue disciplinary action based on the record.

Obviously, I have no idea what the CPCUs in question might have done, so I cannot refer to any specific parts of the Code that might apply to your charges. However, as you consider the possibility of filing a formal complaint, I'd like to call your attention to Guideline G9.2. The integrity of the *Code of Professional Ethics* is best served if the *Code* is enforced, and this can be achieved only if *Code* violations are promptly brought to the attention of the proper officials. However, whether a CPCU should *volunteer* adverse information is left to the judgment of the CPCU. I mention this not to discourage you from pursuing a complaint, but because there has been some misinformation suggesting that CPCUs are ethically required to report Rules violations by other CPCUs. As G9.2 indicates, reporting is encouraged, but it is still voluntary.

I hope this responds to your immediate questions. Please let me know how I can be of further assistance.

Sincerely,

Ethics Counsel

American Institute for CPCU/Insurance Institute of America

Key Words and Phrases

Define or describe each of the words and phrases listed below.

Cancellation (p. 13.6)

Nonrenewal (p. 13.6)

Policy termination (p. 13.6)

Anniversary date (p. 13.6)

Changes provision (p. 13.8)

Liberalization clause (p. 13.9)

Examination of books and records provision (p. 13.10)

Premium audit (p. 13.10)

Inspection and surveys provision (p. 13.11)

Increase in hazard provision (p. 13.13)

Protective safeguards provision (p. 13.16)

Abandonment provision (p. 13.20)

Bankruptcy provision (p. 13.23)

Review Questions

1. List six examples of widely used policy conditions in property and liability insurance policies. (p. 13.3)

2. List the two policy conditions designed to elicit accurate information from the insured both before and after losses occur. (p. 13.4)

3. Explain the purpose of the concealment, misrepresentation, or fraud provision. (p. 13.4)

4. Give an example of how examining patterns in insurance claims can identify an increased likelihood of concealment, misrepresentation, or fraud. (p. 13.4)

5. List five policy provisions that are commonly grouped as coverage maintenance provisions. (p. 13.5)

6. Explain how coverage maintenance provisions help the insurer avoid both moral hazard and adverse selection. (p. 13.5)

7. Differentiate between cancellation and nonrenewal. (p. 13.6)

8. Explain the purpose of the liberalization clause. (p. 13.9)

9. Explain the purpose of the examination of books and records provision. (pp. 13.10–13.11)

10. Explain the purpose of the inspections and surveys provision. (p. 13.11).

11. Describe the effect an increase in hazards provision may have on coverage. (p. 13.13)

12. Describe the insured's two duties in the event of a loss. (pp. 13.17–13.18)

13. Explain how an insured must cooperate with the insurer following a property loss. (p. 13.18)

14. Explain how an insured must cooperate with the insurer following a liability loss. (p. 13.20)

15. Describe the insurer's duties in the event of a property loss. (p. 13.22)

16. Describe the insurer's duties in the event of a liability loss. (p. 13.23)

17. List the common exclusions found in property insurance policies. (p. 13.24)

18. List the common exclusions found in liability insurance policies. (p. 13.24)

19. Compare the exclusions sections of named-perils and "all-risks" property policies. (p. 13.25)

20. Describe the government action exclusion. (p. 13.28)

21. Explain the reasons for the pollution exclusion. (p. 13.29)

22. Should CPCUs or candidates report other CPCUs or candidates who have violated one or more Rules under the Code? Explain. (*Code*, pp. 2.63–2.64)

23. Are CPCUs required to cooperate in the investigation of any CPCU or candidate who has been charged with a Code violation? (*Code*, pp. 2.63–2.64)

24. Why are CPCUs or candidates required to report any person who is not a CPCU (or is not yet a CPCU) but is using the CPCU designation? (*Code*, p. 2.65)

25. How can a person who is considering a formal complaint against a CPCU get some relevant advice without disclosing the complainant's identity? (Course Guide Reading 13-1)

26. Based on HCS-101, did the personnel director violate Rule R9.1 of the Code? (*Code*, pp. 5.2–5.3)

Application Questions

The Barb's Hardware Case. Barbara owns a hardware store, Barb's Hardware. Through her local insurance agent, Barbara has purchased an unendorsed BOP to cover a variety of property and liability loss exposures associated with owning and operating a hardware store. Based on the case below and the businessowners policy (BOP) included in the Appendix to this course guide, find the appropriate policy provision in the BOP (conditions and exclusions sections) and determine the effect that provision has on the each of the following situations.

1. *Barb's Hardware.* Barb's Hardware has had a series of burglaries over the past five years. Barbara, fearful of not being able to find adequate insurance coverage at an affordable premium did not disclose the burglaries to the agent. On April 1, three months after the policy was in force, Barb's Hardware was burglarized again. The insurer became award of the past burglaries through the police reports. (p. 13.4; BOP p. 41)

2. *Barb's Hardware.* In an attempt to keep premiums lower, Barbara tells the insurer that she has installed a state-of-the-art security system. The insurer wants to verify that Barbara has installed the system. (pp. 13.10–13.11; BOP p. 41)

3. *Barb's Hardware.* On May 15, Barbara had forgotten to arm the new security system, and that evening a second burglary occurred. Concerned about the insurer's reaction, Barbara decided not to report the burglary. Two months later (July 22), Barbara had second thoughts and decided to report the burglary to her insurer. (pp. 13.17–13.18; BOP p. 17)

4. *Barb's Hardware*. On August 7, Barbara received a registered
    letter from a local attorney stating that he was representing
    a client who had fallen and been injured in Barb's Hardware
    parking lot after stepping in a large pothole that had been there
    for more than two years. Barbara put the letter in her mail pile
    to forward to her insurer but forgot about it, and the letter was
    never forwarded to her insurer. (p. 13.20; BOP, p. 36)

5. *Barb's Hardware*. On October 3, an earthquake rocked the area
    of the hardware store, causing $50,000 in building damage
    to the Barb's Hardware. An ensuing fire caused by a gas main
    broken by the earthquake caused an additional $150,000 in fire
    damage to the building. (pp. 13.26–13.27; BOP p. 12)

6. *Barb's Hardware*. On the Friday following Thanksgiving, Barb's
    Hardware advertised a number of specials that brought large
    crowds of consumers to her store. An altercation between
    two customers escalated to the point at which Barbara had to
    restrain a customer. The customer later filed a lawsuit against
    Barbara for injuries sustained while being restrained. (p. 13.29;
    BOP p. 28)

Answers to Assignment 13 Questions

NOTE: These answers are provided to give students a basic understanding of acceptable types of responses. They often are not the only valid answers and are not intended to provide an exhaustive response to the questions.

Review Questions

1. Examples of widely used policy conditions are concealment, misrepresentation, or fraud provisions; coverage maintenance provisions; suspension or reduction in coverage provisions; insurer and insured duties in the event of a loss provisions; and dispute resolution, subrogation and salvage provisions.

2. The concealment, misrepresentation, or fraud provisions and the coverage maintenance provisions are designed to elicit accurate information from the insured both before and after losses occur.

3. The concealment, misrepresentation, or fraud provision serves to affirm that the information provided is complete and accurate and that the insurer has used it to issue the policy. It also reinforces the principle of utmost good faith and helps insurers deal with moral hazard concerns regarding insurance policies.

4. Patterns in claim data may indicate an increased likelihood of concealment, misrepresentation, or fraud by the insured. For example, a review of claim data may indicate that the same group of doctors, chiropractors, or lawyers appear repeatedly on suspicious claims. This pattern may indicate that some claimants are misrepresenting their injuries.

5. The following five policy provisions are commonly grouped as coverage maintenance provisions:
   - Cancellation provisions
   - Policy modification provisions
   - Examination of books and record provisions
   - Inspections and surveys provisions
   - Increase in hazards provisions

6. Coverage maintenance provisions help the insurer avoid both moral hazard and adverse selection by granting the insurer access to information to verify data provided by the insured and provide any other relevant information the underwriter may need to properly assess the loss exposure. These provisions also reduce adverse selection by giving the insurer access to information before a loss, for example, by way of an inspection or survey.

7. Cancellation is an action taken by either the insurer or insured to terminate coverage prior to the policy expiration date. Nonrenewal is the action taken by the insurer to terminate coverage on the renewal date. The distinction is important to insureds because an insured who has had an insurance policy canceled often finds obtaining coverage elsewhere difficult.

8. The liberalization clause gives existing insureds the same broadened coverage the insurer offers to new insureds provided the revision occurs during the policy period specified in the clause and the broadened coverage was offered without an additional premium.

9. The examination of books and records provision gives the insurer the right to conduct audits to determine final premium or confirm the amount payable on a claim. This provision ensures that the insurer has access to the information necessary to make these calculations.

10. The inspections and surveys provision gives the insurer the right to conduct loss control inspections and surveys. This provision is most relevant to property insurance policies and gives the insurer the ability to verify the condition of property, safeguards, or presence of hazards that may affect coverage.

11. Policies containing an increase in hazards provision may do the following:
    - Automatically suspend coverage against losses related to the hazard
    - Automatically suspend all coverage
    - Permit the insurer to suspend coverage immediately
    - Automatically limit or reduce coverage

12. The two duties of an insured following a loss are to report losses promptly to the insurer and to cooperate with the insurer in evaluating and settling the claim.

13. Although the specific duties required of an insured following a property loss may vary, cooperation generally takes the form of taking steps to protect property from further damage, providing a list of damaged or destroyed property, giving the insurer access to the damaged or destroyed property, provide sworn testimony, and submitting to an examination under oath.

14. Although the specific duties required of an insured following a liability loss may vary, cooperation generally takes the form of sending copies of any demands or legal papers received, sharing any records or documents related to the claim with the insurer, assisting the insurer in the enforcement of rights against liable parties, and not admitting responsibility or otherwise prejudicing the insurer's opportunity to defend the claim.

15. The insurer's primary duty is payment, which is expressed in the insuring agreement. However, the loss payment provisions provide more detail on the options the insurer has when it comes to payment on property insurance policies. The property insurer has the option to pay the value of the lost or damaged property or the amount spend to repair or replace it, to limit payment to the insured's financial interests, to negotiate settlement with owners of property other than the insured and defend the insured against suits arising from property claims.

16. The two main duties of the insurer in a liability insurance policy are the duty to pay claims and the duty to defend, both of which are covered in the insuring agreement. One condition related to these duties is the bankruptcy provision, which states that the insurer is obligated to pay claims on behalf of an insured who is bankrupt.

17. Common property exclusions include ordinance or law, earth movement, government action, nuclear hazard, utility, war, water, and fungus and bacteria.

18. Common liability exclusions include expected or intended injury, pollution, certified acts of terrorism, and contractual liability.

19. The extent of the exclusions section in a property insurance policy varies depending on whether the policy is a named perils policy or a special coverage form (all-risks policy). A named perils policy lists the causes of loss the policy covers. Its exclusions section is typically not as extensive as that for a special coverage form, in which all losses are covered unless they are specifically excluded. Nonetheless, a named perils coverage form may still have an extensive list of exclusions.

20. The governmental action exclusion wording is broad enough to cover destruction, confiscation, or seizure of property by any governmental or public authority for any reason. Insurers often use this exclusion to avoid paying criminals for property taken because of its use in criminal activity.

21. Pollution loss exposures can be difficult to analyze because they often do not exhibit the definite and measurable characteristics of an ideally insurable loss exposure. Determining exactly when pollution began is often difficult. Furthermore, pollution detection and remediation costs are high and difficult to estimate, complicating the analysis of the potential severity of losses.

22. CPCUs are encouraged to report Code violations by CPCUs or candidates but are generally not required to do so except upon request.

23. Yes, CPCUs are required to cooperate in the investigation of any CPCU or candidate charged with a Code violation. According to Rule R9.2, unless the requested information is privileged, a CPCU shall reveal any information to the proper authority investigating an alleged Code violation.

24. CPCUs are required by the Code of Professional Ethics to report any use of the CPCU designation by someone who is not entitled to do so. This Rule preserves the integrity of the Code by ensuring that only CPCUs use the CPCU credential.

25. It is possible to anonymously discuss an ethics concern with ethics counsel.

26. Based on HCS-101, it does not appear that the personnel director violated R9.1. He did initiate and support Mr. Roe's CPCU candidacy, but he had no reason to suspect that Roe would "engage in" business practices that violate the Code.

Application Questions

1. The following policy provision is most relevant to the case:

   Section III Common Policy Conditions

   C. Concealment, Misrepresentation, or Fraud

   This policy provision gives the insurer the right to void the policy if the insured has misrepresenting material facts related to the policy, the covered property, the insured's interest in the covered property, and any claim under the policy.

2. The following policy provision is most relevant to the case:

   Section III Common Policy Conditions

   E. Inspections and Surveys

   This policy provision gives the insurer the right, but not the obligation, to make inspections and surveys at any time. The insurer may invoke this right to examine the security system that Barbara has installed to determine whether it will affect the coverage offered or the premiums charged.

3. The following policy provision is most relevant to the case:

   E. Property Loss Conditions

   3. Duties In The Event of Loss or Damage

   Under the duties conditions, a. (2) and (3) are most applicable to this case. Barbara did not provide a prompt notice of loss or give a description of how, when, and where the loss or damage occurred. Because she violated one of the policy conditions, the insurer has the right to deny the claim.

4. The following policy provision is most relevant to the case:

    E. Liability and Medical Expenses General Conditions

    2. Duties in the Event of Occurrence, Offense, Claim or Suit

    Barbara may have failed to fulfill duties conditions b. (1) and (2) and c (1). She did not immediately record any specifics about the claim or lawsuit or notify the insurer as soon as practicable. She also failed to send copies of the letter to the insurer. Because she violated one (or more) of the policy conditions, the insurer has the right to deny the claim.

5. The following policy provision is most relevant to the case:

    B. Exclusions

    b. Earth Movement

    According to this property exclusion, the policy does not cover damage related to earthquakes but would cover any damage resulting from a fire or explosion caused by the earthquake. Therefore, the insurer would not pay the $50,000 in damage caused by to the earthquake but would pay the $150,000 in fire damage, subject to policy limits and any coinsurance requirements.

6. The following policy provisions are most relevant to the case:

    B. Exclusions

    1. Applicable to Business Liability Coverage

    a. Expected or Intended Injury

    The liability exclusion precludes from coverage any bodily injury or property damage that could be reasonably expected or intended from an insured's actions. Physically restraining an individual could be reasonably expected to result in bodily injury. However, because Barbara was trying to protect people and property, the exception to this exclusion, the use of reasonable force, may indicate that the policy would provide coverage. Whether Barbara used reasonable force would be a question of fact that the courts may ultimately decide.

Amounts Payable: Property Insurance

Direct Your Learning

Educational Objectives

After learning the content of this assignment, you should be able to:

1. Explain why insurance to value is important to the insured and to the insurer in property insurance, what problems are associated with maintaining insurance to value, and what can be done to minimize these problems.

2. Given a case, apply valuation methods, policy limits, deductibles, and coinsurance or insurance-to-value provisions separately or in combination, to determine the amount payable. In support of this objective:

   - Describe the valuation approaches used in property insurance policies.

   - Explain the reasons for policy limits.

   - Analyze the following types of policy limits used in property insurance: individual property limits, specific limits, blanket limits, sublimits, variable limits, and nondollar limits.

   - Explain why deductibles are applied, how various types of deductibles are applied, and why some policies contain no deductibles.

   - Analyze the purpose and function of coinsurance, insurance-to-value policy provisions, and alternatives to coinsurance.

   - Apply the coinsurance formula.

3. Explain how appraisal provisions aid in resolving disputed claims.

4. Explain how subrogation and salvage provisions can help keep premiums reasonable.

5. Define or describe each of the Key Words and Phrases for this assignment.

Study Materials

Required Reading:

- Foundations of Risk Management and Insurance
  - Chapter 14

Study Aids:

- SMART Practice Exam CD-ROM
- SMART Study Aids Review Notes and Flash Cards— Assignment 14

Outline

- **Insurance to Value**
- **Valuation Methods**
  - A. Actual Cash Value
    1. Replacement Cost Minus Depreciation
    2. Market Value
    3. Broad Evidence Rule
  - B. Replacement Cost
  - C. Actual Loss Sustained
  - D. Other Valuation Methods
    1. Agreed Value Method
    2. Functional Valuation Method
    3. Cost of Reproduction Valuation Method
    4. Pair or Set Clauses Valuation Method
    5. Money and Securities Valuation Method
- **Policy Limits**
  - A. Reasons for Policy Limits
  - B. Individual Property Limits
  - C. Specific Limits
  - D. Blanket Limits
  - E. Sublimits
  - F. Variable Limits
    1. Inflation Guard Protection
    2. Peak Season Endorsement
  - G. Nondollar Limits
- **Deductibles**
  - A. Reasons for Deductibles
    1. Reduce Moral and Morale Hazards and Encourage Loss Control
    2. Reduce Insurer's Costs
  - B. Types of Deductibles
    1. Straight Deductibles
    2. Percentage Deductibles
    3. Time Deductibles

- **Coinsurance and Other Insurance-to-Value Provisions**
  - A. Coinsurance
    1. Coinsurance Clause
    2. Coinsurance Formula
  - B. Insurance-to-Value Provisions in Homeowners and Businessowners Policies
  - C. Alternatives to Coinsurance
    1. Flat Policies
    2. Agreed Value
    3. Monthly Limit of Indemnity
    4. Maximum Period of Indemnity
- **Examples Combining Valuation, Limits, Deductibles, and Coinsurance**
  - A. ACV Valuation/Adequate Insurance Example
  - B. Replacement Cost Valuation/Underinsurance Example
  - C. Blanket Insurance/Underinsurance Example
  - D. Deductible Application Example
- **Disputed Claim Resolution: Appraisal Provisions**
- **Subrogation and Salvage**
- **Summary**

Key Words and Phrases

Define or describe each of the words and phrases listed below.

Insurance to value (p. 14.3)

Actual cash value (ACV) (p. 14.7)

Replacement cost (p. 14.7)

Depreciation (p. 14.7)

Market value (p. 14.8)

Broad evidence rule (p. 14.9)

Actual loss sustained (p. 14.13)

Agreed value method (p. 14.14)

Functional valuation method (p. 14.14)

Pair or set clause (p. 14.15)

Specific limit (p. 14.18)

Blanket limit (p. 14.19)

Sublimit (p. 14.20)

Inflation guard protection (p. 14.21)

Peak season endorsement (p. 14.22)

Deductible (p. 14.23)

Dollar trading (p. 14.24)

Per event deductible (p. 14.26)

Aggregate deductible (p. 14.26)

Straight deductible (p. 14.28)

Split deductible (p. 14.30)

Percentage deductible (p. 14.30)

Time deductible (p. 14.31)

Flat policy (p. 14.38)

Monthly limit of indemnity (p. 14.39)

Maximum period of indemnity (p. 14.40)

Appraisal clause (p. 14.47)

Subrogation (p. 14.48)

Salvage (p. 14.48)

Recovered property provision (p. 14.50)

Review Questions

1. Describe two benefits to the insurer of insuring property policies to value. (p. 14.5)

2. Explain how the insured benefits from insuring property to value. (p. 14.5)

3. Explain why it is difficult to maintain property insurance limits that meet or exceed policy coinsurance or insurance-to-value requirements. (p. 14.6)

4. Describe three common methods of determining ACV for property. (pp. 14.7–14.9)

5. Describe the types of property for which market valuation may be useful. (p. 14.9)

6. Explain why the value of land must be eliminated when determining values for buildings or structures on that land. (p. 14.9)

7. Identify the factors considered when determining a building's ACV under the broad evidence rule. (p. 14.9)

8. Contrast valuation for ACV of residential personal property to that of business personal property based on broad evidence court decisions. (p. 14.10)

9. Explain how insurers reduce the potential moral hazard related to offering coverage on a replacement cost basis. (p. 14.12)

10. Explain why the functional valuation method might be used for some types of property. (p. 14.14)

11. Describe the types of personal property for which the functional valuation method is commonly used. (p. 14.14)

12. Describe circumstances under which the cost of reproduction valuation method for valuable papers and records would not be suitable. (p. 14.15)

13. Explain why the pair or set valuation clause is needed for certain types of property. (p. 14.15)

14. List the four major reasons for including limits in insurance policies. (pp. 14.16–14.17)

15. Contrast scheduled property limits with unscheduled property limits. (p. 14.17)

16. Contrast specific limits with blanket limits. (pp. 14.18–14.19)

17. Explain when it would be helpful for an insured to purchase blanket limits rather than specific limits for owned property. (p. 14.19)

18. Describe two potential disadvantages of inflation guard protection. (p. 14.21)

19. Explain how a peak season endorsement operates as a variable limits method. (p. 14.22)

20. Describe two major disadvantages of the peak season endorsement. (p. 14.22)

21. Describe two ways that deductibles reduce premium costs by requiring insureds to retain a portion of the loss amount. (p. 14.23)

22. Contrast a per event deductible with an aggregate deductible. (p. 14.26)

23. Describe the purpose of including a coinsurance clause in a property insurance policy. (p. 14.32)

24. Explain how insurance-to-value provisions differ from coinsurance provisions in property policies. (p. 14.36)

25. Identify four alternatives to coinsurance that assist policy-holders in avoiding insurance-to-value penalties. (p. 14.38)

26. Describe the operation of the agreed value option under the ISO
    BPP coverage form. (p. 15.39)

27. Explain why a statement of values is required to provide coverage
    on an agreed value basis (p. 14.39)

28. Explain when the appraisal clause would be applied to a
    property insurance loss settlement. (p. 14.47)

29. Contrast the subrogation process with the salvage process for
    property insurance losses. (p. 14.48)

Application Questions

The Smith Case. The Smith family's home is insured under the ISO Homeowners 3 – Special Form Policy shown in the Appendix of this course guide.

1. *Smith.* In the Smiths' homeowners policy, what amount would be payable for each of the following property losses? Ignore any deductible that might apply.

    a. The Smiths' detached garage is destroyed in a windstorm. The replacement cost value of the garage is $15,000; its actual cash value is $12,000. (pp. 14.6–14.12; HO-3 pp. 13–14)

    b. The Smiths' home is burglarized and the following property is taken:

        • Jewelry valued at $4,200

        • A gun collection valued at $3,200 (p. 14.20; HO-3 pp. 3–4)

    c. The grand piano in the Smiths' house is damaged one summer day when a water pipe bursts. The piano was purchased twenty years ago for $6,000, and its current actual cash value is $5,000. The current cost of a new piano of like kind and quality would be $10,000. The cost of repairing the piano is $1,000. (pp. 14.6–14.12; HO-3 pp. 13–14)

2. *Smith*. By referring to the Smiths' homeowners policy, determine whether each of the following property items is covered on a scheduled or an unscheduled basis.(pp. 14.17–14.18)

a. The Smiths' garage

b. A refrigerator in the Smiths' house

c. A piano in the Smiths' house

3. *Smith*. A windstorm damages the roof of the Smith's house. The cost to replace the roof was $3,200. At the time of the loss, the actual cash value of the roof was $2,400. Under the Smith's HO-3 policy, what amount will the insurer pay if, at the time of the loss, the replacement cost value of the house is each of the following? Show your calculations. (pp. 14.36–14.47, HO-3 pp.13–14)

a. $400,000

b. $300,000

c. $250,000

d. $200,000

The Campus Book Store Case. The Campus Book Store is insured under the CPP/ ISO Building and Personal Property Coverage Form shown in the Appendix of this course guide.

4. *Campus Book Store.* In the Campus Book Store policy, what valuation approach would be taken in determining the insurable value of each of the following property items? (pp. 14.6–14.15; BPP pp. 7, 11)

   a.   The Campus Book Store building

   b.   Business personal property, such as display counters and furniture

   c.   Campus Book Store stock that has been sold but has not yet been delivered to the buyer

d. Valuable papers containing customer records

5. *Campus Book Store.* What would the maximum amount payable by the Campus Book Store's insurer be in each of the following situations? Show your calculations, and do not ignore deductibles. (pp. 14.32–14.35; CPP Declarations; BPP pp. 8, 1–12)

a. Total ACV of contents before the loss: $300,000
    ACV of contents loss: $10,000

b. Total ACV of contents before loss: $320,000
    ACV of contents loss: $10,000

c. Total ACV of contents before loss: $320,000
    ACV of contents loss: $320,000

d. Total ACV of contents before loss: $320,000
    ACV of contents loss: $300,000

e. Total ACV of contents before loss: $400,000
    ACV of contents loss: $12,000

f. Total RC of building before loss: $400,000
    RC of building loss: $9,000

g. Total RC of building before loss: $200,000
    RC of building loss: $200,000

6. *Campus Book Store*. Would either of the following variable
   limits options be appropriate for Campus Book Store's business
   personal property coverage? (p. 14.22)

   a. Peak season endorsement

   b. Value reporting form

7. The Stable Environment is a rustic bar and restaurant in a converted horse barn in a highly visible location at an exit ramp of a major highway. Despite its awkward physical layout, business is thriving because The Stable Environment has little competition, and zoning restrictions in the area prohibit new construction.

   a. What are three methods could be used to determine the actual cash value of this property for insurance purposes? (p. 14.7)

   b. Why might insurance on the basis of functional valuation have some appeal for The Stable Environment or its property insurance underwriter? (p. 14.14)

Answers to Assignment 14 Questions

NOTE: These answers are provided to give students a basic understanding of acceptable types of responses. They often are not the only valid answers and are not intended to provide an exhaustive response to the questions.

Review Questions

1. Insurers benefit from insuring property policies to value in the following two ways:

    (1) The premium is adequate to cover potential losses.

    (2) The underwriting process is simplified by reducing the need to determine exact values during underwriting. The determination of underinsurance (not insuring to value) is made at the time of loss; therefore the underwriter does not need to determine whether the property is being underinsured.

2. The insured benefits from insuring property to value because sufficient funds will be available in the event of a total loss and the uncertainty associated with large retained losses is reduced.

3. Maintaining such limits is difficult for the following reasons:

    - The amount of insurance necessary to meet coinsurance requirements is based on the insured property's value at the time of the loss, but the policy limit is selected when the policy is purchased.

    - When selecting insurance limits, an insurance buyer typically estimates property values based on an informed guess.

    - The insurable value at the time of the loss often cannot be precisely measured until the property is actually rebuilt or replaced.

    - Values change over time.

4. The following are three common methods of determining ACV for property:

    (1) Replacement cost minus depreciation.

    (2) Market value. Many courts have ruled that ACV means market value, the price at which a particular piece of property could be sold on the open market by an unrelated buyer and seller.

    (3) The broad evidence rule. Actual cash value is determined based on court decisions that require all relevant factors be considered.

5. Market valuation may be useful when property of like kind and quality is unavailable for purchase, such as with antiques, works of art, and other collectibles. These types of property may be irreplaceable, making replacement cost calculations impossible. Market valuation can also be the most accurate way to determine the value of some older or historic buildings built with obsolete construction methods and materials.

6. Because most insurance policies cover buildings and structures but not land, the land's value must be eliminated in establishing insurable values of property.

7. When the broad evidence rule is used to determine a building's ACV, the following factors are considered:

    - Obsolescence

    - Building's present use and profitability

    - Alternate building uses

    - Present neighborhood characteristics

- Long-term community plans for the area where the building is located, including urban renewal prospects and new roadway plans
- Inflationary or deflationary trends

8. Under the broad evidence rule, courts have decided that residential personal property is valued at its replacement cost new at the time of loss, minus depreciation. Its value in the secondhand market (used furniture and clothing stores) is not the test of its value.

    Business personal property in use (such as furniture, fixtures, and machinery) is generally valued at its replacement cost new at the time of loss, minus depreciation. This class of property has a used market. For secondhand property, the market value of similar property in the same condition is its ACV.

9. To reduce the moral hazard, most replacement cost policies pay out only after the insured has actually replaced the damaged or destroyed property or, in some cases, only if the loss is a relatively low value. Some building policies also require the insured to rebuild the building with identical construction, in the same location, or for the same purpose. Otherwise, depreciation is deducted. In many policies with replacement cost provisions, the insured has the option of settling the claim based on ACV and then has 180 days to refile the claim on the replacement cost basis. This gives the insured the opportunity to obtain funds from the insurer at the time of loss, use those funds to help pay for the rebuilding, and then collect the full replacement cost value on completion.

10. The functional valuation method is sometimes used when replacing buildings or personal property with property of like kind and quality is not practical and when the ACV method does not match insurance needs.

11. The functional valuation method is commonly used with electronics and computers, because new computers may be more functional but less expensive than the models that have to be replaced.

12. The cost of reproduction is not a suitable valuation method for papers and records that could never be restored, such as the only copy of a photograph of a person who is no longer living.

13. A matched pair or set valuation clause is needed for certain types of property because replacement cost, actual cash value, and the other valuation methods do not specify how to deal with the loss of part of a matched pair or set, such as a pair of earrings or a set of silverware. With matched pairs or sets, the loss of one item affects the value of the remaining items.

14. The four major reasons that policies contain limits are as follows:
    (1) To limit the insurer's obligations
    (2) To accommodate consumer preferences
    (3) To reflect insurer financial capacity
    (4) As a substitute for exclusions

15. Property is said to be "scheduled" when the policy covers a list (schedule) of particular property items. Each scheduled item is listed and precisely identified with descriptions, serial numbers, or other identifying marks or characteristics. Each item of scheduled property typically is subject to a limit that reflects the amount of insurance applying only to that property. Most property insurance policies have unscheduled property limits and do not individually list, or schedule, personal property items. For these policies, the policy limits apply to all unscheduled items of covered property as a group.

16. A specific limit is the maximum dollar amount the insurer will pay, per item or per occurrence, for each loss of a particular item or class of property. Specific limits can apply to either a single item of property (such as a building) or a class of property (such as business personal property). A

blanket limit is the maximum dollar amount the insurer will pay for two or more items or classes of property at one or more locations. This means that the property owner would purchase a single limit that would apply to both the building and its business personal property.

17. A blanket limit is especially helpful when the total value of an insured's movable property is fairly constant, but the values may shift between covered locations.

18. The following are two potential disadvantages of inflation guard protection:
    (1) If the property is not adequately insured at the outset, inflation guard protection does not correct the basic coverage inadequacy.
    (2) The inflation percentage selected might bear little or no relationship to actual inflation rates.

19. A peak season endorsement covers the fluctuating values of business personal property by providing differing amounts of insurance for certain periods during the overall policy period. The peak season endorsement adjusts policy limits according to a specified schedule, regardless of policy inception and expiration dates.

20. The following are two major disadvantages of a peak season endorsement:
    (1) The endorsement depends on an advance estimate of the pattern of variable values during a future policy period.
    (2) The endorsement does not respond to any unprojected changes.

21. Deductibles reduce premium costs to the insured because they achieve the following:
    (1) Reduce moral and morale hazard incentives and encourage risk control by the insured
    (2) Eliminate the need for the insurer to process small losses, thereby reducing the insurer's loss costs and loss adjustment expenses.

22. A per event deductible applies to each item, each location, each claim, or each occurrence. Per event deductibles can be variously expressed as dollar amounts, percentages of some value, or time periods. These deductibles are the most common deductibles found in property insurance policies but can leave the insured exposed to substantial retained losses if many covered losses occur within a short period. An aggregate deductible applies collectively to all losses occurring during a specific period, typically a policy year. Aggregate deductibles are usually stated as a dollar figure. An aggregate deductible minimizes retained losses resulting from a high frequency of small losses because all losses that occur during the specified period are accumulated. After the insured has retained losses in the amount of the aggregate, the insurer begins to pay any subsequent losses.

23. Coinsurance is a requirement in most property insurance policies that makes the insured responsible for part of a loss if the property is underinsured below some specified percentage of the property's insurable value. Coinsurance may be described as a penalty the insurer imposes for not buying enough insurance or as a reward for insuring property to full value. If the insured insures the property to full value, then the insurer agrees to waive the insured's participation in the loss, except to the extent of the deductible.

24. The insurance-to-value provision is different from coinsurance provisions. With insurance-to-value provisions, the amount payable by the insurer will not be less than the ACV (subject to policy limits). These provisions are found within a loss payment or loss settlement condition that resembles the coinsurance provision. Unlike policies containing coinsurance provisions, policies containing insurance-to-value provisions do not give the insured a choice of percentages. With coinsurance provisions, the insured can choose from a variety of percentages; in contrast, the insurance-to-value provision has a stated 80 percent requirement.

25. Four alternatives to coinsurance are as follows:
    (1) Flat policies
    (2) Agreed value
    (3) Monthly limit of indemnity
    (4) Maximum period of indemnity

26. The agreed value coverage under the ISO BPP Coverage Form operates as follows:
    - The insurer and the insured agree to what amount of insurance is sufficient to meet the "should" requirement of the coinsurance clause.
    - If the insured carries an amount of insurance at least equal to that agreed value, the insurer will not impose a coinsurance penalty at the time of the loss.
    - A rate increase, typically 5 percent (compared with the rate charged on a policy with 80 percent coinsurance), is applied when premiums are calculated.

27. The statement of values, which must be submitted by the insured and acceptable to the insurer, specifies the full ACV or replacement cost of the covered property. Many insurers require an appraisal to support the statement of values submitted by the insured. The policy's coinsurance percentage is applied to the full ACV or replacement cost to produce the agreed value. The coinsurance clause is suspended if the amount of insurance equals or exceeds the agreed value.

28. The appraisal clause would be applied when the insurer and the insured agree that a given property loss is covered but cannot agree on the property's value or the loss amount, or when the insured thinks the claim is worth more than the insurer is willing to pay.

29. Subrogation is the process by which an insurer recovers payment from a liable third party who has caused a property or liability loss that the insurer has paid to, or on behalf of, an insured. Salvage is the process by which an insurer takes possession of damaged property for which it has paid a total loss and recovers a portion of the loss payment by selling the damaged property. Policy provisions outline how these provisions operate.

Application Questions

Answers in calculations may vary slightly because numbers are rounded.

1. Amounts payable under the Smiths' homeowners policy are as follows:
   a. Garage, $15,000
   b. Jewelry, $1,500
      Gun collection, $2,500
   c. Grand piano, $1,000

2. Under the Smiths' homeowners policy, the bases of coverage are as follows:
   a. Garage, unscheduled
   b. Refrigerator, unscheduled
   c. Piano, unscheduled

3. The insurer would pay the following amounts for windstorm damage to the roof of the Smiths' house, based on the respective replacement costs and the policy's insurance-to-value provision:

a.
$$\text{Did} = \$200,000.$$
$$\text{Should} = \$400,000 \times 0.80 = \$320,000.$$

Did the Smiths meet the insurance-to-value provisions? No.

Therefore the amount payable is the *greater* of the ACV (in this case, $2,400) subject to policy limits and deductibles, calculated as follows:

$$\text{ACV} = \text{Loss amount} - \text{Deductible}$$
$$= \$2400 - \$250$$
$$= \$2,150.$$

or the amount calculated on a replacement costs (RC) basis, subject to policy limits and deductibles, calculated as follows:

$$\text{Amount payable} = \left[\left(\frac{\text{Did}}{\text{Should}} \times \text{Loss amount} \right) - \text{Deductible} \right] \text{ subject to policy limits.}$$

$$= \left(\frac{\$200,000}{\$320,000} \times \$3,200 \right) - \$250$$

$$= (0.625 \times \$3,200) - \$250$$

$$= \$2,000 - 250$$

$$= \$1,750.$$

Because the ACV is greater, the amount payable is $2,150.

b.
$$\text{Did} = \$200,000.$$
$$\text{Should} = \$300,000 \times 0.80 = \$240,000.$$

Did the Smiths meet the insurance-to-value provisions? No.

Therefore the amount payable is the *greater* of the ACV (in this case, $2,400), subject to policy limits and deductibles, calculated as follows:

$$\text{ACV} = \text{Loss amount} - \text{Deductible}$$
$$= \$2,400 - \$250$$
$$= \$2,150.$$

or the amount calculated on a replacement costs (RC) basis, subject to policy limits and deductibles, calculated as follows:

$$\text{Amount payable} = \left[\left(\frac{\text{Did}}{\text{Should}} \times \text{Loss amount} \right) - \text{Deductible} \right] \text{ subject to policy limits.}$$

$$= \left(\frac{\$200,000}{\$240,000} \times \$3,200 \right) - \$250$$

$$= (0.833 \times \$3,200) - \$250$$

$$= \$2,667 - \$250$$

$$= \$2,417.$$

Because the amount calculated on the RC basis is greater, the amount payable is $2,417.

c.
$$\text{Did} = \$200{,}000.$$
$$\text{Should} = \$250{,}000 \times 0.80 = \$200{,}000.$$

Did the Smiths meet the insurance-to-value provisions? Yes.

Therefore the amount payable equals the loss amount on an RC basis, subject to policy limits and deductibles.

$$\text{Amount payable} = \text{Loss amount} - \text{Deductible}$$
$$= \$3{,}200 - \$250$$
$$= \$2{,}950.$$

d.
$$\text{Did} = \$200{,}000.$$
$$\text{Should} = \$200{,}000 \times 0.80 = \$160{,}000.$$

Did the Smiths meet the insurance-to-value provisions? Yes.

Therefore the amount payable equals the loss amount on an RC basis, subject to policy limits and deductibles.

$$\text{Amount payable} = \text{Loss amount} - \text{Deductible}$$
$$= \$3{,}200 - 250$$
$$= \$2{,}950.$$

4. Valuation approaches for Campus Book Store losses are as follows:
   a. Building, replacement cost
   b. Personal property, actual cash value
   c. Stock, selling price less discounts and expenses the insured would otherwise have had
   d. Papers containing customer records, cost of reproduction (that is, the cost of blank materials and the labor to transcribe or copy records when there is a duplicate)

5. Maximum amounts payable for Campus Book Store's losses in each situation, using the policy's 90 percent coinsurance provision, are as follows:
   a.
   $$\text{Did} = \$300{,}000.$$
   $$\text{Should} = \$300{,}000 \times 0.90 = \$270{,}00.$$

   Did Campus Book Store meet the coinsurance requirement? Yes.

   Therefore the amount payable equals the loss amount subject to policy limits and deductibles.

   $$\text{Amount payable} = \text{Loss amount} - \text{Deductible}$$
   $$= \$10{,}000 - \$250$$
   $$= \$9{,}750.$$

   b.
   $$\text{Did} = \$300{,}000.$$
   $$\text{Should} = \$320{,}000 \times 0.90 = \$288{,}000.$$

   Did Campus Book Store meet the coinsurance requirement? Yes.

   Therefore the amount payable equals the loss amount subject to policy limits and deductibles.

   $$\text{Amount payable} = \text{Loss amount} - \text{Deductible}$$
   $$= \$10{,}000 - \$250$$
   $$= \$9{,}750.$$

c. $$\text{Did} = \$300,000.$$
$$\text{Should} = \$320,000 \times 0.90 = \$288,000.$$
Did Campus Book Store meet the coinsurance requirement? Yes.

Therefore the amount payable equals the loss amount subject to policy limits and deductibles.
$$\text{Amount payable} = \text{Loss amount} - \text{Deductible}$$
$$= \$320,000 - \$250$$
$$= \$319,750 \text{ subject to policy limit of}$$
$$\$300,000 = \$300,000.$$

d. $$\text{Did} = \$300,000.$$
$$\text{Should} = \$320,000 \times 0.90 = \$288,000.$$
Did Campus Book Store meet the coinsurance requirement? Yes.

Therefore the amount payable equals the loss amount subject to policy limits and deductibles.
$$\text{Amount payable} = \text{Loss amount} - \text{Deductible}$$
$$= \$300,000 - \$250$$
$$= \$299,750.$$

e. $$\text{Did} = \$200,000.$$
$$\text{Should} = \$400,000 \times 0.90 = \$360,000.$$
Did Campus Book Store meet the coinsurance requirement? No.

Therefore the amount payable equals the loss amount subject to policy limits and deductibles

$$\text{Amount payable} = \left[\left(\frac{\text{Did}}{\text{Should}} \times \text{Loss amount}\right) - \text{Deductible}\right] \text{ subject to policy limits.}$$
$$= \left(\frac{\$300,000}{\$360,000} \times \$12,000\right) - \$250$$
$$= (0.833 \times \$12,000) - \$250$$
$$= \$10,000 - \$250$$
$$= \$9,750.$$

f. $$\text{Did} = \$200,000.$$
$$\text{Should} = \$400,000 \times 0.90 = \$360,000.$$
Did Campus Book Store meet the coinsurance requirement? No.

Therefore the amount payable $= \left[\left(\frac{\text{Did}}{\text{Should}} \times \text{Loss amount}\right) - \text{Deductible}\right]$ subject to policy limits and deductibles.

$$\text{Amount payable} = \left[\left(\frac{\text{Did}}{\text{Should}} \times \text{Loss amount}\right) - \text{Deductible}\right] \text{ subject to policy limits.}$$
$$= \left(\frac{\$300,000}{\$360,000} \times \$9,000\right) - \$250$$
$$= (0.556 \times \$9,000) - \$250$$
$$= \$5,000 - \$250$$
$$= \$4,750.$$

g.
$$\text{Did} = \$200,000.$$
$$\text{Should} = \$200,000 \times 0.90 = \$180,000.$$

Did Campus Book Store meet the coinsurance requirement? Yes.

Therefore the amount payable equals the loss amount subject to policy limits and deductibles

$$\text{Amount payable} = \text{Loss amount} - \text{Deductible}$$
$$= \$200,000 - \$25$$
$$= \$199,750.$$

6. a. A peak season endorsement covers the fluctuating values of business personal property by providing differing amounts of insurance for certain periods during the overall policy period. This endorsement would be appropriate for Campus Book Store. If the store experiences a large increase in stock at the beginning of the school term, the peak season could provide one policy limit for November through July, and a higher limit for August through October.

   b. The value reporting form bases the insured's premium on the business personal property values that the insured reports to the insurer periodically during the policy period. This endorsement is probably not appropriate for Campus Book Store unless the store experienced fluctuations in business personal property values throughout the year.

7. a. ACV has traditionally been based on replacement cost minus depreciation. Other methods of determining ACV include the use of market value and the broad evidence rule.

   b. The Stable Environment was originally constructed as a barn, but it is being used as a bar and restaurant. If part of the original barn is damaged, The Stable Environment might prefer to reconstruct it using modern, lower-cost materials that serve the same restaurant function rather than the materials used in constructing the original barn.

Amounts Payable: Liability Insurance and Other Sources of Recovery

Direct Your Learning

Assignment

15

Study Materials

Required Reading:

- Foundations of Risk Management and Insurance
  - Chapter 15

Study Aids:

- SMART Practice Exam CD-ROM
- SMART Study Aids Review Notes and Flash Cards— Assignment 15

Educational Objectives

After learning the content of this assignment, you should be able to:

1. Explain why determining adequate liability policy limits is difficult.

2. Given a liability insurance claim, apply policy limits and valuation provisions to determine the amounts payable.

   - Explain how liability losses are valued and how that affects amounts payable after a loss.

   - Describe the following types of liability policy limits and their effects on the amounts payable after a loss: single limits, split limits, aggregate limits, limits for defense costs, limits for nonfault-based coverages, and limits on workers' compensation.

3. Explain when and why deductibles and self-insured retentions are applied to liability insurance policies.

4. Explain how arbitration is used to settle disputed liability claims.

5. Describe the following five other sources of recovery that affect amounts payable:

   - Noninsurance agreements

   - Negligent third parties

   - Other insurance in the same policy

   - Other insurance in a similar policy

   - Other insurance in dissimilar policies

6. Describe the three types of other-insurance provisions.

7. Explain how conflicts are resolved for other-insurance provisions.

8. Define or describe each of the Key Words and Phrases for this assignment.

Outline

- **Amounts Payable: Liability Insurance**
  - A. Adequate Policy Limits
  - B. Valuation of Liability Losses
    1. Relevant Policy Provisions
    2. Extent of Damages
  - C. Policy Limits
    1. Single Limit
    2. Split Limits
    3. Aggregate Limits
  - D. Other Policy Limits
    1. Limits for Defense Costs
    2. Limits for Nonfault-Based Coverages
    3. Limits for Workers' Compensation
  - E. Deductibles and Self-Insured Retentions
  - F. Disputed Claims Resolution: Arbitration Provisions

- **Other Sources of Recovery**
  - A. Noninsurance Agreements
  - B. Third-Party Liability
  - C. Other Insurance in the Same Policy
  - D. Other Insurance in a Similar Policy
  - E. Other Insurance in Dissimilar Policies

- **Other-Insurance Provisions**
  - A. Types of Other-Insurance Provisions
    1. Primary/Excess Provisions
    2. Proportional Provisions
    3. Escape Clauses
  - B. Conflict Resolution for Other-Insurance Provisions
    1. Guiding Principles
    2. Court Resolution

- **Summary**

Use the SMART Practice Exam CD-ROM to self-test. The CD-ROM constructs individual assignment or comprehensive sample exams, allowing you to test your recall of important information. Feedback is provided, targeting the areas requiring further review.

Key Words and Phrases

Define or describe each of the words and phrases listed below.

Single limit (p. 15.8)

Split limits (p. 15.10)

Aggregate limit (p. 15.11)

Primary coverage provision (p. 15.23)

Excess coverage provision (p. 15.23)

Proportional other-insurance provision (p. 15.23)

Contribution by equal shares (p. 15.24)

Escape clause (p. 15.25)

Review Questions

1. List the factors that can affect the amount payable under a liability insurance contract. (p.15.3)

2. Explain whether each of the following can be insured to value in a liability insurance policy. (pp. 15.4–15.5)

   a. Property damage

   b. Bodily injury

3. Explain why liability insurance is often purchased in layers. (p. 15.5)

4. List the two factors that affect the determination of amounts payable under a liability insurance policy. (p. 15.6)

5. Explain how the compensable amount of the loss is determined under a liability insurance policy. (p. 15.6)

6. Describe the factors that determine the extent of damages related to each of the following types of claim. (pp. 15.7–15.8)

   a. Property damage claim

   b. Bodily injury claim

7. Describe the ways that policy limits are generally expressed in liability insurance policies. (pp. 15.8–15.12)

8. Describe the three types of limits typically included in policies that contain split limits. (p. 15.10)

9. Explain how defense costs are related to policy limits in liability insurance policies. (p. 15.12)

10. Explain why insurers are willing to pay certain claims regardless of fault (nonfault-based coverages). (p. 15.13)

11. Describe the effectiveness of deductibles in liability insurance policies. (p. 15.15)

12. Compare deductibles and self-insured retentions. (p. 15.16)

13. Describe the types of disagreements that can be resolved through arbitration. (p. 15.16)

14. List the five other sources of recovery that liability insurance policy provisions address. (pp. 15.17–15.18)

15. Explain how subrogation addresses third-party liability and the rights to recovery. (p. 15.19)

16. Explain how duplicate coverage may arise in a package policy. (p. 15.19)

17. Describe the three types of other-insurance provisions. (pp. 15.22–15.25)

18. Describe situations in which insurers share loss amounts proportionally. (p. 15.23)

19. Describe the two crucial points to understanding proportional other-insurance provisions. (p. 15.23)

20. Describe the four types of escape clauses. (p. 15.25)

21. Describe the methods of conflict resolution for other-insurance provisions available to insurers. (p. 15.27)

22. Describe the Guiding Principles that relate to conflict resolution of other-insurance principles. (p. 15.27)

Application Questions

An ISO HO-3 homeowners policy and an ISO Businessowners policy are included in the Appendix in this course guide, and they are used as the bases for Application Questions 1 through 5.

1. In the homeowners policy, what type of limit is each of the following? (pp. 15.8–15.15; HO-3 p. 16)

   a. The bodily injury and property damage limit of liability

   b. The medical payments to others limit of liability

   c. The damage to property of others limit of liability

2. What type of other-insurance provision is applicable to the property section of the homeowners policy? (pp. 15.22–15.27, HO-3 p. 14)

3. Explain how the other-insurance provisions of the liability section of the homeowners policy would apply to a loss involving both this policy and a personal umbrella liability policy. (pp. 15.22–15.27, HO-3 p. 21)

4. What limits apply to defense and supplementary payments under the businessowners policy? (pp. 15.12–15.15, HO-3 p. 27)

5. What types of other-insurance provisions appear in the businessowners policy? (pp. 15.22–15.27, HO-3 p. 42)

6. For each of the following other-insurance situations, determine how much of the loss would be paid by each insurer. (pp. 15.22–15.25)

   a. All policies specify proration by policy limits. $10,000 loss.

       • Policy from Insurer A has a $50,000 limit.

       • Policy from Insurer B has a $40,000 limit.

- Policy from Insurer C has a $10,000 limit that is uncollectible because Insurer C is insolvent.

b. Both policies specify contribution by equal shares. $200,000 loss.

- Policy from Insurer A has a $50,000 limit.

- Policy from Insurer B has a $500,000 limit.

c. Excess/primary provisions. $500,000 loss.

- Policy from Insurer A provides primary coverage with a $300,000 limit.

- Policy from Insurer B provides excess coverage with a $1,000,000 limit.

   d.   Excess provision only. $50,000 loss.

       •   Policy from Insurer A provides coverage in a policy with an excess other-insurance provision and a limit of $100,000. No other insurance applies.

7. While driving Bruce's auto with his permission, Alfred struck and injured a pedestrian who subsequently was awarded a $125,000 judgment against Alfred. Alfred has an auto policy providing $100,000 in liability coverage. This policy covers Alfred while operating a nonowned vehicle such as Bruce's.

Alfred's auto policy contains the following other-insurance provision:

> If there is other applicable liability insurance, we will pay only our share of the loss. Our share is the proportion that our limit of liability bears to the total of all applicable limits. However, any insurance we provide for a vehicle you do not own shall be excess over any other valid and collectible insurance.

What dollar amount, if any, will be paid under Alfred's policy in each of the following situations? Explain your answers. (pp. 15.22–15.25)

   a.   No other auto liability insurance applies.

b. Bruce's car is covered under an auto liability policy. Bruce is the named insured under this policy. Alfred is also an insured because he was using Bruce's car with his permission.

(1) Bruce's policy provides 50/100/25 liability coverage and contains the same other-insurance provisions as Alfred's policy.

(2) Bruce's policy provides $500,000 in liability coverage and contains the following other-insurance provision:

For any covered auto you own, this coverage form provides primary insurance. For any covered auto you do not own, the insurance provided by this coverage form is excess over any other insurance.

Answers to Assignment 15 Questions

NOTE: These answers are provided to give students a basic understanding of acceptable types of responses. They often are not the only valid answers and are not intended to provide an exhaustive response to the questions.

Review Questions

1. Factors that can affect the amount payable include policy limits, the valuation of losses, and the amount of deductibles or self-insured retentions.

2. Some liability loss exposures can be insured to value.

    a. The maximum potential loss for liability loss exposures involving possible damage or destruction to specific property items (property of others) can be determined and insured to value.

    b. Liability claims arising from bodily injury, wrongful death, emotional distress, and so on are more difficult to value, and therefore to insure to value. Limits typically vary based on the individual's or organization's activities, income, and asset level.

3. Liability insurance is often purchased in layers because individuals and organizations need high limits of liability coverage that may not be available from a single insurer. Therefore, a primary insurer will often provide a working layer of coverage with excess layers above.

4. Among the many factors that determine the amounts payable under a liability policy are the relevant policy provisions and the extent of the bodily injury and/or property damage to others.

5. The compensable amount of the loss can be determined by negotiations between the liability insurer and the claimant if the claim can be settled out of court. If a settlement cannot be reached by the parties involved, the liability claim will go to trial and the extent of the insured's liability is then based on legal principles.

6. The factors that determine the extent of damages are as follows:

    a. Property damage—The owner may recover the reasonable cost to repair the property or replace the property if it cannot be economically repaired. When the property must be replaced, the owner is entitled to the property's reasonable market value before damage or destruction and may also recover damages to compensate for the loss of use of the property.

    b. Bodily injury—A broader range of factors applies, including the following:

        • Reasonable and necessary medical expenses

        • Type of bodily injury

        • Lost wages and loss of earning capacity

        • Other out-of-pocket expenses, such as household assistance

        • Current and future pain and suffering resulting from the bodily injury

        • Extent and permanency of disability and impairment

        • Disfigurement resulting from bodily injury

        • Preexisting conditions that could have contributed to the bodily injury

7. In liability insurance, policy limits are generally expressed in one of the following three ways:

    (1) Single limit—one limit that applies to all bodily injury and property damage from a single occurrence, a single person incurring a loss, or a single claim

    (2) Split limits—separate limits for bodily injury claims and for property damage claims

    (3) Aggregate limit—a specific limit on the maximum amount an insurer will pay for all covered occurrences during the covered period

8. Policies containing split limits usually contain the following three types of limits:

    (1) Bodily injury limit applicable to each injured person

    (2) Bodily injury limit applicable to two or more injured persons

    (3) Property damage limit

9. As part of the duty to defend, the insurer also agrees to pay the costs of defending the insured. These defense costs can be paid within or in addition to the policy limits. Knowing whether defense costs are paid either within or in addition to the policy limits is important because the amount of insurance available to pay damages can be significantly reduced when defense costs are paid within the policy limits.

10. Nominal limits for nonfault-based coverages, such as medical payments, enable an insurer to pay small claims in a way that eliminates the need for litigation and preserves the insured's goodwill, while preserving the insurer's defenses in the event of a larger liability claim.

11. Deductibles in liability policies are not as effective as they are in property insurance policies. Liability insurers want to control liability claims from the outset, therefore they want to be involved in even small liability claims that may be less than the deductible amount. In addition, for most liability policies, deductibles would not noticeably reduce premiums because relatively few liability claims involve small amounts that an insurer would be able to avoid with a deductible. Finally, the insurer generally has to pay the third-party claimant the full settlement amount and then try to collect the deductible from the insured who may be unwilling or unable to make the payment.

12. The difference between a deductible and a self-insured retention (SIR) are as follows:

    • With a liability insurance deductible, the insurer defends on a first-dollar basis, pays all covered losses, and then bills the insured for the amount of losses up to the deductible.

    • With an SIR, the insurer pays only losses that exceed the SIR amount. The insurer does not defend claims below the SIR amount. Consequently, the organization is responsible for adjusting and paying its own losses up to the SIR amount.

13. The arbitration process outlines a specific procedure for resolving the following two types of disagreements:

    (1) Disagreements about whether the insured is legally entitled to recover damages

    (2) Disagreements about the amount of damages

14. A multiple-recovery rule applies to other sources against which the insured has a legally enforceable right, including the following five sources:

    (1) Noninsurance agreements

    (2) Negligent third parties

    (3) Other insurance in the same policy

    (4) Other insurance in a similar policy

    (5) Other insurance in a dissimilar policy

15. An insured's recovery from a third party (or a third party's liability insurer) could overlap with the insured's own property insurance coverage. Subrogation policy provisions allow an injured party to file a claim with his/her first party insurer, who can then attempt to collect from the responsible third party.

16. Property and/or liability insurance policies may provide two or more coverages under the same policy. When these package policies are used, a given loss may be covered by more than one of the coverages offered.

17. The three types of other-insurance provisions are as follows:
    (1) Primary/excess provision—specifies that the policy's coverage pays the loss amount either before other applicable policies (primary) or only after the primary limits have been exhausted (excess).
    (2) Proportional provision—limits the insurer's obligation to some portion of the overall loss.
    (3) Escape clause—relieves the insurer of any obligation to pay losses if other insurance is in effect.

18. Insurers typically share the loss amount proportionally when two policies both state that they are primary, when both state that they are excess, or when no statement of primary/excess coverage is indicated.

19. The following two points are crucial to understanding proportional other-insurance provisions:
    (1) An other-insurance provision affects only the policy in which it appears. One insurer's policy cannot specify the coverage that will be provide by another insurer.
    (2) A proportional provision limits an insurer's amount payable but does not reduce coverage. If losses exceed the total policy limits available, each insurer pays its full policy limit, barring indications to the contrary elsewhere in the policy.

20. Escape clauses generally function in one of the following four ways:
    (1) Prohibitions—forbidding other insurance
    (2) Exclusions—excluding property or activities covered by other insurance
    (3) Disclaimers—denying responsibility if other insurance applies
    (4) Offsets—reducing the coverage limit by the amount of other insurance.

21. Sometimes insurers disagree about each insurer's amounts payable when overlapping coverage exists, especially when neither policy's other-insurance provision clearly addresses the situation. The most common resolution is an agreement or a compromise between the two insurers. In cases of severe disagreement, arbitration may be used. Other procedures that can be used to resolve such differences include application of the Guiding Principles or resolution in court.

22. The Guiding Principles were developed by industry-wide associations in the 1960s. They apply when other-insurance provisions are contradictory or when other-insurance provisions do not exist. These principles operate only when more than one policy covers a loss and none of the other policies' other-insurance provisions resolve how the respective coverages should apply.

Application Questions

Answers in calculations may vary slightly because numbers were rounded.

1. The type of homeowners policy limit for each limit named is as follows:
   a. The bodily injury and property damage limit of liability—combined single limit that applies to each occurrence
   b. The medical payments to others limit of liability—separate limit that applies to each person
   c. The damage to property of others limit of liability—separate limit that applies to each occurrence

2. Proration by policy limits applies to the property section of this homeowners policy. However, when the loss is covered by an association or a corporation of property owners, the coverage is excess.

3. Because an umbrella policy is specifically written to provide excess insurance, the homeowners policy would be primary and the umbrella would be excess.

4. The following businessowners policy limits apply:
   - No dollar limit applies to defense costs. Coverage of defense costs ends when the applicable limit of liability is exhausted.
   - Supplementary payments cover the described expenses in full (such as claim expenses the insurer incurs or the cost of release attachment bonds) or cover the expenses subject to stated dollar sublimits ($250 for the cost of bail bonds or $250 per day for lost earnings).

5. The other-insurance clause states that the businessowners policy is excess of the amount due from other insurance and that the insurer will have no duty to defend if another insurer has that duty.

6. The insurers' respective shares of the losses are as follows:
   a. $10,000 loss:
      - Insurer A pays $5,000

$$\frac{\$50,000}{(\$50,000 + \$40,000 + \$10,000)} \times \$10,000$$

$$= \frac{50,000}{100,000} \times 10,000$$

$$= 0.5 \times 10,000$$

$$= \$5,000.$$

      - Insurer B pays $4,000

$$\frac{\$40,000}{(\$50,000 + \$40,000 + \$10,000)} \times \$10,000$$

$$= \frac{40,000}{100,000} \times 10,000$$

$$= 0.4 \times 10,000$$

$$= \$4,000.$$

      - Insurer C owes $1,000

$$\frac{\$10,000}{(\$50,000 + \$40,000 + \$10,000)} \times \$10,000$$

$$= \frac{10,000}{100,000} \times 10,000$$

$$= 0.1 \times 10,000$$

$$= \$1,000.$$

      Insurer C should pay $1,000, but Insurer C is insolvent.
   b. $200,000 loss:
      - Insurer A pays $50,000 (the limit on Insurer A's policy).
      - Insurer B pays $150,000. Both Insurer A and Insurer B pay $50,000, which is the limit on Insurer A's policy. Insurer B then covers the remaining unpaid loss of $100,000, which is within its policy limit.

c. $500,000 loss:
- Insurer A pays $300,000.
- Insurer B pays $200,000.

d. $50,000 loss:
- Insurer A pays $50,000.

7. a. Alfred's policy will pay $100,000. No other insurance applies, and the limit on Alfred's policy is $100,000.

b. (1) Alfred's policy will pay $75,000. Bruce's 50/100/25 split limits cover up to $50,000 per person for bodily injury, and Bruce's insurer will pay the first $50,000. Because the car involved is Bruce's, Bruce's policy is primary and Alfred's policy is excess.

(2) Alfred's policy will pay $0. Bruce's policy is primary and covers the entire amount.

About Institute Exams

Exam questions are based on the educational objectives stated in the course guide. The exam is designed to measure whether you have met those educational objectives. The exam does not test every educational objective. Instead, it tests over a balanced sample of educational objectives.

How to Pass Institute Exams

What can you do to make sure you pass an Institute exam? Students who successfully pass Institute exams do the following:

- Use the assigned study materials. Focus your study on the educational objectives presented at the beginning of each course guide assignment. Thoroughly read the textbook and any other assigned materials, and then complete the course guide exercises. Choose a study method that best suits your needs; for example, participate in a traditional class, online class, or informal study group; or study on your own. Use the Institutes' SMART Study Aids (if available) for practice and review.

- Become familiar with the types of test questions. The practice exam in this course guide will help you understand the different types of questions you will encounter on the exam.

- Maximize test-taking time. Successful students also use the sample exam to practice pacing themselves. Learning how to manage your time during the exam ensures that you will complete all of the test questions in the time allotted.

Types of Exam Questions

The exam contains a variety of questions based on the course's educational objectives. *Using This Course Guide*, on page v, lists and defines many of the action words used in the educational objectives for this course. The same action words are used in the exam questions. Become familiar with these action words before the exam so that you will know how to approach a question that asks you to *apply* a principle, *illustrate* a concept, or *evaluate* a plan. Each of these action words requires a different type of answer. Be prepared to take your cue from the action word before you start to compose your answer.

Most questions can be answered briefly in one or two paragraphs or less. Always be as responsive as possible to the question that is asked but do not pad your answer. Direct answers that focus on the action word, contain the correct information, and end when the question has been answered are the ones that earn full credit on the exam. However, the graders often can and do give partial credit when students provide a part of the correct answer.

CPCU 510 Sample Exam

The following sample exam consists of two sections—Part A and Part B—totaling 100 points. On the actual exam, you must answer all questions in both Part A and Part B of the exam. Each Part A question should be answered independently of the others.

Part B questions may include or make reference to specific facts, case situations, or exhibits. In Part B, your answers must be based on the information provided. When several questions are based on the same set of facts during a computer-administered exam, those facts will appear in a separate window and remain in view for the duration of the questions.

Part A

1. (2 points)

   Joe Jones, a CPCU candidate, is aware of the Code of Professional Ethics and believes that his boss, Whitney Smith, CPCU, has violated a Rule. What process should Joe follow if he decides to file a complaint against Whitney?

2. (6 points)

   During the past five years, eleven medical professional liability claims have been made against Millbourne Memorial Hospital, with each claim resulting in the payment of damages from $1,000,000 to $5,000,000.

   a.   What is the mean frequency of claims per year?

   b.   What is the range of severity of these claims?

c.   What limitations should be considered in using these data to predict Millbourne Memorial Hospital's future medical professional liability losses?

3. (3 points)

Pooling is a risk management arrangement by which several persons or organizations combine their resources to reduce the risks of each participant. Why is pooling more effective in reducing risks for independent, or uncorrelated, risks than for correlated risks?

4. (2 points)

What sanction is automatically imposed on a CPCU who violates Rule R3.3 of the Code of Professional Ethics of the American Institute for CPCU: "A CPCU shall not violate any law or regulation relating to professional activities or commit any felony"?

5. (3 points)

Coverage under a liability insurance policy will not apply unless an event involved all five elements of an insured event. Two of the elements are a covered location and a covered time period. Identify the other *three* elements of an insured event for liability insurance.

6. (3 points)

It is often difficult to calculate the true cost of risk to an individual or organization. Therefore, insurance and risk management professionals often focus on the financial consequences of risk. Describe the three components of the financial consequences of risk.

7. (2 points)

Risk maps are enterprise risk management (ERM) tools often used to help break down the departmentalization of risk that occurred under a traditional risk management program. Describe *two* other functions that risk maps can serve in an ERM program.

8. (3 points)

Separation is a risk control technique that disperses a particular asset or activity over several locations and regularly relies on that asset or activity as part of the organization's working resources. Explain the effect that separation has on the frequency and severity of losses associated with a loss exposure.

9. (4 points)

The risk financing goal of managing cash flow variability addresses the residual uncertainty component of the financial consequences of risk. List and describe the *three* risk financing goals that address the expected costs of losses component of the financial consequences of risk.

10. (2 points)

What information would you expect to find in a policy condition titled *liberalization*?

11. (2 points)

Explain *two* purposes served by policy limits in insurance policies.

12. (2 points)

What is the purpose of the *Guiding Principles—Casualty, Fidelity, Inland Marine—First-Party Property Losses and Claims*, usually referred to as the *Guiding Principles*?

13. (2 points)

In selecting a liability insurance policy and choosing appropriate limits, why is it important for a risk manager to determine whether defense costs are paid within or in addition to policy limits?

14. (5 points)

Music Recording Company (MRC) derives its income from the sale of compact discs (CDs) and audiotapes. One of MRC's loss exposures arises out of the possibility that people might distribute illegal copies of its copyrighted music.

a. Identify each of the *four* dimensions of this loss exposure and explain why each is relevant.

b. Explain whether this loss exposure involves pure or speculative risks.

15. (2 points)

A new edition of a popular personal insurance policy is being introduced this year. Does the Code of Professional Ethics of the American Institute for CPCU obligate all CPCUs who are subject to the Code to remain informed regarding coverage changes in this policy? Explain the provisions of the Code that support your answer.

16. (4 points)

Evaluate the insurability of earthquake damage in policies providing property insurance on private residences. Your answer should take into account the ideal characteristics of an insurable loss exposure.

17. (4 points)

To some extent, all exclusions help to keep insurance premiums reasonable. Explain *one* additional purpose for each of the following types of exclusions in insurance contracts.

a. Exclusion of intentional injury in the Commercial General Liability Coverage Form

b. Exclusion in homeowners policies of loss by freezing unless the pipes have been drained or the owner attempted to maintain heat.

18. (2 points)

Risk management program goals may sometimes conflict with one another. Give *two* examples of post-loss goals that may conflict with the pre-loss goal of economy of operations.

19. (2 points)

Not all of the risk control techniques are effective in managing every type of loss exposure. List the *three* loss control techniques that are most effective in controlling liability loss exposures.

20. (3 points)

Corporate governance dictates that organizations be careful in selecting a domicile if forming a captive. List the four factors an organization should consider in selecting a domicile.

21. (2 points)

Not all insureds obtain insurance in the admitted market. Describe two choices an insurance consumer may have if he or she is unable to obtain insurance in the admitted market.

22. (2 points)

Insurance provides a variety of benefits to individuals, organizations and society. Explain how insurance promotes loss control activities.

23. (3 points)

One of the rationales for government involvement in insurance is to fill insurance needs that are unmet by private insurers. List the other *three* rationales for government involvement in insurance.

24. (3 points)

    Insurance policies generally exclude most intentional torts. Give *three* examples of intentional torts.

25. (2 points)

    Describe the effect on competition that the number and size of competing insurers has in a market.

Part B

26. (4 points)

Mary Sullivan, CPCU, a reinsurance underwriter for ABC Insurance Company, receives the following e-mail message from Josh Davis, who used to work for ABC. Josh is now a facultative reinsurance underwriter for XYZ Reinsurance Company:

> Hi Mary!
>
> I remember you used to underwrite the Crowley account. I just got an application to quote on some reinsurance through a different insurer, and this is really a rush job. Can you save me some time and tell me how you felt about Crowley? Did it seem like a well-managed operation? Were there any major problems? Thanks—I owe you one.
>
> Josh

Having recently underwritten the Crowley account, Mary has some private information that would help Josh make an appropriate underwriting decision, and she thinks he might be able to help her with a similar problem in the future. However, she wonders whether sharing the information she has would violate her responsibilities as a CPCU. Paraphrase a Rule of the Code of Professional Ethics that applies to this situation, and explain how it should guide Mary's decision.

27. (4 points)

Eleanor has commercial property insurance covering the contents of her store. Eleanor's policy was written on an actual cash value (ACV) basis with a $100,000 limit and a 100 percent coinsurance clause. Ignoring any deductible that might apply, how much would she recover in each of the following situations? *Show your calculations or explain your answer.*

a. Personal property ACV at time of loss was $125,000, and the ACV of the loss was $10,000.

b. Personal property ACV at time of loss was $125,000, and the ACV of the loss was $112,500.

28. (7 points)

Kenneth Kane, an active CPCU, is the owner of an independent insurance agency. Kenneth is eager to give as much visibility as possible to the CPCU designation. Briefly explain whether each of the following ways in which Kenneth uses the designation violates the Rules of the Code of Professional Ethics of the American Institute.

a. His business correspondence is signed, "Kenneth Kane." Below this signature is a typed line reading "Kenneth Kane, CPCU."

b. His business card carries the agency name, Kane, CPCU Agency.

c. His business stationery includes an oversized CPCU key in the lower right hand corner.

d. He occasionally wears a T-shirt with the caption "CPCUs know it all."

Orange City Zoo Case. Orange City Zoo's new building, now under construction, will be named in honor of Dr. Stuart, a famous zoo employee. The dedication ceremony will coincide with Dr. Stuart's retirement next year. The $500,000 building project has been funded entirely through individual and corporate donations to the nonprofit Foundation established for that purpose by local business leaders. The Stuart building is being constructed by Construction Company. Following the dedication ceremony, the Foundation will dissolve and turn the building over to Orange City Zoo.

As the Stuart building nears completion, bids for property insurance on the completed structure are solicited. Several insurers provide bids for replacement cost coverage on a policy with an 80 percent coinsurance provision, but Dan Atkinson, the sales representative with the lowest bid, recommends actual cash value coverage with a 100 percent coinsurance provision.

29. (3 points)

Orange City Zoo. Explain why each of the following parties does or does not currently have an insurable interest in the Stuart Building.

a. Dr. Stuart

b. Construction Company

c. Foundation

30. (4 points)

   Orange City Zoo. Do you agree with each of the following statements made by Mr. Atkinson? Justify your answers.

   a. "On a brand new building, there is virtually no difference between the actual cash value and the replacement cost."

   b. "As the building ages, the insured with actual cash value coverage will not need to keep increasing the policy limits to meet coinsurance requirements."

31. (4 points)

   Gary was waterskiing behind his boat, the *Angel*, when it struck and damaged *Water Fun*, an unoccupied boat resting at anchor. At the time of the accident, Gary's friend, Becky, was at the controls of the *Angel*. Nobody was injured in the accident. However, the owner of *Water Fun* has sued both Gary and Becky to pay for the damage to it. Gary is the named insured on the declarations of a boatowners liability policy that describes the *Angel* in the Declarations. Gary's policy includes the following provisions.

   WHAT IS COVERED

   "We" will pay all sums which an "insured" becomes legally obligated to pay as damages due to bodily injury or property damage arising out of the ownership, maintenance, or use of the described vessel.

   WHAT IS NOT COVERED

   "We" do not cover liability arising from the ownership, maintenance, or use of the described vessel:

   1. That results from an intentional act of an insured.
   2. That results from "bodily injury" to persons while they are being towed by the described vessel while water skiing, aquaplaning, or involved in similar water sports.

DEFINITIONS

1. The words "you" and 'your" mean the persons named in the Declarations.

2. The words "we," "us," and "our" mean the company providing this insurance.

3. "Bodily injury" means bodily harm, sickness, or disease to a person.

4. "Insured" means "you" and

   a. "your" spouse

   b. "Your" relatives if residents of your household

   c. persons under the age of 21 in "your" care

   d. a person who operates a covered vessel with your permission.

   This does not include the liability of these "insureds" to "you" or to other "insureds."

5. "Property damage" means an injury to or destruction of property. This includes loss of use.

Based on the preceding information, explain whether Gary's boat-owners policy provides coverage for each of the following against the claim for damages by the owner of the *Water Fun*.

a. Gary

b. Becky

Jack's Bar Case. Wilson, a customer of Jack's Bar, is accused of accidentally starting a fire that causes $30,000 in damage to Jack's business and personal property. Wilson is the named insured under a homeowners policy that includes $300,000 of personal liability coverage that applies to this incident.

Jack's business personal property is covered under two property insurance policies. Insurer A provides $200,000 of coverage, and Insurer B provides $100,000 of coverage. Except for the limits and the name of the insurer, both policies are identical and include the following provisions:

OTHER INSURANCE

1. You may have other insurance subject to the same plan, terms, conditions and provisions as the insurance under this Coverage Part. If you do, we will pay our share of the covered loss or damage. Our share is the proportion that the applicable Limit of Insurance bears to the Limits of Insurance of all insurance covering on the same basis.

2. If there is other insurance covering the same loss or damage, other than that described in 1 above, we will pay only for the amount of covered loss or damage in excess of the amount due from that other insurance, whether you can collect on it or not. But we will not pay more than the applicable Limit of Insurance.

The liability section of Wilson's homeowners policy includes the following condition:

OTHER INSURANCE

This insurance is excess over other valid and collectible insurance except insurance written specifically to cover as excess over the limits of liability that apply in this policy.

32. (1 point)

   Jack's Bar Case. Give an example of a question of fact that courts could be asked to answer in this case.

33. (3 points)

Jacks's Bar Case. Jack's Bar submits a fire claim to both Insurer A and Insurer B. Explain the amount, if any, that each insurer would be obligated to pay. Ignore any coinsurance requirement or deductible that might apply.

34. (3 points)

Jack's Bar Case. Jack's property insurance policy does not explain that he has another option to recover for this loss, besides reporting the claim to Wilson's property insurance policy. Explain this other option.

Answers to CPCU 510 Sample Exam

Note: The following answers represent the type of answers that earn full credit on the examination. They are not intended to be a complete or exhaustive treatment of topics covered in the questions. However, they can help in your review for the exam, and they illustrate how much detail you must provide to earn full credit. Other answers could also earn full credit.

Part A

1. Joe should submit a complaint, alleging the violation, in writing, to the ethics counsel.

2. a.   The hospital's mean frequency of claims per year is: $11 \div 5 = 2.2$.

   b.   The range of severity of the hospital's claims is $4 million ($5,000,000 – $1,000,000).

   c.   Gathering data on past losses is not always an ideal way to determine future loss exposures. The past data must be relevant, complete, consistent, and organized. The past data also must be sufficient, and the quality of the past data must be adequate to produce reliable analysis

3. Pooling reduces risks because the participants that have few or no losses help pay the losses of the participant that does have losses, and vice versa. One participant's good luck offsets another participant's bad luck. When losses are correlated, the participants are more likely to have losses at the same time, and this offsetting effect is absent.

4. The designation of a CPCU who has violated a law relating to professional activities or committed a felony is automatically suspended.

5. The other three elements of an insured event for liability insurance are as follows:
   * Covered activity
   * Alleged legal responsibility to pay covered damages
   * Covered consequences

6. The three components of the financial consequences of risk are as follows:
   * The expected costs of loss or gains—includes both direct and indirect losses associated with the loss exposures.
   * Expenditures on risk management—includes expenditures on risk control and risk financing activities.
   * Cost of residual uncertainty—is the level of risk that remains after individuals or organizations implement their risk management plans.

7. Risk maps are effective communication tools to help senior management better understand the risk inherent to an organization. Risk maps, if tailored to key business goals, can rank risks based on their relative effect on those goals.

8. The intent of separation is to reduce the severity of an individual loss at a single location. However, by creating multiple locations, separation most likely increases loss frequency.

9. The following are the three risk financing goals that address the expected cost of losses component of the financial consequences of risk:
   * Pay for losses—ensure that the funds are available to pay for losses when they occur.
   * Maintain an appropriate level of liquidity—ensure that the level of cash liquidity is related to the retention levels that the individual or organization has assumed.

- Comply with legal requirements—some laws, such as financial responsibility laws, are designed to ensure that the responsible party has the financial ability to compensate (pay for the losses) any injured parties.

10. A liberalization provision states that if a revised policy edition is introduced that has more liberal terms than the existing policy, but no premium increase, this policy is automatically amended to include the broader coverage.

11. Two purposes served by policy limits are the following:
    - To give insurance buyers a choice of how much insurance they want relative to how much they are willing to pay
    - To set a maximum on the insurer's obligations

12. The purpose of the *Guiding Principles* is to help resolve disputes resulting from overlapping coverages.

13. When defense costs are paid in addition to policy limits, the full limits are available to pay damages. When defense costs are paid within limits, the limit applies to both the payment of damages and defense costs combined, with the result that less money is available to pay damages. The risk manager might want a higher limit when purchasing a policy that includes defense costs within limits.

14. a. The four dimensions of a loss exposure and their relevance are as follows:
    - Loss frequency—indicates the number of losses within a specified time period.
    - Loss severity—indicates the amount of each loss.
    - Total dollar losses—indicate the total amount of all losses as a result of the combined effect of loss frequency and severity,
    - Timing—indicates both when losses occur and when they are paid.
    b. The exposure to lost revenue is a business risk that is speculative.

15. No, the clause does not require all CPCUs to be informed about every policy change. CPCUs are obligated to keep informed of technical matters, such as the new policy language, if these matters are essential to their professional duties. A CPCU who does not deal with personal insurance is not obligated under the Code of Ethics to be familiar with details of this change.

16. The insurability of the earthquake damage under the policy, considered in the context of the ideal characteristics of an insurable loss exposure, is as follows:
    - Pure risk—earthquake qualifies
    - Fortuitous—earthquake qualifies
    - Definite in time and measurable—earthquake qualifies
    - Large number of similar independent exposures—earthquake qualifies
    - Independent and not catastrophic—flood can be catastrophic depending on the geographic diversification of the insurer's portfolio.
    - Economically feasible to insure—depends on the location of the property.

17. a. The CGL exclusion regarding intentional injury would assist in managing moral hazards because the insured should be held financially responsible for intentional acts.
    b. This exclusion regarding loss by freezing would assist in managing morale hazards because the insured should be careful enough to do what it takes to maintain enough heat in the house to keep the pipes from freezing.

18. Achieving any post-loss goal involves expending risk management resources that may conflict with the pre-loss goal of economy of operations. The economy of operations goal may conflict with tolerable uncertainty. Spending less on risk management would help meet the economy of operations goal but would increase uncertainty. The legality and social responsibility goals may also conflict with the economy of operations goal. The costs of meeting legal or social requirements conflict with operating economically.

19. The three risk control techniques that are most effective at controlling liability loss exposures are avoidance, loss prevention and loss reduction.

20. When selecting the domicile for a captive, the captive's parents should consider the following:
    - Initial capital requirements, taxes, and annual fees
    - Reputation and regulatory requirements
    - Premium and investment restrictions
    - Support of infrastructure in terms of services provided within the domicile

21. If an insurance consumer cannot obtain coverage in the admitted market, he or she may purchase insurance from a nonadmitted insurer through a surplus lines intermediary or may purchase insurance through the state-run residual market or assigned risk pool, if available.

22. Insurance policies may provide insureds with incentives to undertake loss control activities as a result of policy requirements (such as deductibles) or premium savings incentives (such as discounts for safety measures).

23. One of the reasons state or federal governments are involved in insurance is to fill unmet needs. The other three reasons are as follows:
    - To compel people to buy a particular type of insurance
    - To obtain greater efficiency and/or provide convenience to insurance buyers
    - To achieve collateral social purposes

24. The following are three examples of intentional torts:
    - Defamation
    - Fraud
    - Bad faith

25. The number and size of insurers competing in the insurance market greatly influence how competitive the market will be. In general, the larger the number of insurers competing, the greater competition. Furthermore, if the competing insurers are roughly the same size, the market is more competitive.

Part B

26. Several Rules might apply to this situation, but the one most directly relevant is the Rule against disclosing confidential information except when the disclosure is required by law or is made to a person who must have the information for legitimate business reasons. Although Josh might have a "legitimate business reason" to want the information Mary can provide, the information was entrusted to Mary in confidence, and it would be a breach of ethics for her to share it with Josh. The assumption that he might owe her a similar favor in another case only compounds the problem; it does not justify a breach of confidence by Mary.

27. Eleanor will receive the following:

   a. $\dfrac{\$100,000}{\$125,000} \times \$10,000 = \$8,000.$

   b. $\dfrac{\$100,000}{\$125,000} \times \$112,500 = \$90,000.$

28. Ken's use of the CPCU designation could result in the following:

   a. Use with signature in business correspondence: no violation; this usage is consistent with the Code. CPCUs are allowed to use the initials CPCU after their names in business correspondence.

   b. Use as part of his business's name on his business card: violates a Guideline that is incorporated into a Rule of the Code. CPCUs are not allowed to include the CPCU initials in a business name.

   c. Use of the enlarged key on stationery: Violates a Guideline that is incorporated into a Rule of the Code. CPCUs may imprint the key on business stationery but only at actual or reduced size.

   d. Use on a T-shirt: Violates two Rules of the Code. CPCUs are not allowed to indicate that they are more knowledgeable than others simply because they have the designation. Displaying the CPCU designation in this undignified manner also qualifies as an inappropriate use of the designation.

29. a. Dr. Stuart has no insurable interest because he would suffer no financial loss if the building were damaged or destroyed.

   b. Construction Company has an insurable interest in the building. Construction Company apparently would suffer a financial loss if the building were damaged or destroyed before it is completed and turned over to Foundation.

   c. Foundation has an insurable interest in the building. Foundation apparently has ownership rights in the property and would suffer a financial loss if the building were damaged or destroyed.

30. a. This statement is essentially accurate. ACV is generally considered to equal replacement cost minus depreciation, and a new building has had no chance to depreciate.

   b. This statement is not accurate. Actual cash value equals replacement cost minus depreciation. If the replacement cost of the building increases more rapidly than its depreciation, the actual cash value of the building will increase. If the building is insured to 100% of its ACV when the initial policy is sold and subject to a 100% coinsurance clause, any increase in the ACV of the building will result in failure to meet the coinsurance "requirement."

31. a. Gary is covered as named insured and owner of the *Angel*.

   b. Becky is covered as a person using the boat with the owner's permission.

32. Courts could be asked to determine the facts that led up to Wilson's being accused of accidentally starting the fire. They could be asked to determine Wilson's actions (or inactions) immediately before the fire started.

33. Insurer A would pay $20,000 and Insurer B would pay $10,000. Both policies are subject to the same plan, terms, conditions, and provisions; therefore, the first other-insurance provision, which specifies proration by policy limits, would apply.

34. Rather than pursuing a first-party property insurance claim, Jack could make a third-party liability claim against Wilson. This alternative might be expedient in this case if Wilson is clearly at fault, Wilson has adequate liability insurance, and Wilson's insurer would not subtract a deductible before paying Jack.

Appendix—Sample Policies and Forms

Homeowners Policy Declarations

POLICYHOLDER: Peter and Jennifer Smith
(Named Insured)   1008 N. Monroe Street
Anytown, USA 40000

POLICY NUMBER: 542 H 235668

POLICY PERIOD: **Inception:** April 30, 2005   Policy period begins 12:01 A.M. standard time
Expiration: April 30, 2006   at the residence premises.

FIRST MORTGAGEE AND MAILING ADDRESS:

State Local Mortgage Assn.
C/O Mortgagee, Inc.
P.O. Box 2000
Businesstown, USA 55000

We will provide the insurance described in this policy in return for the premium and compliance with all applicable
policy provisions.

SECTION I COVERAGES	LIMIT	
A—Dwelling	$ 200,000	**SECTION I DEDUCTIBLE:** $ 250
B—Other Structures	$ 20,000	**(In case of loss under Section I, we cover**
C—Personal Property	$ 100,000	**only that part of the loss over the**
D—Loss of Use	$ 60,000	**deductible amount shown above.)**

SECTION II COVERAGES	LIMIT	
E—Personal Liability	$ 100,000	**Each Occurrence**
F—Medical Payments to Others	$ 1,000	**Each Person**

CONSTRUCTION: Masonry Veneer   **NO. FAMILIES:** One   **TYPE ROOF:** Approved

YEAR BUILT: 1990   **PROTECTION CLASS:** 7   **FIRE DISTRICT:** Cook Township

NOT MORE THAN 1000 FEET FROM HYDRANT

NOT MORE THAN 5 MILES FROM FIRE DEPT.

FORMS AND ENDORSEMENTS IN POLICY: HO 00 03, HO 04 61

POLICY PREMIUM: $ 857.00 **COUNTERSIGNATURE DATE:** April 30, 2005   **AGENT:** W.R. Vincent

HOMEOWNERS 3 – SPECIAL FORM

AGREEMENT

We will provide the insurance described in this policy in return for the premium and compliance with all applicable provisions of this policy.

DEFINITIONS

A. In this policy, "you" and "your" refer to the "named insured" shown in the Declarations and the spouse if a resident of the same household. "We", "us" and "our" refer to the Company providing this insurance.

B. In addition, certain words and phrases are defined as follows:

1. "Aircraft Liability", "Hovercraft Liability", "Motor Vehicle Liability" and "Watercraft Liability", subject to the provisions in **b.** below, mean the following:

   a. Liability for "bodily injury" or "property damage" arising out of the:

   (1) Ownership of such vehicle or craft by an "insured";

   (2) Maintenance, occupancy, operation, use, loading or unloading of such vehicle or craft by any person;

   (3) Entrustment of such vehicle or craft by an "insured" to any person;

   (4) Failure to supervise or negligent supervision of any person involving such vehicle or craft by an "insured"; or

   (5) Vicarious liability, whether or not imposed by law, for the actions of a child or minor involving such vehicle or craft.

   b. For the purpose of this definition:

   (1) Aircraft means any contrivance used or designed for flight except model or hobby aircraft not used or designed to carry people or cargo;

   (2) Hovercraft means a self-propelled motorized ground effect vehicle and includes, but is not limited to, flarecraft and air cushion vehicles;

   (3) Watercraft means a craft principally designed to be propelled on or in water by wind, engine power or electric motor; and

   (4) Motor vehicle means a "motor vehicle" as defined in **7.** below.

2. "Bodily injury" means bodily harm, sickness or disease, including required care, loss of services and death that results.

3. "Business" means:

   a. A trade, profession or occupation engaged in on a full-time, part-time or occasional basis; or

   b. Any other activity engaged in for money or other compensation, except the following:

   (1) One or more activities, not described in (2) through (4) below, for which no "insured" receives more than $2,000 in total compensation for the 12 months before the beginning of the policy period;

   (2) Volunteer activities for which no money is received other than payment for expenses incurred to perform the activity;

   (3) Providing home day care services for which no compensation is received, other than the mutual exchange of such services; or

   (4) The rendering of home day care services to a relative of an "insured".

4. "Employee" means an employee of an "insured", or an employee leased to an "insured" by a labor leasing firm under an agreement between an "insured" and the labor leasing firm, whose duties are other than those performed by a "residence employee".

5. "Insured" means:

   a. You and residents of your household who are:

   (1) Your relatives; or

   (2) Other persons under the age of 21 and in the care of any person named above;

   b. A student enrolled in school full time, as defined by the school, who was a resident of your household before moving out to attend school, provided the student is under the age of:

   (1) 24 and your relative; or

   (2) 21 and in your care or the care of a person described in **a.(1)** above; or

c. Under Section **II:**

(1) With respect to animals or watercraft to which this policy applies, any person or organization legally responsible for these animals or watercraft which are owned by you or any person included in **a.** or **b.** above. "Insured" does not mean a person or organization using or having custody of these animals or watercraft in the course of any "business" or without consent of the owner; or

(2) With respect to a "motor vehicle" to which this policy applies:

(a) Persons while engaged in your employ or that of any person included in **a.** or **b.** above; or

(b) Other persons using the vehicle on an "insured location" with your consent.

Under both Sections **I** and **II**, when the word an immediately precedes the word "insured", the words an "insured" together mean one or more "insureds".

6. "Insured location" means:

a. The "residence premises";

b. The part of other premises, other structures and grounds used by you as a residence; and

(1) Which is shown in the Declarations; or

(2) Which is acquired by you during the policy period for your use as a residence;

c. Any premises used by you in connection with a premises described in **a.** and **b.** above;

d. Any part of a premises:

(1) Not owned by an "insured"; and

(2) Where an "insured" is temporarily residing;

e. Vacant land, other than farm land, owned by or rented to an "insured";

f. Land owned by or rented to an "insured" on which a one, two, three or four family dwelling is being built as a residence for an "insured";

g. Individual or family cemetery plots or burial vaults of an "insured"; or

h. Any part of a premises occasionally rented to an "insured" for other than "business" use.

7. "Motor vehicle" means:

a. A self-propelled land or amphibious vehicle; or

b. Any trailer or semitrailer which is being carried on, towed by or hitched for towing by a vehicle described in **a.** above.

8. "Occurrence" means an accident, including continuous or repeated exposure to substantially the same general harmful conditions, which results, during the policy period, in:

a. "Bodily injury"; or

b. "Property damage".

9. "Property damage" means physical injury to, destruction of, or loss of use of tangible property.

10. "Residence employee" means:

a. An employee of an "insured", or an employee leased to an "insured" by a labor leasing firm, under an agreement between an "insured" and the labor leasing firm, whose duties are related to the maintenance or use of the "residence premises", including household or domestic services; or

b. One who performs similar duties elsewhere not related to the "business" of an "insured".

A "residence employee" does not include a temporary employee who is furnished to an "insured" to substitute for a permanent "residence employee" on leave or to meet seasonal or short-term workload conditions.

11. "Residence premises" means:

a. The one family dwelling where you reside;

b. The two, three or four family dwelling where you reside in at least one of the family units; or

c. That part of any other building where you reside;

and which is shown as the "residence premises" in the Declarations.

"Residence premises" also includes other structures and grounds at that location.

DEDUCTIBLE

Unless otherwise noted in this policy, the following deductible provision applies:

Subject to the policy limits that apply, we will pay only that part of the total of all loss payable under Section I that exceeds the deductible amount shown in the Declarations.

SECTION I – PROPERTY COVERAGES

A. Coverage A – Dwelling

1. We cover:

   a. The dwelling on the "residence premises" shown in the Declarations, including structures attached to the dwelling; and

   b. Materials and supplies located on or next to the "residence premises" used to construct, alter or repair the dwelling or other structures on the "residence premises".

2. We do not cover land, including land on which the dwelling is located.

B. Coverage B – Other Structures

1. We cover other structures on the "residence premises" set apart from the dwelling by clear space. This includes structures connected to the dwelling by only a fence, utility line, or similar connection.

2. We do not cover:

   a. Land, including land on which the other structures are located;

   b. Other structures rented or held for rental to any person not a tenant of the dwelling, unless used solely as a private garage;

   c. Other structures from which any "business" is conducted; or

   d. Other structures used to store "business" property. However, we do cover a structure that contains "business" property solely owned by an "insured" or a tenant of the dwelling provided that "business" property does not include gaseous or liquid fuel, other than fuel in a permanently installed fuel tank of a vehicle or craft parked or stored in the structure.

3. The limit of liability for this coverage will not be more than 10% of the limit of liability that applies to Coverage A. Use of this coverage does not reduce the Coverage A limit of liability.

C. Coverage C – Personal Property

1. **Covered Property**

   We cover personal property owned or used by an "insured" while it is anywhere in the world. After a loss and at your request, we will cover personal property owned by:

   a. Others while the property is on the part of the "residence premises" occupied by an "insured"; or

   b. A guest or a "residence employee", while the property is in any residence occupied by an "insured".

2. **Limit For Property At Other Residences**

   Our limit of liability for personal property usually located at an "insured's" residence, other than the "residence premises", is 10% of the limit of liability for Coverage C, or $1,000, whichever is greater. However, this limitation does not apply to personal property:

   a. Moved from the "residence premises" because it is being repaired, renovated or rebuilt and is not fit to live in or store property in; or

   b. In a newly acquired principal residence for 30 days from the time you begin to move the property there.

3. **Special Limits Of Liability**

   The special limit for each category shown below is the total limit for each loss for all property in that category. These special limits do not increase the Coverage C limit of liability.

   a. $200 on money, bank notes, bullion, gold other than goldware, silver other than silverware, platinum other than platinumware, coins, medals, scrip, stored value cards and smart cards.

   b. $1,500 on securities, accounts, deeds, evidences of debt, letters of credit, notes other than bank notes, manuscripts, personal records, passports, tickets and stamps. This dollar limit applies to these categories regardless of the medium (such as paper or computer software) on which the material exists.

   This limit includes the cost to research, replace or restore the information from the lost or damaged material.

c. $1,500 on watercraft of all types, including their trailers, furnishings, equipment and outboard engines or motors.

d. $1,500 on trailers or semitrailers not used with watercraft of all types.

e. $1,500 for loss by theft of jewelry, watches, furs, precious and semiprecious stones.

f. $2,500 for loss by theft of firearms and related equipment.

g. $2,500 for loss by theft of silverware, silver-plated ware, goldware, gold-plated ware, platinumware, platinum-plated ware and pewterware. This includes flatware, hollow-ware, tea sets, trays and trophies made of or including silver, gold or pewter.

h. $2,500 on property, on the "residence premises", used primarily for "business" purposes.

i. $500 on property, away from the "residence premises", used primarily for "business" purposes. However, this limit does not apply to loss to electronic apparatus and other property described in Categories **j.** and **k.** below.

j. $1,500 on electronic apparatus and accessories, while in or upon a "motor vehicle", but only if the apparatus is equipped to be operated by power from the "motor vehicle's" electrical system while still capable of being operated by other power sources.

Accessories include antennas, tapes, wires, records, discs or other media that can be used with any apparatus described in this Category **j.**

k. $1,500 on electronic apparatus and accessories used primarily for "business" while away from the "residence premises" and not in or upon a "motor vehicle". The apparatus must be equipped to be operated by power from the "motor vehicle's" electrical system while still capable of being operated by other power sources.

Accessories include antennas, tapes, wires, records, discs or other media that can be used with any apparatus described in this Category **k.**

4. Property Not Covered

We do not cover:

a. Articles separately described and specifically insured, regardless of the limit for which they are insured, in this or other insurance;

b. Animals, birds or fish;

c. "Motor vehicles".

(1) This includes:

(a) Their accessories, equipment and parts; or

(b) Electronic apparatus and accessories designed to be operated solely by power from the electrical system of the "motor vehicle". Accessories include antennas, tapes, wires, records, discs or other media that can be used with any apparatus described above.

The exclusion of property described in **(a)** and **(b)** above applies only while such property is in or upon the "motor vehicle".

(2) We do cover "motor vehicles" not required to be registered for use on public roads or property which are:

(a) Used solely to service an "insured's" residence; or

(b) Designed to assist the handicapped;

d. Aircraft meaning any contrivance used or designed for flight including any parts whether or not attached to the aircraft.

We do cover model or hobby aircraft not used or designed to carry people or cargo;

e. Hovercraft and parts. Hovercraft means a self-propelled motorized ground effect vehicle and includes, but is not limited to, flarecraft and air cushion vehicles;

f. Property of roomers, boarders and other tenants, except property of roomers and boarders related to an "insured";

g. Property in an apartment regularly rented or held for rental to others by an "insured", except as provided in **E.10.** Landlord's Furnishings under Section I – Property Coverages;

h. Property rented or held for rental to others off the "residence premises";

i. "Business" data, including such data stored in:

(1) Books of account, drawings or other paper records; or

(2) Computers and related equipment.

We do cover the cost of blank recording or storage media, and of prerecorded computer programs available on the retail market;

 HO 00 03 10 00

j. Credit cards, electronic fund transfer cards or access devices used solely for deposit, withdrawal or transfer of funds except as provided in **E.6.** Credit Card, Electronic Fund Transfer Card Or Access Device, Forgery And Counterfeit Money under Section **I** – Property Coverages; or

k. Water or steam.

D. Coverage D – Loss Of Use

The limit of liability for Coverage **D** is the total limit for the coverages in **1.** Additional Living Expense, **2.** Fair Rental Value and **3.** Civil Authority Prohibits Use below.

1. Additional Living Expense

If a loss covered under Section **I** makes that part of the "residence premises" where you reside not fit to live in, we cover any necessary increase in living expenses incurred by you so that your household can maintain its normal standard of living.

Payment will be for the shortest time required to repair or replace the damage or, if you permanently relocate, the shortest time required for your household to settle elsewhere.

2. Fair Rental Value

If a loss covered under Section **I** makes that part of the "residence premises" rented to others or held for rental by you not fit to live in, we cover the fair rental value of such premises less any expenses that do not continue while it is not fit to live in.

Payment will be for the shortest time required to repair or replace such premises.

3. Civil Authority Prohibits Use

If a civil authority prohibits you from use of the "residence premises" as a result of direct damage to neighboring premises by a Peril Insured Against, we cover the loss as provided in **1.** Additional Living Expense and **2.** Fair Rental Value above for no more than two weeks.

4. Loss Or Expense Not Covered

We do not cover loss or expense due to cancellation of a lease or agreement.

The periods of time under **1.** Additional Living Expense, **2.** Fair Rental Value and **3.** Civil Authority Prohibits Use above are not limited by expiration of this policy.

E. Additional Coverages

1. Debris Removal

a. We will pay your reasonable expense for the removal of:

(1) Debris of covered property if a Peril Insured Against that applies to the damaged property causes the loss; or

(2) Ash, dust or particles from a volcanic eruption that has caused direct loss to a building or property contained in a building.

This expense is included in the limit of liability that applies to the damaged property. If the amount to be paid for the actual damage to the property plus the debris removal expense is more than the limit of liability for the damaged property, an additional 5% of that limit is available for such expense.

b. We will also pay your reasonable expense, up to $1,000, for the removal from the "residence premises" of:

(1) Your tree(s) felled by the peril of Windstorm or Hail or Weight of Ice, Snow or Sleet; or

(2) A neighbor's tree(s) felled by a Peril Insured Against under Coverage **C**;

provided the tree(s):

(3) Damage(s) a covered structure; or

(4) Does not damage a covered structure, but:

(a) Block(s) a driveway on the "residence premises" which prevent(s) a "motor vehicle", that is registered for use on public roads or property, from entering or leaving the "residence premises"; or

(b) Block(s) a ramp or other fixture designed to assist a handicapped person to enter or leave the dwelling building.

The $1,000 limit is the most we will pay in any one loss regardless of the number of fallen trees. No more than $500 of this limit will be paid for the removal of any one tree.

This coverage is additional insurance.

2. Reasonable Repairs

a. We will pay the reasonable cost incurred by you for the necessary measures taken solely to protect covered property that is damaged by a Peril Insured Against from further damage.

b. If the measures taken involve repair to other damaged property, we will only pay if that property is covered under this policy and the damage is caused by a Peril Insured Against. This coverage does not:

  (1) Increase the limit of liability that applies to the covered property; or

  (2) Relieve you of your duties, in case of a loss to covered property, described in **B.4.** under Section I – Conditions.

3. Trees, Shrubs And Other Plants

We cover trees, shrubs, plants or lawns, on the "residence premises", for loss caused by the following Perils Insured Against:

  a. Fire or Lightning;

  b. Explosion;

  c. Riot or Civil Commotion;

  d. Aircraft;

  e. Vehicles not owned or operated by a resident of the "residence premises";

  f. Vandalism or Malicious Mischief; or

  g. Theft.

We will pay up to 5% of the limit of liability that applies to the dwelling for all trees, shrubs, plants or lawns. No more than $500 of this limit will be paid for any one tree, shrub or plant. We do not cover property grown for "business" purposes.

This coverage is additional insurance.

4. Fire Department Service Charge

We will pay up to $500 for your liability assumed by contract or agreement for fire department charges incurred when the fire department is called to save or protect covered property from a Peril Insured Against. We do not cover fire department service charges if the property is located within the limits of the city, municipality or protection district furnishing the fire department response.

This coverage is additional insurance. No deductible applies to this coverage.

5. Property Removed

We insure covered property against direct loss from any cause while being removed from a premises endangered by a Peril Insured Against and for no more than 30 days while removed.

This coverage does not change the limit of liability that applies to the property being removed.

6. Credit Card, Electronic Fund Transfer Card Or Access Device, Forgery And Counterfeit Money

  a. We will pay up to $500 for:

  (1) The legal obligation of an "insured" to pay because of the theft or unauthorized use of credit cards issued to or registered in an "insured's" name;

  (2) Loss resulting from theft or unauthorized use of an electronic fund transfer card or access device used for deposit, withdrawal or transfer of funds, issued to or registered in an "insured's" name;

  (3) Loss to an "insured" caused by forgery or alteration of any check or negotiable instrument; and

  (4) Loss to an "insured" through acceptance in good faith of counterfeit United States or Canadian paper currency.

  All loss resulting from a series of acts committed by any one person or in which any one person is concerned or implicated is considered to be one loss.

  This coverage is additional insurance. No deductible applies to this coverage.

  b. We do not cover:

  (1) Use of a credit card, electronic fund transfer card or access device:

    (a) By a resident of your household;

    (b) By a person who has been entrusted with either type of card or access device; or

    (c) If an "insured" has not complied with all terms and conditions under which the cards are issued or the devices accessed; or

  (2) Loss arising out of "business" use or dishonesty of an "insured".

  c. If the coverage in **a.** above applies, the following defense provisions also apply:

  (1) We may investigate and settle any claim or suit that we decide is appropriate. Our duty to defend a claim or suit ends when the amount we pay for the loss equals our limit of liability.

  (2) If a suit is brought against an "insured" for liability under **a.(1)** or **(2)** above, we will provide a defense at our expense by counsel of our choice.

  (3) We have the option to defend at our expense an "insured" or an "insured's" bank against any suit for the enforcement of payment under **a.(3)** above.

7. Loss Assessment

   a. We will pay up to $1,000 for your share of loss assessment charged during the policy period against you, as owner or tenant of the "residence premises", by a corporation or association of property owners. The assessment must be made as a result of direct loss to property, owned by all members collectively, of the type that would be covered by this policy if owned by you, caused by a Peril Insured Against under Coverage **A**, other than:

      (1) Earthquake; or

      (2) Land shock waves or tremors before, during or after a volcanic eruption.

      The limit of $1,000 is the most we will pay with respect to any one loss, regardless of the number of assessments. We will only apply one deductible, per unit, to the total amount of any one loss to the property described above, regardless of the number of assessments.

   b. We do not cover assessments charged against you or a corporation or association of property owners by any governmental body.

   c. Paragraph **P.** Policy Period under Section **I** – Conditions does not apply to this coverage.

This coverage is additional insurance.

8. Collapse

   a. With respect to this Additional Coverage:

      (1) Collapse means an abrupt falling down or caving in of a building or any part of a building with the result that the building or part of the building cannot be occupied for its current intended purpose.

      (2) A building or any part of a building that is in danger of falling down or caving in is not considered to be in a state of collapse.

      (3) A part of a building that is standing is not considered to be in a state of collapse even if it has separated from another part of the building.

      (4) A building or any part of a building that is standing is not considered to be in a state of collapse even if it shows evidence of cracking, bulging, sagging, bending, leaning, settling, shrinkage or expansion.

   b. We insure for direct physical loss to covered property involving collapse of a building or any part of a building if the collapse was caused by one or more of the following:

      (1) The Perils Insured Against named under Coverage **C;**

      (2) Decay that is hidden from view, unless the presence of such decay is known to an "insured" prior to collapse;

      (3) Insect or vermin damage that is hidden from view, unless the presence of such damage is known to an "insured" prior to collapse;

      (4) Weight of contents, equipment, animals or people;

      (5) Weight of rain which collects on a roof; or

      (6) Use of defective material or methods in construction, remodeling or renovation if the collapse occurs during the course of the construction, remodeling or renovation.

   c. Loss to an awning, fence, patio, deck, pavement, swimming pool, underground pipe, flue, drain, cesspool, septic tank, foundation, retaining wall, bulkhead, pier, wharf or dock is not included under **b.(2)** through **(6)** above, unless the loss is a direct result of the collapse of a building or any part of a building.

   d. This coverage does not increase the limit of liability that applies to the damaged covered property.

9. Glass Or Safety Glazing Material

   a. We cover:

      (1) The breakage of glass or safety glazing material which is part of a covered building, storm door or storm window;

      (2) The breakage of glass or safety glazing material which is part of a covered building, storm door or storm window when caused directly by earth movement; and

      (3) The direct physical loss to covered property caused solely by the pieces, fragments or splinters of broken glass or safety glazing material which is part of a building, storm door or storm window.

b. This coverage does not include loss:

   (1) To covered property which results because the glass or safety glazing material has been broken, except as provided in **a.(3)** above; or

   (2) On the "residence premises" if the dwelling has been vacant for more than 60 consecutive days immediately before the loss, except when the breakage results directly from earth movement as provided in **a.(2)** above. A dwelling being constructed is not considered vacant.

c. This coverage does not increase the limit of liability that applies to the damaged property.

10. Landlord's Furnishings

We will pay up to $2,500 for your appliances, carpeting and other household furnishings, in each apartment on the "residence premises" regularly rented or held for rental to others by an "insured", for loss caused by a Peril Insured Against in Coverage **C,** other than Theft.

This limit is the most we will pay in any one loss regardless of the number of appliances, carpeting or other household furnishings involved in the loss.

This coverage does not increase the limit of liability applying to the damaged property.

11. Ordinance Or Law

a. You may use up to 10% of the limit of liability that applies to Coverage **A** for the increased costs you incur due to the enforcement of any ordinance or law which requires or regulates:

   (1) The construction, demolition, remodeling, renovation or repair of that part of a covered building or other structure damaged by a Peril Insured Against;

   (2) The demolition and reconstruction of the undamaged part of a covered building or other structure, when that building or other structure must be totally demolished because of damage by a Peril Insured Against to another part of that covered building or other structure; or

   (3) The remodeling, removal or replacement of the portion of the undamaged part of a covered building or other structure necessary to complete the remodeling, repair or replacement of that part of the covered building or other structure damaged by a Peril Insured Against.

b. You may use all or part of this ordinance or law coverage to pay for the increased costs you incur to remove debris resulting from the construction, demolition, remodeling, renovation, repair or replacement of property as stated in **a.** above.

c. We do not cover:

   (1) The loss in value to any covered building or other structure due to the requirements of any ordinance or law; or

   (2) The costs to comply with any ordinance or law which requires any "insured" or others to test for, monitor, clean up, remove, contain, treat, detoxify or neutralize, or in any way respond to, or assess the effects of, pollutants in or on any covered building or other structure.

   Pollutants means any solid, liquid, gaseous or thermal irritant or contaminant, including smoke, vapor, soot, fumes, acids, alkalis, chemicals and waste. Waste includes materials to be recycled, reconditioned or reclaimed.

This coverage is additional insurance.

12. Grave Markers

We will pay up to $5,000 for grave markers, including mausoleums, on or away from the "residence premises" for loss caused by a Peril Insured Against under Coverage **C.**

This coverage does not increase the limits of liability that apply to the damaged covered property.

SECTION I – PERILS INSURED AGAINST

A. Coverage A – Dwelling And Coverage B – Other Structures

  1. We insure against risk of direct physical loss to property described in Coverages **A** and **B.**

  2. We do not insure, however, for loss:

    a. Excluded under Section I – Exclusions;

    b. Involving collapse, except as provided in **E.8.** Collapse under Section I – Property Coverages; or

    c. Caused by:

     (1) Freezing of a plumbing, heating, air conditioning or automatic fire protective sprinkler system or of a household appliance, or by discharge, leakage or overflow from within the system or appliance caused by freezing. This provision does not apply if you have used reasonable care to:

      (a) Maintain heat in the building; or

    HO 00 03 10 00

(b) Shut off the water supply and drain all systems and appliances of water.

However, if the building is protected by an automatic fire protective sprinkler system, you must use reasonable care to continue the water supply and maintain heat in the building for coverage to apply.

For purposes of this provision a plumbing system or household appliance does not include a sump, sump pump or related equipment or a roof drain, gutter, downspout or similar fixtures or equipment;

(2) Freezing, thawing, pressure or weight of water or ice, whether driven by wind or not, to a:

(a) Fence, pavement, patio or swimming pool;

(b) Footing, foundation, bulkhead, wall, or any other structure or device that supports all or part of a building, or other structure;

(c) Retaining wall or bulkhead that does not support all or part of a building or other structure; or

(d) Pier, wharf or dock;

(3) Theft in or to a dwelling under construction, or of materials and supplies for use in the construction until the dwelling is finished and occupied;

(4) Vandalism and malicious mischief, and any ensuing loss caused by any intentional and wrongful act committed in the course of the vandalism or malicious mischief, if the dwelling has been vacant for more than 60 consecutive days immediately before the loss. A dwelling being constructed is not considered vacant;

(5) Mold, fungus or wet rot. However, we do insure for loss caused by mold, fungus or wet rot that is hidden within the walls or ceilings or beneath the floors or above the ceilings of a structure if such loss results from the accidental discharge or overflow of water or steam from within:

(a) A plumbing, heating, air conditioning or automatic fire protective sprinkler system, or a household appliance, on the "residence premises"; or

(b) A storm drain, or water, steam or sewer pipes, off the "residence premises".

For purposes of this provision, a plumbing system or household appliance does not include a sump, sump pump or related equipment or a roof drain, gutter, downspout or similar fixtures or equipment; or

(6) Any of the following:

(a) Wear and tear, marring, deterioration;

(b) Mechanical breakdown, latent defect, inherent vice, or any quality in property that causes it to damage or destroy itself;

(c) Smog, rust or other corrosion, or dry rot;

(d) Smoke from agricultural smudging or industrial operations;

(e) Discharge, dispersal, seepage, migration, release or escape of pollutants unless the discharge, dispersal, seepage, migration, release or escape is itself caused by a Peril Insured Against named under Coverage **C**.

Pollutants means any solid, liquid, gaseous or thermal irritant or contaminant, including smoke, vapor, soot, fumes, acids, alkalis, chemicals and waste. Waste includes materials to be recycled, reconditioned or reclaimed;

(f) Settling, shrinking, bulging or expansion, including resultant cracking, of bulkheads, pavements, patios, footings, foundations, walls, floors, roofs or ceilings;

(g) Birds, vermin, rodents, or insects; or

(h) Animals owned or kept by an "insured".

Exception To c.(6)

Unless the loss is otherwise excluded, we cover loss to property covered under Coverage **A** or **B** resulting from an accidental discharge or overflow of water or steam from within a:

(i) Storm drain, or water, steam or sewer pipe, off the "residence premises"; or

(ii) Plumbing, heating, air conditioning or automatic fire protective sprinkler system or household appliance on the "residence premises". This includes the cost to tear out and replace any part of a building, or other structure, on the "residence premises", but only when necessary to repair the system or appliance. However, such tear out and replacement coverage only applies to other structures if the water or steam causes actual damage to a building on the "residence premises".

We do not cover loss to the system or appliance from which this water or steam escaped.

For purposes of this provision, a plumbing system or household appliance does not include a sump, sump pump or related equipment or a roof drain, gutter, down spout or similar fixtures or equipment.

Section I – Exclusion **A.3.** Water Damage, Paragraphs **a.** and **c.** that apply to surface water and water below the surface of the ground do not apply to loss by water covered under **c.(5)** and **(6)** above.

Under **2.b.** and **c.** above, any ensuing loss to property described in Coverages **A** and **B** not precluded by any other provision in this policy is covered.

B. Coverage C – Personal Property

We insure for direct physical loss to the property described in Coverage **C** caused by any of the following perils unless the loss is excluded in Section I – Exclusions.

1. **Fire Or Lightning**

2. **Windstorm Or Hail**

   This peril includes loss to watercraft of all types and their trailers, furnishings, equipment, and outboard engines or motors, only while inside a fully enclosed building.

   This peril does not include loss to the property contained in a building caused by rain, snow, sleet, sand or dust unless the direct force of wind or hail damages the building causing an opening in a roof or wall and the rain, snow, sleet, sand or dust enters through this opening.

3. **Explosion**

4. **Riot Or Civil Commotion**

5. **Aircraft**

   This peril includes self-propelled missiles and spacecraft.

6. **Vehicles**

7. **Smoke**

   This peril means sudden and accidental damage from smoke, including the emission or puffback of smoke, soot, fumes or vapors from a boiler, furnace or related equipment.

   This peril does not include loss caused by smoke from agricultural smudging or industrial operations.

8. **Vandalism Or Malicious Mischief**

9. **Theft**

   a. This peril includes attempted theft and loss of property from a known place when it is likely that the property has been stolen.

   b. This peril does not include loss caused by theft:

   (1) Committed by an "insured";

   (2) In or to a dwelling under construction, or of materials and supplies for use in the construction until the dwelling is finished and occupied;

   (3) From that part of a "residence premises" rented by an "insured" to someone other than another "insured"; or

   (4) That occurs off the "residence premises" of:

   (a) Trailers, semitrailers and campers;

   (b) Watercraft of all types, and their furnishings, equipment and outboard engines or motors; or

   (c) Property while at any other residence owned by, rented to, or occupied by an "insured", except while an "insured" is temporarily living there. Property of an "insured" who is a student is covered while at the residence the student occupies to attend school as long as the student has been there at any time during the 60 days immediately before the loss.

10. **Falling Objects**

    This peril does not include loss to property contained in a building unless the roof or an outside wall of the building is first damaged by a falling object. Damage to the falling object itself is not included.

11. **Weight Of Ice, Snow Or Sleet**

    This peril means weight of ice, snow or sleet which causes damage to property contained in a building.

HO 00 03 10 00

12. Accidental Discharge Or Overflow Of Water Or Steam

   a. This peril means accidental discharge or overflow of water or steam from within a plumbing, heating, air conditioning or automatic fire protective sprinkler system or from within a household appliance.

   b. This peril does not include loss:

   (1) To the system or appliance from which the water or steam escaped;

   (2) Caused by or resulting from freezing except as provided in Peril Insured Against **14.** Freezing;

   (3) On the "residence premises" caused by accidental discharge or overflow which occurs off the "residence premises"; or

   (4) Caused by mold, fungus or wet rot unless hidden within the walls or ceilings or beneath the floors or above the ceilings of a structure.

   c. In this peril, a plumbing system or household appliance does not include a sump, sump pump or related equipment or a roof drain, gutter, downspout or similar fixtures or equipment.

   d. Section I – Exclusion **A.3.** Water Damage, Paragraphs **a.** and **c.** that apply to surface water and water below the surface of the ground do not apply to loss by water covered under this peril.

13. Sudden And Accidental Tearing Apart, Cracking, Burning Or Bulging

   This peril means sudden and accidental tearing apart, cracking, burning or bulging of a steam or hot water heating system, an air conditioning or automatic fire protective sprinkler system, or an appliance for heating water.

   We do not cover loss caused by or resulting from freezing under this peril.

14. Freezing

   a. This peril means freezing of a plumbing, heating, air conditioning or automatic fire protective sprinkler system or of a household appliance but only if you have used reasonable care to:

   (1) Maintain heat in the building; or

   (2) Shut off the water supply and drain all systems and appliances of water.

   However, if the building is protected by an automatic fire protective sprinkler system, you must use reasonable care to continue the water supply and maintain heat in the building for coverage to apply.

   b. In this peril, a plumbing system or household appliance does not include a sump, sump pump or related equipment or a roof drain, gutter, downspout or similar fixtures or equipment.

15. Sudden And Accidental Damage From Artificially Generated Electrical Current

   This peril does not include loss to tubes, transistors, electronic components or circuitry that are a part of appliances, fixtures, computers, home entertainment units or other types of electronic apparatus.

16. Volcanic Eruption

   This peril does not include loss caused by earthquake, land shock waves or tremors.

SECTION I – EXCLUSIONS

A. We do not insure for loss caused directly or indirectly by any of the following. Such loss is excluded regardless of any other cause or event contributing concurrently or in any sequence to the loss. These exclusions apply whether or not the loss event results in widespread damage or affects a substantial area.

1. Ordinance Or Law

   Ordinance Or Law means any ordinance or law:

   a. Requiring or regulating the construction, demolition, remodeling, renovation or repair of property, including removal of any resulting debris. This Exclusion **A.1.a.** does not apply to the amount of coverage that may be provided for in **E.11.** Ordinance Or Law under Section I – Property Coverages;

   b. The requirements of which result in a loss in value to property; or

   c. Requiring any "insured" or others to test for, monitor, clean up, remove, contain, treat, detoxify or neutralize, or in any way respond to, or assess the effects of, pollutants.

   Pollutants means any solid, liquid, gaseous or thermal irritant or contaminant, including smoke, vapor, soot, fumes, acids, alkalis, chemicals and waste. Waste includes materials to be recycled, reconditioned or reclaimed.

   This Exclusion **A.1.** applies whether or not the property has been physically damaged.

2. Earth Movement

   Earth Movement means:

   a. Earthquake, including land shock waves or tremors before, during or after a volcanic eruption;

b. Landslide, mudslide or mudflow;

c. Subsidence or sinkhole; or

d. Any other earth movement including earth sinking, rising or shifting;

caused by or resulting from human or animal forces or any act of nature unless direct loss by fire or explosion ensues and then we will pay only for the ensuing loss.

This Exclusion **A.2.** does not apply to loss by theft.

3. Water Damage

Water Damage means:

a. Flood, surface water, waves, tidal water, overflow of a body of water, or spray from any of these, whether or not driven by wind;

b. Water or water-borne material which backs up through sewers or drains or which overflows or is discharged from a sump, sump pump or related equipment; or

c. Water or water-borne material below the surface of the ground, including water which exerts pressure on or seeps or leaks through a building, sidewalk, driveway, foundation, swimming pool or other structure;

caused by or resulting from human or animal forces or any act of nature.

Direct loss by fire, explosion or theft resulting from water damage is covered.

4. Power Failure

Power Failure means the failure of power or other utility service if the failure takes place off the "residence premises". But if the failure results in a loss, from a Peril Insured Against on the "residence premises", we will pay for the loss caused by that peril.

5. Neglect

Neglect means neglect of an "insured" to use all reasonable means to save and preserve property at and after the time of a loss.

6. War

War includes the following and any consequence of any of the following:

a. Undeclared war, civil war, insurrection, rebellion or revolution;

b. Warlike act by a military force or military personnel; or

c. Destruction, seizure or use for a military purpose.

Discharge of a nuclear weapon will be deemed a warlike act even if accidental.

7. Nuclear Hazard

This Exclusion **A.7.** pertains to Nuclear Hazard to the extent set forth in **M.** Nuclear Hazard Clause under Section I – Conditions.

8. Intentional Loss

Intentional Loss means any loss arising out of any act an "insured" commits or conspires to commit with the intent to cause a loss.

In the event of such loss, no "insured" is entitled to coverage, even "insureds" who did not commit or conspire to commit the act causing the loss.

9. Governmental Action

Governmental Action means the destruction, confiscation or seizure of property described in Coverage **A, B** or **C** by order of any governmental or public authority.

This exclusion does not apply to such acts ordered by any governmental or public authority that are taken at the time of a fire to prevent its spread, if the loss caused by fire would be covered under this policy.

B. We do not insure for loss to property described in Coverages **A** and **B** caused by any of the following. However, any ensuing loss to property described in Coverages **A** and **B** not precluded by any other provision in this policy is covered.

1. Weather conditions. However, this exclusion only applies if weather conditions contribute in any way with a cause or event excluded in **A.** above to produce the loss.

2. Acts or decisions, including the failure to act or decide, of any person, group, organization or governmental body.

3. Faulty, inadequate or defective:

a. Planning, zoning, development, surveying, siting;

b. Design, specifications, workmanship, repair, construction, renovation, remodeling, grading, compaction;

c. Materials used in repair, construction, renovation or remodeling; or

d. Maintenance;

of part or all of any property whether on or off the "residence premises".

SECTION I – CONDITIONS

A. Insurable Interest And Limit Of Liability

Even if more than one person has an insurable interest in the property covered, we will not be liable in any one loss:

1. To an "insured" for more than the amount of such "insured's" interest at the time of loss; or

2. For more than the applicable limit of liability.

B. Duties After Loss

In case of a loss to covered property, we have no duty to provide coverage under this policy if the failure to comply with the following duties is prejudicial to us. These duties must be performed either by you, an "insured" seeking coverage, or a representative of either:

1. Give prompt notice to us or our agent;

2. Notify the police in case of loss by theft;

3. Notify the credit card or electronic fund transfer card or access device company in case of loss as provided for in **E.6.** Credit Card, Electronic Fund Transfer Card Or Access Device, Forgery And Counterfeit Money under Section I – Property Coverages;

4. Protect the property from further damage. If repairs to the property are required, you must:

   a. Make reasonable and necessary repairs to protect the property; and

   b. Keep an accurate record of repair expenses;

5. Cooperate with us in the investigation of a claim;

6. Prepare an inventory of damaged personal property showing the quantity, description, actual cash value and amount of loss. Attach all bills, receipts and related documents that justify the figures in the inventory;

7. As often as we reasonably require:

   a. Show the damaged property;

   b. Provide us with records and documents we request and permit us to make copies; and

   c. Submit to examination under oath, while not in the presence of another "insured", and sign the same;

8. Send to us, within 60 days after our request, your signed, sworn proof of loss which sets forth, to the best of your knowledge and belief:

   a. The time and cause of loss;

   b. The interests of all "insureds" and all others in the property involved and all liens on the property;

   c. Other insurance which may cover the loss;

d. Changes in title or occupancy of the property during the term of the policy;

e. Specifications of damaged buildings and detailed repair estimates;

f. The inventory of damaged personal property described in **6.** above;

g. Receipts for additional living expenses incurred and records that support the fair rental value loss; and

h. Evidence or affidavit that supports a claim under **E.6.** Credit Card, Electronic Fund Transfer Card Or Access Device, Forgery And Counterfeit Money under Section I – Property Coverages, stating the amount and cause of loss.

C. Loss Settlement

In this Condition **C.**, the terms "cost to repair or replace" and "replacement cost" do not include the increased costs incurred to comply with the enforcement of any ordinance or law, except to the extent that coverage for these increased costs is provided in **E.11.** Ordinance Or Law under Section I – Property Coverages. Covered property losses are settled as follows:

1. Property of the following types:

   a. Personal property;

   b. Awnings, carpeting, household appliances, outdoor antennas and outdoor equipment, whether or not attached to buildings;

   c. Structures that are not buildings; and

   d. Grave markers, including mausoleums;

   at actual cash value at the time of loss but not more than the amount required to repair or replace.

2. Buildings covered under Coverage **A** or **B** at replacement cost without deduction for depreciation, subject to the following:

   a. If, at the time of loss, the amount of insurance in this policy on the damaged building is 80% or more of the full replacement cost of the building immediately before the loss, we will pay the cost to repair or replace, after application of any deductible and without deduction for depreciation, but not more than the least of the following amounts:

      (1) The limit of liability under this policy that applies to the building;

      (2) The replacement cost of that part of the building damaged with material of like kind and quality and for like use; or

      (3) The necessary amount actually spent to repair or replace the damaged building.

If the building is rebuilt at a new premises, the cost described in **(2)** above is limited to the cost which would have been incurred if the building had been built at the original premises.

b. If, at the time of loss, the amount of insurance in this policy on the damaged building is less than 80% of the full replacement cost of the building immediately before the loss, we will pay the greater of the following amounts, but not more than the limit of liability under this policy that applies to the building:

(1) The actual cash value of that part of the building damaged; or

(2) That proportion of the cost to repair or replace, after application of any deductible and without deduction for depreciation, that part of the building damaged, which the total amount of insurance in this policy on the damaged building bears to 80% of the replacement cost of the building.

c. To determine the amount of insurance required to equal 80% of the full replacement cost of the building immediately before the loss, do not include the value of:

(1) Excavations, footings, foundations, piers, or any other structures or devices that support all or part of the building, which are below the undersurface of the lowest basement floor;

(2) Those supports described in **(1)** above which are below the surface of the ground inside the foundation walls, if there is no basement; and

(3) Underground flues, pipes, wiring and drains.

d. We will pay no more than the actual cash value of the damage until actual repair or replacement is complete. Once actual repair or replacement is complete, we will settle the loss as noted in **2.a.** and **b.** above.

However, if the cost to repair or replace the damage is both:

(1) Less than 5% of the amount of insurance in this policy on the building; and

(2) Less than $2,500;

we will settle the loss as noted in **2.a.** and **b.** above whether or not actual repair or replacement is complete.

e. You may disregard the replacement cost loss settlement provisions and make claim under this policy for loss to buildings on an actual cash value basis. You may then make claim for any additional liability according to the provisions of this Condition **C.** Loss Settlement, provided you notify us of your intent to do so within 180 days after the date of loss.

D. Loss To A Pair Or Set

In case of loss to a pair or set we may elect to:

1. Repair or replace any part to restore the pair or set to its value before the loss; or

2. Pay the difference between actual cash value of the property before and after the loss.

E. Appraisal

If you and we fail to agree on the amount of loss, either may demand an appraisal of the loss. In this event, each party will choose a competent and impartial appraiser within 20 days after receiving a written request from the other. The two appraisers will choose an umpire. If they cannot agree upon an umpire within 15 days, you or we may request that the choice be made by a judge of a court of record in the state where the "residence premises" is located. The appraisers will separately set the amount of loss. If the appraisers submit a written report of an agreement to us, the amount agreed upon will be the amount of loss. If they fail to agree, they will submit their differences to the umpire. A decision agreed to by any two will set the amount of loss.

Each party will:

1. Pay its own appraiser; and

2. Bear the other expenses of the appraisal and umpire equally.

F. Other Insurance And Service Agreement

If a loss covered by this policy is also covered by:

1. Other insurance, we will pay only the proportion of the loss that the limit of liability that applies under this policy bears to the total amount of insurance covering the loss; or

2. A service agreement, this insurance is excess over any amounts payable under any such agreement. Service agreement means a service plan, property restoration plan, home warranty or other similar service warranty agreement, even if it is characterized as insurance.

G. Suit Against Us

No action can be brought against us unless there has been full compliance with all of the terms under Section I of this policy and the action is started within two years after the date of loss.

 HO 00 03 10 00

H. Our Option

If we give you written notice within 30 days after we receive your signed, sworn proof of loss, we may repair or replace any part of the damaged property with material or property of like kind and quality.

I. Loss Payment

We will adjust all losses with you. We will pay you unless some other person is named in the policy or is legally entitled to receive payment. Loss will be payable 60 days after we receive your proof of loss and:

1. Reach an agreement with you;

2. There is an entry of a final judgment; or

3. There is a filing of an appraisal award with us.

J. Abandonment Of Property

We need not accept any property abandoned by an "insured".

K. Mortgage Clause

1. If a mortgagee is named in this policy, any loss payable under Coverage **A** or **B** will be paid to the mortgagee and you, as interests appear. If more than one mortgagee is named, the order of payment will be the same as the order of precedence of the mortgages.

2. If we deny your claim, that denial will not apply to a valid claim of the mortgagee, if the mortgagee:

   a. Notifies us of any change in ownership, occupancy or substantial change in risk of which the mortgagee is aware;

   b. Pays any premium due under this policy on demand if you have neglected to pay the premium; and

   c. Submits a signed, sworn statement of loss within 60 days after receiving notice from us of your failure to do so. Paragraphs **E.** Appraisal, **G.** Suit Against Us and **I.** Loss Payment under Section I – Conditions also apply to the mortgagee.

3. If we decide to cancel or not to renew this policy, the mortgagee will be notified at least 10 days before the date cancellation or nonrenewal takes effect.

4. If we pay the mortgagee for any loss and deny payment to you:

   a. We are subrogated to all the rights of the mortgagee granted under the mortgage on the property; or

b. At our option, we may pay to the mortgagee the whole principal on the mortgage plus any accrued interest. In this event, we will receive a full assignment and transfer of the mortgage and all securities held as collateral to the mortgage debt.

5. Subrogation will not impair the right of the mortgagee to recover the full amount of the mortgagee's claim.

L. No Benefit To Bailee

We will not recognize any assignment or grant any coverage that benefits a person or organization holding, storing or moving property for a fee regardless of any other provision of this policy.

M. Nuclear Hazard Clause

1. "Nuclear Hazard" means any nuclear reaction, radiation, or radioactive contamination, all whether controlled or uncontrolled or however caused, or any consequence of any of these.

2. Loss caused by the nuclear hazard will not be considered loss caused by fire, explosion, or smoke, whether these perils are specifically named in or otherwise included within the Perils Insured Against.

3. This policy does not apply under Section I to loss caused directly or indirectly by nuclear hazard, except that direct loss by fire resulting from the nuclear hazard is covered.

N. Recovered Property

If you or we recover any property for which we have made payment under this policy, you or we will notify the other of the recovery. At your option, the property will be returned to or retained by you or it will become our property. If the recovered property is returned to or retained by you, the loss payment will be adjusted based on the amount you received for the recovered property.

O. Volcanic Eruption Period

One or more volcanic eruptions that occur within a 72 hour period will be considered as one volcanic eruption.

P. Policy Period

This policy applies only to loss which occurs during the policy period.

Q. Concealment Or Fraud

We provide coverage to no "insureds" under this policy if, whether before or after a loss, an "insured" has:

1. Intentionally concealed or misrepresented any material fact or circumstance;

2. Engaged in fraudulent conduct; or

3. Made false statements;

relating to this insurance.

R. Loss Payable Clause

If the Declarations show a loss payee for certain listed insured personal property, the definition of "insured" is changed to include that loss payee with respect to that property.

If we decide to cancel or not renew this policy, that loss payee will be notified in writing.

SECTION II – LIABILITY COVERAGES

A. Coverage E – Personal Liability

If a claim is made or a suit is brought against an "insured" for damages because of "bodily injury" or "property damage" caused by an "occurrence" to which this coverage applies, we will:

1. Pay up to our limit of liability for the damages for which an "insured" is legally liable. Damages include prejudgment interest awarded against an "insured"; and

2. Provide a defense at our expense by counsel of our choice, even if the suit is groundless, false or fraudulent. We may investigate and settle any claim or suit that we decide is appropriate. Our duty to settle or defend ends when our limit of liability for the "occurrence" has been exhausted by payment of a judgment or settlement.

B. Coverage F – Medical Payments To Others

We will pay the necessary medical expenses that are incurred or medically ascertained within three years from the date of an accident causing "bodily injury". Medical expenses means reasonable charges for medical, surgical, x-ray, dental, ambulance, hospital, professional nursing, prosthetic devices and funeral services. This coverage does not apply to you or regular residents of your household except "residence employees". As to others, this coverage applies only:

1. To a person on the "insured location" with the permission of an "insured"; or

2. To a person off the "insured location", if the "bodily injury":

a. Arises out of a condition on the "insured location" or the ways immediately adjoining;

b. Is caused by the activities of an "insured";

c. Is caused by a "residence employee" in the course of the "residence employee's" employment by an "insured"; or

d. Is caused by an animal owned by or in the care of an "insured".

SECTION II – EXCLUSIONS

A. "Motor Vehicle Liability"

1. Coverages **E** and **F** do not apply to any "motor vehicle liability" if, at the time and place of an "occurrence", the involved "motor vehicle":

a. Is registered for use on public roads or property;

b. Is not registered for use on public roads or property, but such registration is required by a law, or regulation issued by a government agency, for it to be used at the place of the "occurrence"; or

c. Is being:

(1) Operated in, or practicing for, any prearranged or organized race, speed contest or other competition;

(2) Rented to others;

(3) Used to carry persons or cargo for a charge; or

(4) Used for any "business" purpose except for a motorized golf cart while on a golfing facility.

2. If Exclusion **A.1.** does not apply, there is still no coverage for "motor vehicle liability" unless the "motor vehicle" is:

a. In dead storage on an "insured location";

b. Used solely to service an "insured's" residence;

c. Designed to assist the handicapped and, at the time of an "occurrence", it is:

(1) Being used to assist a handicapped person; or

(2) Parked on an "insured location";

d. Designed for recreational use off public roads and:

(1) Not owned by an "insured"; or

(2) Owned by an "insured" provided the "occurrence" takes place on an "insured location" as defined in Definitions **B. 6.a., b., d., e.** or **h.;** or

e. A motorized golf cart that is owned by an "insured", designed to carry up to 4 persons, not built or modified after manufacture to exceed a speed of 25 miles per hour on level ground and, at the time of an "occurrence", is within the legal boundaries of:

(1) A golfing facility and is parked or stored there, or being used by an "insured" to:

(a) Play the game of golf or for other recreational or leisure activity allowed by the facility;

(b) Travel to or from an area where "motor vehicles" or golf carts are parked or stored; or

(c) Cross public roads at designated points to access other parts of the golfing facility; or

(2) A private residential community, including its public roads upon which a motorized golf cart can legally travel, which is subject to the authority of a property owners association and contains an "insured's" residence.

B. "Watercraft Liability"

1. Coverages **E** and **F** do not apply to any "watercraft liability" if, at the time of an "occurrence", the involved watercraft is being:

a. Operated in, or practicing for, any prearranged or organized race, speed contest or other competition. This exclusion does not apply to a sailing vessel or a predicted log cruise;

b. Rented to others;

c. Used to carry persons or cargo for a charge; or

d. Used for any "business" purpose.

2. If Exclusion **B.1.** does not apply, there is still no coverage for "watercraft liability" unless, at the time of the "occurrence", the watercraft:

a. Is stored;

b. Is a sailing vessel, with or without auxiliary power, that is:

(1) Less than 26 feet in overall length; or

(2) 26 feet or more in overall length and not owned by or rented to an "insured"; or

c. Is not a sailing vessel and is powered by:

(1) An inboard or inboard-outdrive engine or motor, including those that power a water jet pump, of:

(a) 50 horsepower or less and not owned by an "insured"; or

(b) More than 50 horsepower and not owned by or rented to an "insured"; or

(2) One or more outboard engines or motors with:

(a) 25 total horsepower or less;

(b) More than 25 horsepower if the outboard engine or motor is not owned by an "insured";

(c) More than 25 horsepower if the outboard engine or motor is owned by an "insured" who acquired it during the policy period; or

(d) More than 25 horsepower if the outboard engine or motor is owned by an "insured" who acquired it before the policy period, but only if:

(i) You declare them at policy inception; or

(ii) Your intent to insure them is reported to us in writing within 45 days after you acquire them.

The coverages in **(c)** and **(d)** above apply for the policy period.

Horsepower means the maximum power rating assigned to the engine or motor by the manufacturer.

C. "Aircraft Liability"

This policy does not cover "aircraft liability".

D. "Hovercraft Liability"

This policy does not cover "hovercraft liability".

E. Coverage E – Personal Liability And Coverage F – Medical Payments To Others

Coverages **E** and **F** do not apply to the following:

1. Expected Or Intended Injury

"Bodily injury" or "property damage" which is expected or intended by an "insured" even if the resulting "bodily injury" or "property damage":

a. Is of a different kind, quality or degree than initially expected or intended; or

b. Is sustained by a different person, entity, real or personal property, than initially expected or intended.

However, this Exclusion **E.1.** does not apply to "bodily injury" resulting from the use of reasonable force by an "insured" to protect persons or property;

2. "Business"

a. "Bodily injury" or "property damage" arising out of or in connection with a "business" conducted from an "insured location" or engaged in by an "insured", whether or not the "business" is owned or operated by an "insured" or employs an "insured".

This Exclusion **E.2.** applies but is not limited to an act or omission, regardless of its nature or circumstance, involving a service or duty rendered, promised, owed, or implied to be provided because of the nature of the "business".

b. This Exclusion **E.2.** does not apply to:

(1) The rental or holding for rental of an "insured location";

(a) On an occasional basis if used only as a residence;

(b) In part for use only as a residence, unless a single family unit is intended for use by the occupying family to lodge more than two roomers or boarders; or

(c) In part, as an office, school, studio or private garage; and

(2) An "insured" under the age of 21 years involved in a part-time or occasional, self-employed "business" with no employees;

3. Professional Services

"Bodily injury" or "property damage" arising out of the rendering of or failure to render professional services;

4. "Insured's" Premises Not An "Insured Location"

"Bodily injury" or "property damage" arising out of a premises:

a. Owned by an "insured";

b. Rented to an "insured"; or

c. Rented to others by an "insured";

that is not an "insured location";

5. War

"Bodily injury" or "property damage" caused directly or indirectly by war, including the following and any consequence of any of the following:

a. Undeclared war, civil war, insurrection, rebellion or revolution;

b. Warlike act by a military force or military personnel; or

c. Destruction, seizure or use for a military purpose.

Discharge of a nuclear weapon will be deemed a warlike act even if accidental;

6. Communicable Disease

"Bodily injury" or "property damage" which arises out of the transmission of a communicable disease by an "insured";

7. Sexual Molestation, Corporal Punishment Or Physical Or Mental Abuse

"Bodily injury" or "property damage" arising out of sexual molestation, corporal punishment or physical or mental abuse; or

8. Controlled Substance

"Bodily injury" or "property damage" arising out of the use, sale, manufacture, delivery, transfer or possession by any person of a Controlled Substance as defined by the Federal Food and Drug Law at 21 U.S.C.A. Sections 811 and 812. Controlled Substances include but are not limited to cocaine, LSD, marijuana and all narcotic drugs. However, this exclusion does not apply to the legitimate use of prescription drugs by a person following the orders of a licensed physician.

Exclusions **A.** "Motor Vehicle Liability", **B.** "Watercraft Liability", **C.** "Aircraft Liability", **D.** "Hovercraft Liability" and **E.4.** "Insured's" Premises Not An "Insured Location" do not apply to "bodily injury" to a "residence employee" arising out of and in the course of the "residence employee's" employment by an "insured".

F. Coverage E – Personal Liability

Coverage **E** does not apply to:

1. Liability:

a. For any loss assessment charged against you as a member of an association, corporation or community of property owners, except as provided in **D.** Loss Assessment under Section **II** – Additional Coverages;

b. Under any contract or agreement entered into by an "insured". However, this exclusion does not apply to written contracts:

(1) That directly relate to the ownership, maintenance or use of an "insured location"; or

(2) Where the liability of others is assumed by you prior to an "occurrence";

unless excluded in **a.** above or elsewhere in this policy;

2. "Property damage" to property owned by an "insured". This includes costs or expenses incurred by an "insured" or others to repair, replace, enhance, restore or maintain such property to prevent injury to a person or damage to property of others, whether on or away from an "insured location";

3. "Property damage" to property rented to, occupied or used by or in the care of an "insured". This exclusion does not apply to "property damage" caused by fire, smoke or explosion;

4. "Bodily injury" to any person eligible to receive any benefits voluntarily provided or required to be provided by an "insured" under any:

a. Workers' compensation law;

    b. Non-occupational disability law; or

    c. Occupational disease law;

  5. "Bodily injury" or "property damage" for which an "insured" under this policy:

    a. Is also an insured under a nuclear energy liability policy issued by the:

      (1) Nuclear Energy Liability Insurance Association;

      (2) Mutual Atomic Energy Liability Underwriters;

      (3) Nuclear Insurance Association of Canada;

      or any of their successors; or

    b. Would be an insured under such a policy but for the exhaustion of its limit of liability; or

  6. "Bodily injury" to you or an "insured" as defined under Definitions **5.a.** or **b.**

    This exclusion also applies to any claim made or suit brought against you or an "insured":

    a. To repay; or

    b. Share damages with;

    another person who may be obligated to pay damages because of "bodily injury" to an "insured".

G. Coverage F – Medical Payments To Others

Coverage **F** does not apply to "bodily injury":

  1. To a "residence employee" if the "bodily injury":

    a. Occurs off the "insured location"; and

    b. Does not arise out of or in the course of the "residence employee's" employment by an "insured";

  2. To any person eligible to receive benefits voluntarily provided or required to be provided under any:

    a. Workers' compensation law;

    b. Non-occupational disability law; or

    c. Occupational disease law;

  3. From any:

    a. Nuclear reaction;

    b. Nuclear radiation; or

    c. Radioactive contamination;

    all whether controlled or uncontrolled or however caused; or

    d. Any consequence of any of these; or

  4. To any person, other than a "residence employee" of an "insured", regularly residing on any part of the "insured location".

SECTION II – ADDITIONAL COVERAGES

We cover the following in addition to the limits of liability:

A. Claim Expenses

We pay:

  1. Expenses we incur and costs taxed against an "insured" in any suit we defend;

  2. Premiums on bonds required in a suit we defend, but not for bond amounts more than the Coverage **E** limit of liability. We need not apply for or furnish any bond;

  3. Reasonable expenses incurred by an "insured" at our request, including actual loss of earnings (but not loss of other income) up to $250 per day, for assisting us in the investigation or defense of a claim or suit; and

  4. Interest on the entire judgment which accrues after entry of the judgment and before we pay or tender, or deposit in court that part of the judgment which does not exceed the limit of liability that applies.

B. First Aid Expenses

We will pay expenses for first aid to others incurred by an "insured" for "bodily injury" covered under this policy. We will not pay for first aid to an "insured".

C. Damage To Property Of Others

  1. We will pay, at replacement cost, up to $1,000 per "occurrence" for "property damage" to property of others caused by an "insured".

  2. We will not pay for "property damage":

    a. To the extent of any amount recoverable under Section **I**;

    b. Caused intentionally by an "insured" who is 13 years of age or older;

    c. To property owned by an "insured";

    d. To property owned by or rented to a tenant of an "insured" or a resident in your household; or

    e. Arising out of:

      (1) A "business" engaged in by an "insured";

      (2) Any act or omission in connection with a premises owned, rented or controlled by an "insured", other than the "insured location"; or

      (3) The ownership, maintenance, occupancy, operation, use, loading or unloading of aircraft, hovercraft, watercraft or "motor vehicles".

This exclusion **e.(3)** does not apply to a "motor vehicle" that:

(a) Is designed for recreational use off public roads;

(b) Is not owned by an "insured"; and

(c) At the time of the "occurrence", is not required by law, or regulation issued by a government agency, to have been registered for it to be used on public roads or property.

D. Loss Assessment

1. We will pay up to $1,000 for your share of loss assessment charged against you, as owner or tenant of the "residence premises", during the policy period by a corporation or association of property owners, when the assessment is made as a result of:

a. "Bodily injury" or "property damage" not excluded from coverage under Section II – Exclusions; or

b. Liability for an act of a director, officer or trustee in the capacity as a director, officer or trustee, provided such person:

(1) Is elected by the members of a corporation or association of property owners; and

(2) Serves without deriving any income from the exercise of duties which are solely on behalf of a corporation or association of property owners.

2. Paragraph I. Policy Period under Section II – Conditions does not apply to this Loss Assessment Coverage.

3. Regardless of the number of assessments, the limit of $1,000 is the most we will pay for loss arising out of:

a. One accident, including continuous or repeated exposure to substantially the same general harmful condition; or

b. A covered act of a director, officer or trustee. An act involving more than one director, officer or trustee is considered to be a single act.

4. We do not cover assessments charged against you or a corporation or association of property owners by any governmental body.

SECTION II – CONDITIONS

A. Limit Of Liability

Our total liability under Coverage **E** for all damages resulting from any one "occurrence" will not be more than the Coverage **E** limit of liability shown in the Declarations. This limit is the same regardless of the number of "insureds", claims made or persons injured. All "bodily injury" and "property damage" resulting from any one accident or from continuous or repeated exposure to substantially the same general harmful conditions shall be considered to be the result of one "occurrence".

Our total liability under Coverage **F** for all medical expense payable for "bodily injury" to one person as the result of one accident will not be more than the Coverage **F** limit of liability shown in the Declarations.

B. Severability Of Insurance

This insurance applies separately to each "insured". This condition will not increase our limit of liability for any one "occurrence".

C. Duties After "Occurrence"

In case of an "occurrence", you or another "insured" will perform the following duties that apply. We have no duty to provide coverage under this policy if your failure to comply with the following duties is prejudicial to us. You will help us by seeing that these duties are performed:

1. Give written notice to us or our agent as soon as is practical, which sets forth:

a. The identity of the policy and the "named insured" shown in the Declarations;

b. Reasonably available information on the time, place and circumstances of the "occurrence"; and

c. Names and addresses of any claimants and witnesses;

2. Cooperate with us in the investigation, settlement or defense of any claim or suit;

3. Promptly forward to us every notice, demand, summons or other process relating to the "occurrence";

4. At our request, help us:

a. To make settlement;

b. To enforce any right of contribution or indemnity against any person or organization who may be liable to an "insured";

 HO 00 03 10 00

  c. With the conduct of suits and attend hearings and trials; and

  d. To secure and give evidence and obtain the attendance of witnesses;

5. With respect to **C.** Damage To Property Of Others under Section **II** – Additional Coverages, submit to us within 60 days after the loss, a sworn statement of loss and show the damaged property, if in an "insured's" control;

6. No "insured" shall, except at such "insured's" own cost, voluntarily make payment, assume obligation or incur expense other than for first aid to others at the time of the "bodily injury".

D. Duties Of An Injured Person – Coverage F – Medical Payments To Others

1. The injured person or someone acting for the injured person will:

   a. Give us written proof of claim, under oath if required, as soon as is practical; and

   b. Authorize us to obtain copies of medical reports and records.

2. The injured person will submit to a physical exam by a doctor of our choice when and as often as we reasonably require.

E. Payment Of Claim – Coverage F – Medical Payments To Others

Payment under this coverage is not an admission of liability by an "insured" or us.

F. Suit Against Us

1. No action can be brought against us unless there has been full compliance with all of the terms under this Section **II.**

2. No one will have the right to join us as a party to any action against an "insured".

3. Also, no action with respect to Coverage **E** can be brought against us until the obligation of such "insured" has been determined by final judgment or agreement signed by us.

G. Bankruptcy Of An "Insured"

Bankruptcy or insolvency of an "insured" will not relieve us of our obligations under this policy.

H. Other Insurance

This insurance is excess over other valid and collectible insurance except insurance written specifically to cover as excess over the limits of liability that apply in this policy.

I. Policy Period

This policy applies only to "bodily injury" or "property damage" which occurs during the policy period.

J. Concealment Or Fraud

We do not provide coverage to an "insured" who, whether before or after a loss, has:

1. Intentionally concealed or misrepresented any material fact or circumstance;

2. Engaged in fraudulent conduct; or

3. Made false statements;

relating to this insurance.

SECTIONS I AND II – CONDITIONS

A. Liberalization Clause

If we make a change which broadens coverage under this edition of our policy without additional premium charge, that change will automatically apply to your insurance as of the date we implement the change in your state, provided that this implementation date falls within 60 days prior to or during the policy period stated in the Declarations.

This Liberalization Clause does not apply to changes implemented with a general program revision that includes both broadenings and restrictions in coverage, whether that general program revision is implemented through introduction of:

1. A subsequent edition of this policy; or

2. An amendatory endorsement.

B. Waiver Or Change Of Policy Provisions

A waiver or change of a provision of this policy must be in writing by us to be valid. Our request for an appraisal or examination will not waive any of our rights.

C. Cancellation

1. You may cancel this policy at any time by returning it to us or by letting us know in writing of the date cancellation is to take effect.

2. We may cancel this policy only for the reasons stated below by letting you know in writing of the date cancellation takes effect. This cancellation notice may be delivered to you, or mailed to you at your mailing address shown in the Declarations. Proof of mailing will be sufficient proof of notice.

   a. When you have not paid the premium, we may cancel at any time by letting you know at least 10 days before the date cancellation takes effect.

   b. When this policy has been in effect for less than 60 days and is not a renewal with us, we may cancel for any reason by letting you know at least 10 days before the date cancellation takes effect.

c. When this policy has been in effect for 60 days or more, or at any time if it is a renewal with us, we may cancel:

(1) If there has been a material misrepresentation of fact which if known to us would have caused us not to issue the policy; or

(2) If the risk has changed substantially since the policy was issued.

This can be done by letting you know at least 30 days before the date cancellation takes effect.

d. When this policy is written for a period of more than one year, we may cancel for any reason at anniversary by letting you know at least 30 days before the date cancellation takes effect.

3. When this policy is canceled, the premium for the period from the date of cancellation to the expiration date will be refunded pro rata.

4. If the return premium is not refunded with the notice of cancellation or when this policy is returned to us, we will refund it within a reasonable time after the date cancellation takes effect.

D. Nonrenewal

We may elect not to renew this policy. We may do so by delivering to you, or mailing to you at your mailing address shown in the Declarations, written notice at least 30 days before the expiration date of this policy. Proof of mailing will be sufficient proof of notice.

E. Assignment

Assignment of this policy will not be valid unless we give our written consent.

F. Subrogation

An "insured" may waive in writing before a loss all rights of recovery against any person. If not waived, we may require an assignment of rights of recovery for a loss to the extent that payment is made by us.

If an assignment is sought, an "insured" must sign and deliver all related papers and cooperate with us.

Subrogation does not apply to Coverage **F** or Paragraph **C.** Damage To Property Of Others under Section **II** – Additional Coverages.

G. Death

If any person named in the Declarations or the spouse, if a resident of the same household, dies, the following apply:

1. We insure the legal representative of the deceased but only with respect to the premises and property of the deceased covered under the policy at the time of death; and

2. "Insured" includes:

a. An "insured" who is a member of your household at the time of your death, but only while a resident of the "residence premises"; and

b. With respect to your property, the person having proper temporary custody of the property until appointment and qualification of a legal representative.

BUSINESSOWNERS COVERAGE FORM

Various provisions in this policy restrict coverage. Read the entire policy carefully to determine rights, duties and what is and is not covered.

Throughout this Coverage Form the words "you" and "your" refer to the Named Insured shown in the Declarations. The words "we", "us" and "our" refer to the Company providing this insurance.

In **Section II – Liability,** the word "insured" means any person or organization qualifying as such under Paragraph **C** – Who Is An Insured.

Other words and phrases that appear in quotation marks have special meaning. Refer to Paragraph **H.** Property Definitions in **Section I – Property** and Paragraph **F.** Liability And Medical Expenses Definitions in **Section II – Liability.**

SECTION I – PROPERTY

A. Coverage

We will pay for direct physical loss of or damage to Covered Property at the premises described in the Declarations caused by or resulting from any Covered Cause of Loss.

1. Covered Property

Covered Property includes Buildings as described under Paragraph **a.** below, Business Personal Property as described under Paragraph **b.** below, or both, depending on whether a Limit of Insurance is shown in the Declarations for that type of property. Regardless of whether coverage is shown in the Declarations for Buildings, Business Personal Property, or both, there is no coverage for property described under Paragraph **2.** Property Not Covered.

a. Buildings, meaning the buildings and structures at the premises described in the Declarations, including:

(1) Completed additions;

(2) Fixtures, including outdoor fixtures;

(3) Permanently installed:

  (a) Machinery; and

  (b) Equipment;

(4) Your personal property in apartments, rooms or common areas furnished by you as landlord;

(5) Personal property owned by you that is used to maintain or service the buildings or structures or the premises, including:

  (a) Fire extinguishing equipment;

  (b) Outdoor furniture;

  (c) Floor coverings; and

  (d) Appliances used for refrigerating, ventilating, cooking, dishwashing or laundering;

(6) If not covered by other insurance:

  (a) Additions under construction, alterations and repairs to the buildings or structures;

  (b) Materials, equipment, supplies and temporary structures, on or within 100 feet of the described premises, used for making additions, alterations or repairs to the buildings or structures.

b. Business Personal Property located in or on the buildings at the described premises or in the open (or in a vehicle) within 100 feet of the described premises, including:

(1) Property you own that is used in your business;

(2) Property of others that is in your care, custody or control, except as otherwise provided in Loss Payment Property Loss Condition Paragraph **E.6.d.(3)(b);**

(3) Tenant's improvements and betterments. Improvements and betterments are fixtures, alterations, installations or additions:

  (a) Made a part of the building or structure you occupy but do not own; and

  (b) You acquired or made at your expense but cannot legally remove; and

(4) Leased personal property for which you have a contractual responsibility to insure, unless otherwise provided for under Paragraph **1.b.(2).**

(5) Exterior building glass, if you are a tenant and no Limit of Insurance is shown in the Declarations for Building property. The glass must be owned by you or in your care, custody or control.

2. Property Not Covered

Covered Property does not include:

a. Aircraft, automobiles, motortrucks and other vehicles subject to motor vehicle registration;

b. "Money" or "securities" except as provided in the:

    (1) Money and Securities Optional Coverage; or

    (2) Employee Dishonesty Optional Coverage;

c. Contraband, or property in the course of illegal transportation or trade;

d. Land (including land on which the property is located), water, growing crops or lawns;

e. Outdoor fences, radio or television antennas (including satellite dishes) and their lead-in wiring, masts or towers, signs (other than signs attached to buildings), trees, shrubs or plants, all except as provided in the:

    (1) Outdoor Property Coverage Extension; or

    (2) Outdoor Signs Optional Coverage;

f. Watercraft (including motors, equipment and accessories) while afloat.

g. Accounts, bills, food stamps, other evidences of debt, accounts receivable or "valuable papers and records"; except as otherwise provided in this policy.

h. "Computer(s)" which are permanently installed or designed to be permanently installed in any aircraft, watercraft, motortruck or other vehicle subject to motor vehicle registration. This paragraph does not apply to "computer(s)" while held as "stock".

3. Covered Causes Of Loss

Risks of direct physical loss unless the loss is:

a. Excluded in Paragraph **B.** Exclusions in Section **I**; or

b. Limited in Paragraph **4.** Limitations in Section **I.**

4. Limitations

a. We will not pay for loss of or damage to:

    (1) Steam boilers, steam pipes, steam engines or steam turbines caused by or resulting from any condition or event inside such equipment. But we will pay for loss of or damage to such equipment caused by or resulting from an explosion of gases or fuel within the furnace of any fired vessel or within the flues or passages through which the gases of combustion pass.

    (2) Hot water boilers or other water heating equipment caused by or resulting from any condition or event inside such boilers or equipment, other than an explosion.

    (3) Property that is missing, where the only evidence of the loss or damage is a shortage disclosed on taking inventory, or other instances where there is no physical evidence to show what happened to the property. This limitation does not apply to the Optional Coverage for Money and Securities.

    (4) Property that has been transferred to a person or to a place outside the described premises on the basis of unauthorized instructions.

    (5) The interior of any building or structure caused by or resulting from rain, snow, sleet, ice, sand or dust, whether driven by wind or not, unless:

        (a) The building or structure first sustains damage by a Covered Cause of Loss to its roof or walls through which the rain, snow, sleet, ice, sand or dust enters; or

        (b) The loss or damage is caused by or results from thawing of snow, sleet or ice on the building or structure.

b. We will not pay for loss of or damage to fragile articles such as glassware, statuary, marbles, chinaware and porcelains, if broken, unless caused by the "specified causes of loss" or building glass breakage. This restriction does not apply to:

    (1) Glass that is part of the exterior or interior of a building or structure;

    (2) Containers of property held for sale; or

    (3) Photographic or scientific instrument lenses.

c. For loss or damage by theft, the following types of property are covered only up to the limits shown:

    (1) $2,500 for furs, fur garments and garments trimmed with fur.

    (2) $2,500 for jewelry, watches, watch movements, jewels, pearls, precious and semi-precious stones, bullion, gold, silver, platinum and other precious alloys or metals. This limit does not apply to jewelry and watches worth $100 or less per item.

    (3) $2,500 for patterns, dies, molds and forms.

BP 00 03 07 02

5. Additional Coverages

a. Debris Removal

(1) Subject to Paragraphs **(3)** and **(4)**, we will pay your expense to remove debris of Covered Property caused by or resulting from a Covered Cause of Loss that occurs during the policy period. The expenses will be paid only if they are reported to us in writing within 180 days of the date of direct physical loss or damage.

(2) Debris Removal does not apply to costs to:

(a) Extract "pollutants" from land or water; or

(b) Remove, restore or replace polluted land or water.

(3) Subject to the exceptions in Paragraph **(4)**, the following provisions apply:

(a) The most that we will pay for the total of direct physical loss or damage plus debris removal expense is the Limit of Insurance applicable to the Covered Property that has sustained loss or damage.

(b) Subject to Paragraph **(a)** above, the amount we will pay for debris removal expense is limited to 25% of the sum of the deductible plus the amount that we pay for direct physical loss or damage to the Covered Property that has sustained loss or damage.

(4) We will pay up to an additional $10,000 for debris removal expense, for each location, in any one occurrence of physical loss or damage to Covered Property, if one or both of the following circumstances apply:

(a) The total of the actual debris removal expense plus the amount we pay for direct physical loss or damage exceeds the Limit of Insurance on the Covered Property that has sustained loss or damage.

(b) The actual debris removal expense exceeds 25% of the sum of the deductible plus the amount that we pay for direct physical loss or damage to the Covered Property that has sustained loss or damage.

Therefore, if Paragraphs **(4)(a)** and/or **(4)(b)** apply, our total payment for direct physical loss or damage and debris removal expense may reach but will never exceed the Limit of Insurance on the Covered Property that has sustained loss or damage, plus $10,000.

(5) Examples

Example #1

Limit of Insurance	$ 90,000
Amount of Deductible	$ 500
Amount of Loss	$ 50,000
Amount of Loss Payable	$ 49,500
	($50,000 – $500)
Debris Removal Expense	$ 10,000
Debris Removal Expense Payable	$ 10,000
($10,000 is 20% of $50,000)	

The debris removal expense is less than 25% of the sum of the loss payable plus the deductible. The sum of the loss payable and the debris removal expense ($49,500 + $10,000 = $59,500) is less than the Limit of Insurance. Therefore the full amount of debris removal expense is payable in accordance with the terms of Paragraph **(3)**.

Example #2

Limit of Insurance	$ 90,000
Amount of Deductible	$ 500
Amount of Loss	$ 80,000
Amount of Loss Payable	$ 79,500
	($80,000 – $500)
Debris Removal Expense	$ 30,000
Debris Removal Expense Payable	
Basic Amount	$ 10,500
Additional Amount	$ 10,000

The basic amount payable for debris removal expense under the terms of Paragraph **(3)** is calculated as follows: $80,000 ($79,500 + $500) x .25 = $20,000; capped at $10,500). The cap applies because the sum of the loss payable ($79,500) and the basic amount payable for debris removal expense ($10,500) cannot exceed the Limit of Insurance ($90,000).

The additional amount payable for debris removal expense is provided in accordance with the terms of Paragraph **(4)**, because the debris removal expense ($30,000) exceeds 25% of the loss payable plus the deductible ($30,000 is 37.5% of $80,000), and because the sum of the loss payable and debris removal expense ($79,500 + $30,000 =$109,500) would exceed the Limit of Insurance ($90,000). The additional amount of covered debris removal expense is $10,000, the maximum payable under Paragraph **(4).** Thus the total payable for debris removal expense in this example is $20,500; $9,500 of the debris removal expense is not covered.

b. Preservation Of Property

If it is necessary to move Covered Property from the described premises to preserve it from loss or damage by a Covered Cause of Loss, we will pay for any direct physical loss of or damage to that property:

(1) While it is being moved or while temporarily stored at another location; and

(2) Only if the loss or damage occurs within 30 days after the property is first moved.

c. Fire Department Service Charge

When the fire department is called to save or protect Covered Property from a Covered Cause of Loss, we will pay up to $1,000 for your liability for fire department service charges:

(1) Assumed by contract or agreement prior to loss; or

(2) Required by local ordinance.

d. Collapse

(1) With respect to buildings:

(a) Collapse means an abrupt falling down or caving in of a building or any part of a building with the result that the building or part of the building cannot be occupied for its intended purpose;

(b) A building or any part of a building that is in danger of falling down or caving in is not considered to be in a state of collapse;

(c) A part of a building that is standing is not considered to be in a state of collapse even if it has separated from another part of the building;

(d) A building that is standing or any part of a building that is standing is not considered to be in a state of collapse even if it shows evidence of cracking, bulging, sagging, bending, leaning, settling, shrinkage or expansion.

(2) We will pay for direct physical loss or damage to Covered Property, caused by collapse of a building or any part of a building that is insured under this policy, if the collapse is caused by one or more of the following:

(a) The "specified causes of loss" or breakage of building glass, all only as insured against in this policy;

(b) Decay that is hidden from view, unless the presence of such decay is known to an insured prior to collapse;

(c) Insect or vermin damage that is hidden from view, unless the presence of such damage is known to an insured prior to collapse;

(d) Weight of people or personal property;

(e) Weight of rain that collects on a roof;

(f) Use of defective material or methods in construction, remodeling or renovation if the collapse occurs during the course of the construction, remodeling or renovation. However, if the collapse occurs after construction, remodeling or renovation is complete and is caused in part by a cause of loss listed in Paragraphs **(a)** through **(e),** we will pay for the loss or damage even if use of defective material or methods in construction, remodeling or renovation, contributes to the collapse.

The criteria set forth in Paragraphs **(1)(a)** through **(1)(d)** do not limit the coverage otherwise provided under this Additional Coverage for the causes of loss listed in Paragraphs **(2)(a), (2)(d)** and **(2)(e).**

(3) With respect to the following property:

(a) Awnings;

(b) Gutters and downspouts;

(c) Yard fixtures;

(d) Outdoor swimming pools;

(e) Piers, wharves and docks;

(f) Beach or diving platforms or appurtenances;

(g) Retaining walls; and

(h) Walks, roadways and other paved surfaces;

if the collapse is caused by a cause of loss listed in Paragraphs **(2)(b)** through **(2)(f),** we will pay for loss or damage to that property only if such loss or damage is a direct result of the collapse of a building insured under this policy and the property is Covered Property under this policy.

(4) If personal property abruptly falls down or caves in and such collapse is not the result of collapse of a building, we will pay for loss or damage to Covered Property caused by such collapse of personal property only if:

(a) The collapse was caused by a cause of loss listed in Paragraphs **(2)(a)** through **(2)(f)** of this Additional Coverage;

(b) The personal property which collapses is inside a building; and

(c) The property which collapses is not of a kind listed in Paragraph **(3)** above, regardless of whether that kind of property is considered to be personal property or real property.

The coverage stated in this Paragraph **(4)** does not apply to personal property if marring and/or scratching is the only damage to that personal property caused by the collapse.

Collapse of personal property does not mean cracking, bulging, sagging, bending, leaning, settling, shrinkage or expansion.

(5) This Additional Coverage, Collapse, will not increase the Limits Of Insurance provided in this policy.

e. Water Damage, Other Liquids, Powder Or Molten Material Damage

If loss or damage caused by or resulting from covered water or other liquid, powder or molten material damage loss occurs, we will also pay the cost to tear out and replace any part of the building or structure to repair damage to the system or appliance from which the water or other substance escapes.

We will not pay the cost to repair any defect that caused the loss or damage; but we will pay the cost to repair or replace damaged parts of fire extinguishing equipment if the damage:

(1) Results in discharge of any substance from an automatic fire protection system; or

(2) Is directly caused by freezing.

f. Business Income

(1) Business Income

(a) We will pay for the actual loss of Business Income you sustain due to the necessary suspension of your "operations" during the "period of restoration". The suspension must be caused by direct physical loss of or damage to property at the described premises. The loss or damage must be caused by or result from a Covered Cause of Loss. With respect to loss of or damage to personal property in the open or personal property in a vehicle, the described premises include the area within 100 feet of the site at which the described premises are located.

With respect to the requirements set forth in the preceding paragraph, if you occupy only part of the site at which the described premises are located, your premises means:

(i) The portion of the building which you rent, lease or occupy; and

(ii) Any area within the building or on the site at which the described premises are located, if that area services, or is used to gain access to, the described premises.

(b) We will only pay for loss of Business Income that you sustain during the "period of restoration" and that occurs within 12 consecutive months after the date of direct physical loss or damage. We will only pay for ordinary payroll expenses for 60 days following the date of direct physical loss or damage, unless a greater number of days is shown in the Declarations.

(c) Business Income means the:

(i) Net Income (Net Profit or Loss before income taxes) that would have been earned or incurred if no physical loss or damage had occurred, but not including any Net Income that would likely have been earned as a result of an increase in the volume of business due to favorable business conditions caused by the impact of the Covered Cause of Loss on customers or on other businesses; and

(ii) Continuing normal operating expenses incurred, including payroll.

(d) Ordinary payroll expenses:

(i) Mean payroll expenses for all your employees except:

i. Officers;

ii. Executives;

iii. Department Managers;

iv. Employees under contract; and

v. Additional Exemptions shown in the Declarations as:

- Job Classifications; or

- Employees.

(ii) Include:

i. Payroll;

ii. Employee benefits, if directly related to payroll;

iii. FICA payments you pay;

iv. Union dues you pay; and

v. Workers' compensation premiums.

(2) Extended Business Income

(a) If the necessary suspension of your "operations" produces a Business Income loss payable under this policy, we will pay for the actual loss of Business Income you incur during the period that:

(i) Begins on the date property except finished stock is actually repaired, rebuilt or replaced and "operations" are resumed; and

(ii) Ends on the earlier of:

i. The date you could restore your "operations", with reasonable speed, to the level which would generate the Business Income amount that would have existed if no direct physical loss or damage had occurred; or

ii. 30 consecutive days after the date determined in Paragraph **(a)(i)** above, unless a greater number of consecutive days is shown in the Declarations.

However, Extended Business Income does not apply to loss of Business Income incurred as a result of unfavorable business conditions caused by the impact of the Covered Cause of Loss in the area where the described premises are located.

(b) Loss of Business Income must be caused by direct physical loss or damage at the described premises caused by or resulting from any Covered Cause of Loss.

(3) With respect to the coverage provided in this Additional Coverage, suspension means:

(a) The partial slowdown or complete cessation of your business activities; and

(b) That a part or all of the described premises is rendered untenantable, if coverage for Business Income applies.

(4) This Additional Coverage is not subject to the Limits of Insurance of **Section I – Property.**

g. Extra Expense

(1) We will pay necessary Extra Expense you incur during the "period of restoration" that you would not have incurred if there had been no direct physical loss or damage to property at the described premises. The loss or damage must be caused by or result from a Covered Cause of Loss. With respect to loss of or damage to personal property in the open or personal property in a vehicle, the described premises include the area within 100 feet of the site at which the described premises are located.

With respect to the requirements set forth in the preceding paragraph, if you occupy only part of the site at which the described premises are located, your premises means:

(a) The portion of the building which you rent, lease or occupy; and

(b) Any area within the building or on the site at which the described premises are located, if that area services, or is used to gain access to, the described premises.

(2) Extra Expense means expense incurred:

(a) To avoid or minimize the suspension of business and to continue "operations":

(i) At the described premises; or

(ii) At replacement premises or at temporary locations, including relocation expenses, and costs to equip and operate the replacement or temporary locations.

(b) To minimize the suspension of business if you cannot continue "operations".

(c) To:

(i) Repair or replace any property; or

(ii) Research, replace or restore the lost information on damaged "valuable papers and records"

to the extent it reduces the amount of loss that otherwise would have been payable under this Additional Coverage or Additional Coverage **f.** Business Income.

(3) With respect to the coverage provided in this Additional Coverage, suspension means:

(a) The partial slowdown or complete cessation of your business activities; and

(b) That a part or all of the described premises is rendered untenantable, if coverage for Business Income applies.

(4) We will only pay for Extra Expense that occurs within 12 consecutive months after the date of direct physical loss or damage. This Additional Coverage is not subject to the Limits of Insurance of **Section I – Property.**

h. Pollutant Clean Up And Removal

We will pay your expense to extract "pollutants" from land or water at the described premises if the discharge, dispersal, seepage, migration, release or escape of the "pollutants" is caused by or results from a Covered Cause of Loss that occurs during the policy period. The expenses will be paid only if they are reported to us in writing within 180 days of the earlier of:

(1) The date of direct physical loss or damage; or

(2) The end of the policy period.

The most we will pay for each location under this Additional Coverage is $10,000 for the sum of all such expenses arising out of Covered Causes of Loss occurring during each separate 12 month period of this policy.

i. Civil Authority

We will pay for the actual loss of Business Income you sustain and necessary Extra Expense caused by action of civil authority that prohibits access to the described premises due to direct physical loss of or damage to property, other than at the described premises, caused by or resulting from any Covered Cause of Loss.

The coverage for Business Income will begin 72 hours after the time of that action and will apply for a period of up to three consecutive weeks after coverage begins.

The coverage for necessary Extra Expense will begin immediately after the time of that action and ends:

(1) 3 consecutive weeks after the time of that action; or

(2) When your Business Income coverage ends;

whichever is later.

The definitions of Business Income and Extra Expense contained in the Business Income and Extra Expense Additional Coverages also apply to this Civil Authority Additional Coverage. The Civil Authority Additional Coverage is not subject to the Limits of Insurance of **Section I – Property.**

j. Money Orders And Counterfeit Paper Currency

We will pay for loss resulting directly from your having accepted in good faith, in exchange for merchandise, "money" or services:

(1) Money orders issued by any post office, express company or bank that are not paid upon presentation; or

(2) "Counterfeit" paper currency that is acquired during the regular course of business.

The most we will pay for any loss under this Additional Coverage is $1,000.

k. Forgery Or Alteration

(1) We will pay for loss resulting directly from forgery or alteration of, any check, draft, promissory note, bill of exchange or similar written promise of payment in "money", that you or your agent has issued, or that was issued by someone who impersonates you or your agent.

(2) If you are sued for refusing to pay the check, draft, promissory note, bill of exchange or similar written promise of payment in "money", on the basis that it has been forged or altered, and you have our written consent to defend against the suit, we will pay for any reasonable legal expenses that you incur in that defense.

(3) The most we will pay for any loss, including legal expenses, under this Additional Coverage is $2,500, unless a higher Limit of Insurance is shown in the Declarations.

l. Increased Cost Of Construction

(1) This Additional Coverage applies only to buildings insured on a replacement cost basis.

(2) In the event of damage by a Covered Cause of Loss to a building that is Covered Property, we will pay the increased costs incurred to comply with enforcement of an ordinance or law in the course of repair, rebuilding or replacement of damaged parts of that property, subject to the limitations stated in Paragraphs **(3)** through **(9)** of this Additional Coverage.

(3) The ordinance or law referred to in Paragraph **(2)** of this Additional Coverage is an ordinance or law that regulates the construction or repair of buildings or establishes zoning or land use requirements at the described premises, and is in force at the time of loss.

(4) Under this Additional Coverage, we will not pay any costs due to an ordinance or law that:

(a) You were required to comply with before the loss, even when the building was undamaged; and

(b) You failed to comply with.

(5) Under this Additional Coverage, we will not pay any costs associated with the enforcement of an ordinance or law which requires any insured or others to test for, monitor, clean up, remove, contain, treat, detoxify or neutralize, or in any way respond to, or assess the effects of "pollutants".

(6) The most we will pay under this Additional Coverage, for each described building insured under **Section I – Property,** is $10,000. If a damaged building(s) is covered under a blanket Limit of Insurance which applies to more than one building or item of property, then the most we will pay under this Additional Coverage, for each damaged building, is $10,000.

The amount payable under this Additional Coverage is additional insurance.

(7) With respect to this Additional Coverage:

(a) We will not pay for the Increased Cost of Construction:

(i) Until the property is actually repaired or replaced, at the same or another premises; and

(ii) Unless the repairs or replacement are made as soon as reasonably possible after the loss or damage, not to exceed two years. We may extend this period in writing during the two years.

(b) If the building is repaired or replaced at the same premises, or if you elect to rebuild at another premises, the most we will pay for the Increased Cost of Construction is the increased cost of construction at the same premises.

(c) If the ordinance or law requires relocation to another premises, the most we will pay for the Increased Cost of Construction is the increased cost of construction at the new premises.

(8) This Additional Coverage is not subject to the terms of the Ordinance or Law Exclusion, to the extent that such Exclusion would conflict with the provisions of this Additional Coverage.

(9) The costs addressed in the Loss Payment Property Loss Condition in **Section I – Property** do not include the increased cost attributable to enforcement of an ordinance or law. The amount payable under this Additional Coverage, as stated in Paragraph **(6)** of this Additional Coverage, is not subject to such limitation.

m. **Business Income From Dependent Properties**

(1) We will pay for the actual loss of Business Income you sustain due to physical loss or damage at the premises of a dependent property caused by or resulting from any Covered Cause of Loss.

The most we will pay under this Additional Coverage is $5,000 unless a higher Limit of Insurance is indicated in the Declarations.

(2) We will reduce the amount of your Business Income loss, other than Extra Expense, to the extent you can resume "operations", in whole or in part, by using any other available:

(a) Source of materials; or

(b) Outlet for your products.

(3) If you do not resume "operations", or do not resume "operations" as quickly as possible, we will pay based on the length of time it would have taken to resume "operations" as quickly as possible.

(4) Dependent property means property owned by others whom you depend on to:

(a) Deliver materials or services to you, or to others for your account. But services does not mean water, communication or power supply services;

(b) Accept your products or services;

(c) Manufacture your products for delivery to your customers under contract for sale; or

(d) Attract customers to your business.

The dependent property must be located in the coverage territory of this policy.

(5) The coverage period for Business Income under this Additional Coverage:

(a) Begins 72 hours after the time of direct physical loss or damage caused by or resulting from any Covered Cause of Loss at the premises of the dependent property; and

(b) Ends on the date when the property at the premises of the dependent property should be repaired, rebuilt or replaced with reasonable speed and similar quality.

(6) The Business Income coverage period, as stated in Paragraph **(5),** does not include any increased period required due to the enforcement of any ordinance or law that:

(a) Regulates the construction, use or repair, or requires the tearing down of any property; or

(b) Requires any insured or others to test for, monitor, clean up, remove, contain, treat, detoxify or neutralize, or in any way respond to, or assess the effects of "pollutants".

The expiration date of this policy will not reduce the Business Income coverage period.

(7) The definition of Business Income contained in the Business Income Additional Coverage also applies to this Business Income From Dependent Properties Additional Coverage.

n. **Glass Expenses**

(1) We will pay for expenses incurred to put up temporary plates or board up openings if repair or replacement of damaged glass is delayed.

(2) We will pay for expenses incurred to remove or replace obstructions when repairing or replacing glass that is part of a building. This does not include removing or replacing window displays.

o. Fire Extinguisher Systems Recharge Expense

(1) We will pay:

(a) The cost of recharging or replacing, whichever is less, your fire extinguishers and fire extinguishing systems (including hydrostatic testing if needed) if they are discharged on or within 100 feet of the described premises; and

(b) For loss or damage to Covered Property if such loss or damage is the result of an accidental discharge of chemicals from a fire extinguisher or a fire extinguishing system.

(2) No coverage will apply if the fire extinguishing system is discharged during installation or testing.

(3) The most we will pay under this Additional Coverage is $5,000 in any one occurrence.

6. Coverage Extensions

In addition to the Limits of Insurance of **Section I – Property,** you may extend the insurance provided by this policy as provided below.

Except as otherwise provided, the following Extensions apply to property located in or on the building described in the Declarations or in the open (or in a vehicle) within 100 feet of the described premises, unless a higher Limit of Insurance is shown in the Declarations.

a. Newly Acquired Or Constructed Property

(1) Buildings

If this policy covers Buildings, you may extend that insurance to apply to:

(a) Your new buildings while being built on the described premises; and

(b) Buildings you acquire at premises other than the one described, intended for:

(i) Similar use as the building described in the Declarations; or

(ii) Use as a warehouse.

The most we will pay for loss or damage under this Extension is $250,000 at each building.

(2) Business Personal Property

(a) If this policy covers Business Personal Property, you may extend that insurance to apply to:

(i) Business Personal Property, including such property that you newly acquire, at any location you acquire.

(ii) Business Personal Property, including such property that you newly acquire, located at your newly constructed or acquired buildings at the location described in the Declarations; or

(iii) Business Personal Property that you newly acquire, located at the described premises.

This Extension does not apply to personal property that you temporarily acquire in the course of installing or performing work on such property or your wholesale activities.

The most we will pay for loss or damage under this Extension is $100,000 at each premises.

(3) Period Of Coverage

With respect to insurance on or at each newly acquired or constructed property, coverage will end when any of the following first occurs:

(a) This policy expires;

(b) 30 days expire after you acquire the property or begin construction of that part of the building that would qualify as covered property; or

(c) You report values to us.

We will charge you additional premium for values reported from the date you acquire the property or begin construction of that part of the building that would qualify as covered property.

b. Personal Property Off Premises

You may extend the insurance that applies to Business Personal Property to apply to covered Business Personal Property, other than "money" and "securities", "valuable papers and records" or accounts receivable, while it is in the course of transit or at a premises you do not own, lease or operate. The most we will pay for loss or damage under this Extension is $5,000.

© ISO Properties, Inc., 2001

c. Outdoor Property

You may extend the insurance provided by this policy to apply to your outdoor fences, radio and television antennas (including satellite dishes), signs (other than signs attached to buildings), trees, shrubs and plants, including debris removal expense, caused by or resulting from any of the following causes of loss:

(1) Fire;

(2) Lightning;

(3) Explosion;

(4) Riot or Civil Commotion; or

(5) Aircraft.

The most we will pay for loss or damage under this Extension is $2,500, but not more than $500 for any one tree, shrub or plant.

d. Personal Effects

You may extend the insurance that applies to Business Personal Property to apply to personal effects owned by you, your officers, your partners or "members", your "managers" or your employees. This extension does not apply to:

(1) Tools or equipment used in your business; or

(2) Loss or damage by theft.

The most we will pay for loss or damage under this Extension is $2,500 at each described premises.

e. Valuable Papers And Records

(1) You may extend the insurance that applies to Business Personal Property to apply to direct physical loss or damage to "valuable papers and records" that you own, or that are in your care, custody or control caused by or resulting from a Covered Cause of Loss. This Coverage Extension includes the cost to research, replace or restore the lost information on "valuable papers and records" for which duplicates do not exist.

(2) This Coverage Extension does not apply to:

(a) Property held as samples or for delivery after sale;

(b) Property in storage away from the premises shown in the Declarations.

(3) The most we will pay under this Coverage Extension for loss or damage to "valuable papers and records" in any one occurrence at the described premises is $10,000, unless a higher Limit of Insurance for "valuable papers and records" is shown in the Declarations.

For "valuable papers and records" not at the described premises, the most we will pay is $5,000.

(4) Paragraph **B. Exclusions** in **Section I – Property** does not apply to this Coverage Extension except for:

(a) Paragraph **B.1.c.,** Governmental Action;

(b) Paragraph **B.1.d.,** Nuclear Hazard;

(c) Paragraph **B.1.f.,** War And Military Action;

(d) Paragraph **B.2.f.,** Dishonesty;

(e) Paragraph **B.2.g.,** False Pretense; and

(f) Paragraph **B.3.**

f. Accounts Receivable

(1) You may extend the insurance that applies to Business Personal Property to apply to accounts receivable. We will pay:

(a) All amounts due from your customers that you are unable to collect;

(b) Interest charges on any loan required to offset amounts you are unable to collect pending our payment of these amounts;

(c) Collection expenses in excess of your normal collection expenses that are made necessary by loss or damage; and

(d) Other reasonable expenses that you incur to re-establish your records of accounts receivable;

that result from direct physical loss or damage by any Covered Cause of Loss to your records of accounts receivable.

(2) The most we will pay under this Coverage Extension for loss or damage in any one occurrence at the described premises is $10,000, unless a higher Limit of Insurance for accounts receivable is shown in the Declarations.

For accounts receivable not at the described premises, the most we will pay is $5,000.

(3) Paragraph **B. Exclusions** in **Section I – Property** does not apply to this Coverage Extension except for:

- **(a)** Paragraph **B.1.c.,** Governmental Action;
- **(b)** Paragraph **B.1.d.,** Nuclear Hazard;
- **(c)** Paragraph **B.1.f.,** War And Military Action;
- **(d)** Paragraph **B.2.f.,** Dishonesty;
- **(e)** Paragraph **B.2.g.,** False Pretense;
- **(f)** Paragraph **B.3.;** and
- **(g)** Paragraph **B.5.** Accounts Receivable Exclusion.

B. Exclusions

1. We will not pay for loss or damage caused directly or indirectly by any of the following. Such loss or damage is excluded regardless of any other cause or event that contributes concurrently or in any sequence to the loss. These exclusions apply whether or not the loss event results in widespread damage or affects a substantial area.

a. Ordinance Or Law

(1) The enforcement of any ordinance or law:

- **(a)** Regulating the construction, use or repair of any property; or
- **(b)** Requiring the tearing down of any property, including the cost of removing its debris.

(2) This exclusion, Ordinance Or Law, applies whether the loss results from:

- **(a)** An ordinance or law that is enforced even if the property has not been damaged; or
- **(b)** The increased costs incurred to comply with an ordinance or law in the course of construction, repair, renovation, remodeling or demolition of property or removal of its debris, following a physical loss to that property.

b. Earth Movement

(1) Earthquake, including any earth sinking, rising or shifting related to such event;

(2) Landslide, including any earth sinking, rising or shifting related to such event;

(3) Mine subsidence, meaning subsidence of a man-made mine, whether or not mining activity has ceased;

(4) Earth sinking (other than sinkhole collapse), rising or shifting including soil conditions which cause settling, cracking or other disarrangement of foundations or other parts of realty. Soil conditions include contraction, expansion, freezing, thawing, erosion, improperly compacted soil and the action of water under the ground surface.

But if Earth Movement, as described in Paragraphs **(1)** through **(4)** above, results in fire or explosion, we will pay for the loss or damage caused by that fire or explosion.

(5) Volcanic eruption, explosion or effusion. But if volcanic eruption, explosion or effusion results in fire, building glass breakage or volcanic action, we will pay for the loss or damage caused by that fire, building glass breakage or volcanic action.

Volcanic action means direct loss or damage resulting from the eruption of a volcano when the loss or damage is caused by:

- **(a)** Airborne volcanic blast or airborne shock waves;
- **(b)** Ash, dust or particulate matter; or
- **(c)** Lava flow.

All volcanic eruptions that occur within any 168-hour period will constitute a single occurrence.

Volcanic action does not include the cost to remove ash, dust or particulate matter that does not cause direct physical loss of or damage to Covered Property.

c. Governmental Action

Seizure or destruction of property by order of governmental authority.

But we will pay for loss or damage caused by or resulting from acts of destruction ordered by governmental authority and taken at the time of a fire to prevent its spread, if the fire would be covered under this policy.

d. Nuclear Hazard

Nuclear reaction or radiation, or radioactive contamination, however caused.

But if nuclear reaction or radiation, or radioactive contamination, results in fire, we will pay for the loss or damage caused by that fire.

e. Power Failure

The failure of power or other utility service supplied to the described premises, however caused, if the failure occurs away from the described premises.

But if the failure of power or other utility service results in a Covered Cause of Loss, we will pay for the loss or damage caused by that Covered Cause of Loss.

This exclusion does not apply to loss or damage to "computer(s)" and "electronic media and records".

f. War And Military Action

(1) War, including undeclared or civil war;

(2) Warlike action by a military force, including action in hindering or defending against an actual or expected attack, by any government, sovereign or other authority using military personnel or other agents; or

(3) Insurrection, rebellion, revolution, usurped power, or action taken by governmental authority in hindering or defending against any of these.

g. Water

(1) Flood, surface water, waves, tides, tidal waves, overflow of any body of water, or their spray, all whether driven by wind or not;

(2) Mudslide or mudflow;

(3) Water that backs up or overflows from a sewer, drain or sump; or

(4) Water under the ground surface pressing on, or flowing or seeping through:

    (a) Foundations, walls, floors or paved surfaces;

    (b) Basements, whether paved or not; or

    (c) Doors, windows or other openings.

But if Water, as described in Paragraphs **(1)** through **(4)**, results in fire, explosion or sprinkler leakage, we will pay for the loss or damage caused by that fire, explosion or sprinkler leakage.

h. Certain Computer-Related Losses

(1) The failure, malfunction or inadequacy of:

    (a) Any of the following, whether belonging to any insured or to others:

        (i) "Computer" hardware, including microprocessors or other electronic data processing equipment as may be described elsewhere in this policy;

        (ii) "Computer" application software or other "electronic media and records" as may be described elsewhere in this policy;

        (iii) "Computer" operating systems and related software;

        (iv) "Computer" networks;

        (v) Microprocessors ("computer" chips) not part of any "computer" system; or

        (vi) Any other computerized or electronic equipment or components; or

    (b) Any other products, and any services, data or functions that directly or indirectly use or rely upon, in any manner, any of the items listed in Paragraph **(a)** above;

due to the inability to correctly recognize, distinguish, interpret or accept one or more dates or times. An example is the inability of computer software to recognize the year 2000.

(2) Any advice, consultation, design, evaluation, inspection, installation, maintenance, repair, replacement or supervision provided or done by you or for you to determine, rectify or test for, any potential or actual problems described in Paragraph **(1)** above.

However, if excluded loss or damage, as described in Paragraph **(1)** above results in a "Specified Cause of Loss" under **Section I – Property,** we will pay only for the loss or damage caused by such "Specified Cause of Loss".

We will not pay for repair, replacement or modification of any items in Paragraphs **(1)(a)** or **(1)(b)** to correct any deficiencies or change any features.

2. We will not pay for loss or damage caused by or resulting from any of the following:

a. Electrical Apparatus

Artificially generated electrical current, including electric arcing, that disturbs electrical devices, appliances or wires.

But if artificially generated electrical current results in fire, we will pay for the loss or damage caused by fire.

We will pay for loss or damage to "computer(s)" due to artificially generated electrical current if such loss or damage is caused by or results from:

(1) An occurrence that took place within 100 feet of the described premises; or

(2) Interruption of electric power supply, power surge, blackout or brownout if the cause of such occurrence took place within 100 feet of the described premises.

b. Consequential Losses

Delay, loss of use or loss of market.

c. Smoke, Vapor, Gas

Smoke, vapor or gas from agricultural smudging or industrial operations.

d. Steam Apparatus

Explosion of steam boilers, steam pipes, steam engines or steam turbines owned or leased by you, or operated under your control. But if explosion of steam boilers, steam pipes, steam engines or steam turbines results in fire or combustion explosion, we will pay for the loss or damage caused by that fire or combustion explosion. We will also pay for loss or damage caused by or resulting from the explosion of gases or fuel within the furnace of any fired vessel or within the flues or passages through which the gases of combustion pass.

e. Frozen Plumbing

Water, other liquids, powder or molten material that leaks or flows from plumbing, heating, air conditioning or other equipment (except fire protective systems) caused by or resulting from freezing, unless:

(1) You do your best to maintain heat in the building or structure; or

(2) You drain the equipment and shut off the supply if the heat is not maintained.

f. Dishonesty

Dishonest or criminal acts by you, anyone else with an interest in the property, or any of your or their partners, "members", officers, "managers", employees, directors, trustees, authorized representatives or anyone to whom you entrust the property for any purpose:

(1) Acting alone or in collusion with others;

(2) Whether or not occurring during the hours of employment.

This exclusion does not apply to acts of destruction by your employees; but theft by employees is not covered.

With respect to accounts receivable and "valuable papers and records", this exclusion does not apply to carriers for hire.

This exclusion does not apply to coverage that is provided under the Employee Dishonesty Optional Coverage.

g. False Pretense

Voluntary parting with any property by you or anyone else to whom you have entrusted the property if induced to do so by any fraudulent scheme, trick, device or false pretense.

h. Exposed Property

Rain, snow, ice or sleet to personal property in the open.

i. Collapse

Collapse, except as provided in the Additional Coverage for Collapse. But if collapse results in a Covered Cause of Loss, we will pay for the loss or damage caused by that Covered Cause of Loss.

j. Pollution

We will not pay for loss or damage caused by or resulting from the discharge, dispersal, seepage, migration, release or escape of "pollutants" unless the discharge, dispersal, seepage, migration, release or escape is itself caused by any of the "specified causes of loss". But if the discharge, dispersal, seepage, migration, release or escape of "pollutants" results in a "specified cause of loss", we will pay for the loss or damage caused by that "specified cause of loss".

k. Neglect

Neglect of an insured to use all reasonable means to save and preserve property from further damage at and after the time of loss.

l. Other Types Of Loss

(1) Wear and tear;

(2) Rust, corrosion, fungus, decay, deterioration, hidden or latent defect or any quality in property that causes it to damage or destroy itself;

(3) Smog;

(4) Settling, cracking, shrinking or expansion;

(5) Nesting or infestation, or discharge or release of waste products or secretions, by insects, birds, rodents or other animals;

(6) Mechanical breakdown, including rupture or bursting caused by centrifugal force.

This exclusion does not apply with respect to the breakdown of "computer(s)";

(7) The following causes of loss to personal property:

(a) Dampness or dryness of atmosphere;

(b) Changes in or extremes of temperature; or

(c) Marring or scratching.

But if an excluded cause of loss that is listed in Paragraphs **(1)** through **(7)** above results in a "specified cause of loss" or building glass breakage, we will pay for the loss or damage caused by that "specified cause of loss" or building glass breakage.

m. Errors Or Omissions

Errors or omissions in:

(1) Programming, processing or storing data, as described under "electronic media and records" or in any "computer" operations; or

(2) Processing or copying "valuable papers and records".

However, we will pay for direct physical loss or damage caused by resulting fire or explosion if these causes of loss would be covered by this coverage form.

n. Installation, Testing, Repair

Errors or deficiency in design, installation, testing, maintenance, modification or repair of your "computer" system including "electronic media and records".

However, we will pay for direct physical loss or damage caused by resulting fire or explosion if these causes of loss would be covered by this coverage form.

o. Electrical Disturbance

Electrical or magnetic injury, disturbance or erasure of "electronic media and records", except as provided for under the Coverage Extensions of **Section I – Property.**

However, we will pay for direct loss or damage caused by lightning.

3. We will not pay for loss or damage caused by or resulting from any of the following Paragraphs **a.** through **c.** But if an excluded cause of loss that is listed in Paragraphs **a.** through **c.** results in a Covered Cause of Loss, we will pay for the loss or damage caused by that Covered Cause of Loss.

a. Weather Conditions

Weather conditions. But this exclusion only applies if weather conditions contribute in any way with a cause or event excluded in Paragraph **B.1.** above to produce the loss or damage.

b. Acts Or Decisions

Acts or decisions, including the failure to act or decide, of any person, group, organization or governmental body.

c. Negligent Work

Faulty, inadequate or defective:

(1) Planning, zoning, development, surveying, siting;

(2) Design, specifications, workmanship, repair, construction, renovation, remodeling, grading, compaction;

(3) Materials used in repair, construction, renovation or remodeling; or

(4) Maintenance;

of part or all of any property on or off the described premises.

4. Business Income And Extra Expense Exclusions

a. We will not pay for:

(1) Any Extra Expense, or increase of Business Income loss, caused by or resulting from:

(a) Delay in rebuilding, repairing or replacing the property or resuming "operations", due to interference at the location of the rebuilding, repair or replacement by strikers or other persons; or

(b) Suspension, lapse or cancellation of any license, lease or contract. But if the suspension, lapse or cancellation is directly caused by the suspension of "operations", we will cover such loss that affects your Business Income during the "period of restoration".

(2) Any other consequential loss.

b. With respect to this exclusion, suspension means:

(1) The partial slowdown or complete cessation of your business activities; and

(2) That a part or all of the described premises is rendered untenantable, if coverage for Business Income applies.

5. Accounts Receivable Exclusion

The following additional exclusion applies to the Accounts Receivable Coverage Extension:

We will not pay for:

a. Loss or damage caused by or resulting from alteration, falsification, concealment or destruction of records of accounts receivable done to conceal the wrongful giving, taking or withholding of "money", "securities" or other property.

This exclusion applies only to the extent of the wrongful giving, taking or withholding.

b. Loss or damage caused by or resulting from bookkeeping, accounting or billing errors or omissions.

c. Any loss or damage that requires any audit of records or any inventory computation to prove its factual existence.

C. Limits Of Insurance

1. The most we will pay for loss or damage in any one occurrence is the applicable Limit of Insurance of **Section I – Property** shown in the Declarations.

2. The most we will pay for loss of or damage to outdoor signs attached to buildings is $1,000 per sign in any one occurrence.

3. The limits applicable to the Coverage Extensions and the Fire Department Service Charge and Pollutant Clean Up and Removal Additional Coverages are in addition to the Limits of Insurance of **Section I – Property.**

4. Building Limit – Automatic Increase

a. The Limit of Insurance for Buildings will automatically increase by the annual percentage shown in the Declarations.

b. The amount of increase will be:

(1) The Building limit that applied on the most recent of the policy inception date, the policy anniversary date, or any other policy change amending the Building limit, times

(2) The percentage of annual increase shown in the Declarations, expressed as a decimal (example: 8% is .08), times

(3) The number of days since the beginning of the current policy year of the effective date of the most recent policy change amending the Building limit, divided by 365.

Example:

If: The applicable Building limit is $100,000. The annual percentage increase is 8%. The number of days since the beginning of the policy year (or last policy change) is 146.

The amount of increase is

$100,000 x .08 x 146 ÷ 365 = $3,200.

5. Business Personal Property Limit – Seasonal Increase

a. The Limit of Insurance for Business Personal Property will automatically increase by 25% to provide for seasonal variations.

b. This increase will apply only if the Limit of Insurance shown for Business Personal Property in the Declarations is at least 100% of your average monthly values during the lesser of:

(1) The 12 months immediately preceding the date the loss or damage occurs; or

(2) The period of time you have been in business as of the date the loss or damage occurs.

D. Deductibles

1. We will not pay for loss or damage in any one occurrence until the amount of loss or damage exceeds the Deductible shown in the Declarations. We will then pay the amount of loss or damage in excess of the Deductible up to the applicable Limit of Insurance of **Section I – Property.**

2. Regardless of the amount of the Deductible, the most we will deduct from any loss or damage for Glass and under all of the following Optional Coverages in any one occurrence is the Optional Coverage/Glass Deductible shown in the Declarations:

a. Money and Securities;

b. Employee Dishonesty; and

c. Outdoor Signs.

© ISO Properties, Inc., 2001   **BP 00 03 07 02**

But this Optional Coverage/Glass Deductible will not increase the Deductible shown in the Declarations. This Deductible will be used to satisfy the requirements of the Deductible in the Declarations.

3. No deductible applies to the following Additional Coverages:

   a. Fire Department Service Charge;

   b. Business Income;

   c. Extra Expense;

   d. Civil Authority; and

   e. Fire Extinguisher Systems Recharge Expense.

E. **Property Loss Conditions**

1. **Abandonment**

   There can be no abandonment of any property to us.

2. **Appraisal**

   If we and you disagree on the amount of loss, either may make written demand for an appraisal of the loss. In this event, each party will select a competent and impartial appraiser. The two appraisers will select an umpire. If they cannot agree, either may request that selection be made by a judge of a court having jurisdiction. The appraisers will state separately the amount of loss. If they fail to agree, they will submit their differences to the umpire. A decision agreed to by any two will be binding. Each party will:

   a. Pay its chosen appraiser; and

   b. Bear the other expenses of the appraisal and umpire equally.

   If there is an appraisal, we will still retain our right to deny the claim.

3. **Duties In The Event Of Loss Or Damage**

   a. You must see that the following are done in the event of loss or damage to Covered Property:

      (1) Notify the police if a law may have been broken.

      (2) Give us prompt notice of the loss or damage. Include a description of the property involved.

      (3) As soon as possible, give us a description of how, when and where the loss or damage occurred.

   (4) Take all reasonable steps to protect the Covered Property from further damage, and keep a record of your expenses necessary to protect the Covered Property, for consideration in the settlement of the claim. This will not increase the Limits of Insurance of **Section I – Property.** However, we will not pay for any subsequent loss or damage resulting from a cause of loss that is not a Covered Cause of Loss. Also, if feasible, set the damaged property aside and in the best possible order for examination.

   (5) At our request, give us complete inventories of the damaged and undamaged property. Include quantities, costs, values and amount of loss claimed.

   (6) As often as may be reasonably required, permit us to inspect the property proving the loss or damage and examine your books and records.

      Also permit us to take samples of damaged and undamaged property for inspection, testing and analysis, and permit us to make copies from your books and records.

   (7) Send us a signed, sworn proof of loss containing the information we request to investigate the claim. You must do this within 60 days after our request. We will supply you with the necessary forms.

   (8) Cooperate with us in the investigation or settlement of the claim.

   (9) Resume all or part of your "operations" as quickly as possible.

   b. We may examine any insured under oath, while not in the presence of any other insured and at such times as may be reasonably required, about any matter relating to this insurance or the claim, including an insured's books and records. In the event of an examination, an insured's answers must be signed.

4. **Legal Action Against Us**

   No one may bring a legal action against us under this insurance unless:

   a. There has been full compliance with all of the terms of this insurance; and

   b. The action is brought within 2 years after the date on which the direct physical loss or damage occurred.

5. Electronic Media And Records Limitation

We will not pay for any loss of Business Income caused by direct physical loss of or damage to "electronic media and records" after the longer of:

a. 60 consecutive days from the date of direct physical loss or damage; or

b. The period, beginning with the date of direct physical loss or damage, necessary to repair, rebuild or replace with reasonable speed and similar quality, other property at the described premises due to loss or damage caused by the same occurrence.

Example #1

A Covered Cause of Loss damages a "computer" on June 1. It takes until September 1 to replace the "computer", and until October 1 to restore the data that was lost when the damage occurred. We will only pay for the Business Income loss sustained during the period June 1 – September 1. Loss during the period September 2 – October 1 is not covered.

Example #2

A Covered Cause of Loss results in the loss of data processing programming records on August 1. The records are replaced on October 15. We will only pay for the Business Income loss sustained during the period August 1 – September 29 (60 consecutive days). Loss during the period September 30 – October 15 is not covered.

6. Loss Payment

In the event of loss or damage covered by this policy:

a. At our option, we will either:

(1) Pay the value of lost or damaged property;

(2) Pay the cost of repairing or replacing the lost or damaged property;

(3) Take all or any part of the property at an agreed or appraised value; or

(4) Repair, rebuild or replace the property with other property of like kind and quality, subject to Paragraph **d.(1)(e)** below.

b. We will give notice of our intentions within 30 days after we receive the sworn proof of loss.

c. We will not pay you more than your financial interest in the Covered Property.

d. Except as provided in Paragraphs **(2)** through **(8)** below, we will determine the value of Covered Property as follows:

(1) At replacement cost without deduction for depreciation, subject to the following:

(a) If, at the time of loss, the Limit of Insurance on the lost or damaged property is 80% or more of the full replacement cost of the property immediately before the loss, we will pay the cost to repair or replace, after application of the deductible and without deduction for depreciation, but not more than the least of the following amounts:

(i) The Limit of Insurance under **Section I – Property** that applies to the lost or damaged property;

(ii) The cost to replace, on the same premises, the lost or damaged property with other property:

i. Of comparable material and quality; and

ii. Used for the same purpose; or

(iii) The amount that you actually spend that is necessary to repair or replace the lost or damaged property.

If a building is rebuilt at a new premises, the cost is limited to the cost which would have been incurred had the building been built at the original premises.

(b) If, at the time of loss, the Limit of Insurance applicable to the lost or damaged property is less than 80% of the full replacement cost of the property immediately before the loss, we will pay the greater of the following amounts, but not more than the Limit of Insurance that applies to the property:

(i) The actual cash value of the lost or damaged property; or

(ii) A proportion of the cost to repair or replace the lost or damaged property, after application of the deductible and without deduction for depreciation. This proportion will equal the ratio of the applicable Limit of Insurance to 80% of the cost of repair or replacement.

               BP 00 03 07 02

(c) You may make a claim for loss or damage covered by this insurance on an actual cash value basis instead of on a replacement cost basis. In the event you elect to have loss or damage settled on an actual cash value basis, you may still make a claim on a replacement cost basis if you notify us of your intent to do so within 180 days after the loss or damage.

(d) We will not pay on a replacement cost basis for any loss or damage:

(i) Until the lost or damaged property is actually repaired or replaced; and

(ii) Unless the repairs or replacement are made as soon as reasonably possible after the loss or damage.

However, if the cost to repair or replace the damaged building property is $2,500 or less, we will settle the loss according to the provisions of Paragraphs **d.(1)(a)** and **d.(1)(b)** above whether or not the actual repair or replacement is complete.

(e) The cost to repair, rebuild or replace does not include the increased cost attributable to enforcement of any ordinance or law regulating the construction, use or repair of any property.

(2) If the "Actual Cash Value – Buildings" option applies, as shown in the Declarations, Paragraph **(1)** above does not apply to Buildings. Instead, we will determine the value of Buildings at actual cash value.

(3) The following property at actual cash value:

(a) Used or second-hand merchandise held in storage or for sale;

(b) Property of others. However, if an item(s) of personal property of others is subject to a written contract which governs your liability for loss or damage to that item(s), then valuation of that item(s) will be based on the amount for which you are liable under such contract, but not to exceed the lesser of the replacement cost of the property or the applicable Limit of Insurance;

(c) Household contents, except personal property in apartments or rooms furnished by you as landlord;

(d) Manuscripts;

(e) Works of art, antiques or rare articles, including etchings, pictures, statuary, marbles, bronzes, porcelains and bric-a-brac.

(4) Glass at the cost of replacement with safety glazing material if required by law.

(5) Tenants' Improvements and Betterments at:

(a) Replacement cost if you make repairs promptly.

(b) A proportion of your original cost if you do not make repairs promptly. We will determine the proportionate value as follows:

(i) Multiply the original cost by the number of days from the loss or damage to the expiration of the lease; and

(ii) Divide the amount determined in **(i)** above by the number of days from the installation of improvements to the expiration of the lease.

If your lease contains a renewal option, the expiration of the renewal option period will replace the expiration of the lease in this procedure.

(c) Nothing if others pay for repairs or replacement.

(6) Loss or damage to "valuable papers and records" will be valued at the cost of restoration or replacement, including the cost of data entry, re-programming, computer consultation services and the media on which the data or programs reside. To the extent that the contents of the "valuable papers and records" are not restored, the "valuable papers and records" will be valued at the cost of replacement with blank materials of substantially identical type.

(7) Applicable only to the Optional Coverages:

(a) "Money" at its face value; and

(b) "Securities" at their value at the close of business on the day the loss is discovered.

(8) Applicable only to Accounts Receivable:

  (a) If you cannot accurately establish the amount of accounts receivable outstanding as of the time of loss or damage:

  (i) We will determine the total of the average monthly amounts of accounts receivable for the 12 months immediately preceding the month in which the loss or damage occurs; and

  (ii) We will adjust that total for any normal fluctuations in the amount of accounts receivable for the month in which the loss or damage occurred or for any demonstrated variance from the average for that month.

  (b) The following will be deducted from the total amount of accounts receivable, however that amount is established:

  (i) The amount of the accounts for which there is no loss or damage;

  (ii) The amount of the accounts that you are able to re-establish or collect;

  (iii) An amount to allow for probable bad debts that you are normally unable to collect; and

  (iv) All unearned interest and service charges.

e. Our payment for loss of or damage to personal property of others will only be for the account of the owners of the property. We may adjust losses with the owners of lost or damaged property if other than you. If we pay the owners, such payments will satisfy your claims against us for the owners' property. We will not pay the owners more than their financial interest in the Covered Property.

f. We may elect to defend you against suits arising from claims of owners of property. We will do this at our expense.

g. We will pay for covered loss or damage within 30 days after we receive the sworn proof of loss, provided you have complied with all of the terms of this policy, and

(1) We have reached agreement with you on the amount of loss; or

(2) An appraisal award has been made.

7. Recovered Property

If either you or we recover any property after loss settlement, that party must give the other prompt notice. At your option, you may retain the property. But then you must return to us the amount we paid to you for the property. We will pay recovery expenses and the expenses to repair the recovered property, subject to the Limits of Insurance of **Section I – Property.**

8. Resumption Of Operations

We will reduce the amount of your:

a. Business Income loss, other than Extra Expense, to the extent you can resume your "operations", in whole or in part, by using damaged or undamaged property (including merchandise or stock) at the described premises or elsewhere.

b. Extra Expense loss to the extent you can return "operations" to normal and discontinue such Extra Expense.

9. Vacancy

  a. Description Of Terms

  (1) As used in this Vacancy Condition, the term building and the term vacant have the meanings set forth in Paragraphs **(a)** and **(b)** below:

  (a) When this policy is issued to a tenant, and with respect to that tenant's interest in Covered Property, building means the unit or suite rented or leased to the tenant. Such building is vacant when it does not contain enough business personal property to conduct customary operations.

  (b) When this policy is issued to the owner or general lessee of a building, building means the entire building. Such building is vacant unless at least 31% of its total square footage is:

  (i) Rented to a lessee or sub-lessee and used by the lessee or sub-lessee to conduct its customary operations; and/or

  (ii) Used by the building owner to conduct customary operations.

  (2) Buildings under construction or renovation are not considered vacant.

BP 00 03 07 02

b. Vacancy Provisions

If the building where loss or damage occurs has been vacant for more than 60 consecutive days before that loss or damage occurs:

(1) We will not pay for any loss or damage caused by any of the following even if they are Covered Causes of Loss:

(a) Vandalism;

(b) Sprinkler leakage, unless you have protected the system against freezing;

(c) Building glass breakage;

(d) Water damage;

(e) Theft; or

(f) Attempted theft.

(2) With respect to Covered Causes of Loss other than those listed in Paragraphs **(1)(a)** through **(1)(f)** above, we will reduce the amount we would otherwise pay for the loss or damage by 15%.

F. Property General Conditions

1. Control Of Property

Any act or neglect of any person other than you beyond your direction or control will not affect this insurance.

The breach of any condition of this Coverage Form at any one or more locations will not affect coverage at any location where, at the time of loss or damage, the breach of condition does not exist.

2. Mortgageholders

a. The term "mortgageholder" includes trustee.

b. We will pay for covered loss of or damage to buildings or structures to each mortgageholder shown in the Declarations in their order of precedence, as interests may appear.

c. The mortgageholder has the right to receive loss payment even if the mortgageholder has started foreclosure or similar action on the building or structure.

d. If we deny your claim because of your acts or because you have failed to comply with the terms of this policy, the mortgageholder will still have the right to receive loss payment if the mortgageholder:

(1) Pays any premium due under this policy at our request if you have failed to do so;

(2) Submits a signed, sworn proof of loss within 60 days after receiving notice from us of your failure to do so; and

(3) Has notified us of any change in ownership, occupancy or substantial change in risk known to the mortgageholder.

All of the terms of this policy will then apply directly to the mortgageholder.

e. If we pay the mortgageholder for any loss or damage and deny payment to you because of your acts or because you have failed to comply with the terms of this policy:

(1) The mortgageholder's rights under the mortgage will be transferred to us to the extent of the amount we pay; and

(2) The mortgageholder's right to recover the full amount of the mortgageholder's claim will not be impaired.

At our option, we may pay to the mortgageholder the whole principal on the mortgage plus any accrued interest. In this event, your mortgage and note will be transferred to us and you will pay your remaining mortgage debt to us.

f. If we cancel this policy, we will give written notice to the mortgageholder at least:

(1) 10 days before the effective date of cancellation if we cancel for your nonpayment of premium; or

(2) 30 days before the effective date of cancellation if we cancel for any other reason.

g. If we elect not to renew this policy, we will give written notice to the mortgageholder at least 10 days before the expiration date of this policy.

3. No Benefit To Bailee

No person or organization, other than you, having custody of Covered Property will benefit from this insurance.

4. Policy Period, Coverage Territory

Under **Section I – Property:**

a. We cover loss or damage commencing:

(1) During the policy period shown in the Declarations; and

(2) Within the coverage territory or, with respect to property in transit, while it is between points in the coverage territory.

b. The coverage territory is:

(1) The United States of America (including its territories and possessions);

(2) Puerto Rico; and

(3) Canada.

G. Optional Coverages

If shown as applicable in the Declarations, the following Optional Coverages also apply. These coverages are subject to the terms and conditions applicable to property coverage in this policy, except as provided below.

1. Outdoor Signs

 a. We will pay for direct physical loss of or damage to all outdoor signs at the described premises:

 (1) Owned by you; or

 (2) Owned by others but in your care, custody or control.

 b. Paragraph **A.3., Covered Causes Of Loss,** and Paragraph **B., Exclusions** in **Section I – Property,** do not apply to this Optional Coverage, except for:

 (1) Paragraph **B.1.c.,** Governmental Action;

 (2) Paragraph **B.1.d.,** Nuclear Hazard; and

 (3) Paragraph **B.1.f.,** War And Military Action.

 c. We will not pay for loss or damage caused by or resulting from:

 (1) Wear and tear;

 (2) Hidden or latent defect;

 (3) Rust;

 (4) Corrosion; or

 (5) Mechanical breakdown.

 d. The most we will pay for loss or damage in any one occurrence is the Limit of Insurance for Outdoor Signs shown in the Declarations.

 e. The provisions of this Optional Coverage supersede all other references to outdoor signs in this policy.

2. Money And Securities

 a. We will pay for loss of "money" and "securities" used in your business while at a bank or savings institution, within your living quarters or the living quarters of your partners or any employee having use and custody of the property, at the described premises, or in transit between any of these places, resulting directly from:

 (1) Theft, meaning any act of stealing;

 (2) Disappearance; or

 (3) Destruction.

 b. In addition to the Limitations and Exclusions applicable to **Section I – Property,** we will not pay for loss:

 (1) Resulting from accounting or arithmetical errors or omissions;

 (2) Due to the giving or surrendering of property in any exchange or purchase; or

 (3) Of property contained in any "money"-operated device unless the amount of "money" deposited in it is recorded by a continuous recording instrument in the device.

 c. The most we will pay for loss in any one occurrence is:

 (1) The limit shown in the Declarations for Inside the Premises for "money" and "securities" while:

 (a) In or on the described premises; or

 (b) Within a bank or savings institution; and

 (2) The limit shown in the Declarations for Outside the Premises for "money" and "securities" while anywhere else.

 d. All loss:

 (1) Caused by one or more persons; or

 (2) Involving a single act or series of related acts;

 is considered one occurrence.

 e. You must keep records of all "money" and "securities" so we can verify the amount of any loss or damage.

3. Employee Dishonesty

 a. We will pay for direct loss of or damage to Business Personal Property and "money" and "securities" resulting from dishonest acts committed by any of your employees acting alone or in collusion with other persons (except you or your partner) with the manifest intent to:

 (1) Cause you to sustain loss or damage; and also

 (2) Obtain financial benefit (other than salaries, commissions, fees, bonuses, promotions, awards, profit sharing, pensions or other employee benefits earned in the normal course of employment) for:

 (a) Any employee; or

 (b) Any other person or organization.

 b. We will not pay for loss or damage:

 (1) Resulting from any dishonest or criminal act that you or any of your partners or "members" commit whether acting alone or in collusion with other persons.

© ISO Properties, Inc., 2001

(2) Resulting from any dishonest act committed by any of your employees (except as provided in Paragraph **a.**), "managers" or directors:

    (a) Whether acting alone or in collusion with other persons; or

    (b) While performing services for you or otherwise.

(3) The only proof of which as to its existence or amount is:

    (a) An inventory computation; or

    (b) A profit and loss computation.

c. The most we will pay for loss or damage in any one occurrence is the Limit of Insurance for Employee Dishonesty shown in the Declarations.

d. All loss or damage:

    (1) Caused by one or more persons; or

    (2) Involving a single act or series of acts;

    is considered one occurrence.

e. If any loss is covered:

    (1) Partly by this insurance; and

    (2) Partly by any prior cancelled or terminated insurance that we or any affiliate had issued to you or any predecessor in interest;

    the most we will pay is the larger of the amount recoverable under this insurance or the prior insurance.

    We will pay only for loss or damage you sustain through acts committed or events occurring during the Policy Period. Regardless of the number of years this policy remains in force or the number of premiums paid, no Limit of Insurance cumulates from year to year or period to period.

f. This Optional Coverage is cancelled as to any employee immediately upon discovery by:

    (1) You; or

    (2) Any of your partners, "members", "managers", officers or directors not in collusion with the employee;

    of any dishonest act committed by that employee before or after being hired by you.

g. We will pay only for covered loss or damage sustained during the policy period and discovered no later than one year from the end of the policy period.

h. If you (or any predecessor in interest) sustained loss or damage during the policy period of any prior insurance that you could have recovered under that insurance except that the time within which to discover loss or damage had expired, we will pay for it under this Optional Coverage, provided:

    (1) This Optional Coverage became effective at the time of cancellation or termination of the prior insurance; and

    (2) The loss or damage would have been covered by this Optional Coverage had it been in effect when the acts or events causing the loss or damage were committed or occurred.

i. The insurance under Paragraph **h.** above is part of, not in addition to, the Limit of Insurance applying to this Optional Coverage and is limited to the lesser of the amount recoverable under:

    (1) This Optional Coverage as of its effective date; or

    (2) The prior insurance had it remained in effect.

4. Mechanical Breakdown

a. We will pay for direct damage to Covered Property caused by an Accident to an Object. The Object must be:

    (1) Owned by you or in your care, custody or control; and

    (2) At the described premises.

b. Accident means a sudden and accidental breakdown of the Object or a part of the Object. At the time the breakdown occurs, it must manifest itself by physical damage to the Object that necessitates repair or replacement.

c. None of the following is an Accident:

    (1) Depletion, deterioration, corrosion or erosion;

    (2) Wear and tear;

    (3) Leakage at any valve, fitting, shaft seal, gland packing, joint or connection;

    (4) Breakdown of any vacuum tube, gas tube or brush;

    (5) Breakdown of any "computer", including "computer(s)" used to operate production type machinery or equipment;

    (6) Breakdown of any structure or foundation supporting the Object or any of its parts;

(7) The functioning of any safety or protective device; or

(8) The explosion of gases or fuel within the furnace of any Object or within the flues or passages through which the gases of combustion pass.

d. Object means any of the following equipment:

(1) Boiler and Pressure Vessels:

(a) Steam heating boilers and condensate return tanks used with them;

(b) Hot water heating boilers and expansion tanks used with them;

(c) Hot water supply boilers;

(d) Other fired or unfired vessels used for maintenance or service of the described premises but not used for processing or manufacturing;

(e) Steam boiler piping, valves, fittings, traps and separators, but only if they:

(i) Are on your premises or between parts of your premises;

(ii) Contain steam or condensate of steam; and

(iii) Are not part of any other vessel or apparatus;

(f) Feed water piping between any steam boiler and a feed pump or injector.

(2) Air Conditioning Units – Any air conditioning unit that has a capacity of 60,000 Btu or more, including:

(a) Inductors, convectors and coils that make use of a refrigerant and form part of a cooling, humidity control or space heating system;

(b) Interconnecting piping, valves and fittings containing only a refrigerant, water, brine or other solution;

(c) Vessels heated directly or indirectly that:

(i) Form part of an absorption type system; and

(ii) Function as a generator, regenerator or concentrator;

(d) Compressors, pumps, fans and blowers used solely with the system together with their driving electric motors; and

(e) Control equipment used solely with the system.

e. Object does not mean:

(1) As Boiler and Pressure Vessels:

(a) Equipment that is not under internal vacuum or internal pressure other than weight of contents;

(b) Boiler settings;

(c) Insulating or refractory material; or

(d) Electrical, reciprocating or rotating apparatus within or forming a part of the boiler or vessel.

(2) As Air Conditioning Units, any:

(a) Vessel, cooling tower, reservoir or other source of cooling water for a condenser or compressor, or any water piping leading to or from that source; or

(b) Wiring or piping leading to or from the unit.

f. We will not pay for an Accident to any Object while being tested.

g. Suspension

Whenever an Object is found to be in, or exposed to, a dangerous condition, any of our representatives may immediately suspend the insurance against loss from an Accident to that Object. This can be done by delivering or mailing a written notice of suspension to:

(1) Your last known address; or

(2) The address where the Object is located.

If we suspend your insurance, you will get a pro rata refund of premium. But the suspension will be effective even if we have not yet made or offered a refund.

H. Property Definitions

1. "Computer" means:

a. Programmable electronic equipment that is used to store, retrieve and process data; and

b. Associated peripheral equipment that provides communication, including input and output functions such as printing and auxiliary functions such as data transmission.

"Computer" does not include those used to operate production type machinery or equipment.

2. "Counterfeit" means an imitation of an actual valid original which is intended to deceive and to be taken as the original.

3. "Electronic media and records" means the following, if owned by you or licensed to you and used in your business:

   a. Media, meaning disks, tapes, film, drums, cells or other media which are used with electronically controlled equipment.

   b. Data, meaning information or facts stored on media described in Paragraph a. above. Data includes "valuable papers and records" converted to data.

   c. "Computer" program, meaning a set of related electronic instructions which direct the operations and functions of a "computer" or a device connected to it, which enable the "computer" or device to receive, process, restore, retrieve or send data.

   d. Software, including systems and applications software.

4. "Manager" means a person serving in a directorial capacity for a limited liability company.

5. "Member" means an owner of a limited liability company represented by its membership interest, who also may serve as a "manager".

6. "Money" means:

   a. Currency, coins and bank notes in current use and having a face value; and

   b. Travelers checks, register checks and money orders held for sale to the public.

7. "Operations" means your business activities occurring at the described premises.

8. "Period of restoration":

   a. Means the period of time that:

      (1) Begins:

         (a) 72 hours after the time of direct physical loss or damage for Business Income Coverage; or

         (b) Immediately after the time of direct physical loss or damage for Extra Expense Coverage;

         caused by or resulting from any Covered Cause of Loss at the described premises; and

      (2) Ends on the earlier of:

         (a) The date when the property at the described premises should be repaired, rebuilt or replaced with reasonable speed and similar quality; or

         (b) The date when business is resumed at a new permanent location.

   b. Does not include any increased period required due to the enforcement of any ordinance or law that:

      (1) Regulates the construction, use or repair, or requires the tearing down of any property; or

      (2) Requires any insured or others to test for, monitor, clean up, remove, contain, treat, detoxify or neutralize, or in any way respond to or assess the effects of "pollutants".

   The expiration date of this policy will not cut short the "period of restoration".

9. "Pollutants" means any solid, liquid, gaseous or thermal irritant or contaminant, including smoke, vapor, soot, fumes, acids, alkalis, chemicals and waste. Waste includes materials to be recycled, reconditioned or reclaimed.

10. "Securities" means negotiable and nonnegotiable instruments or contracts representing either "money" or other property and includes:

    a. Tokens, tickets, revenue and other stamps (whether represented by actual stamps or unused value in a meter) in current use; and

    b. Evidences of debt issued in connection with credit or charge cards, which cards are not issued by you;

    but does not include "money".

11. "Specified Causes of Loss" means the following:

    Fire; lightning; explosion; windstorm or hail; smoke; aircraft or vehicles; riot or civil commotion; vandalism; leakage from fire extinguishing equipment; sinkhole collapse; volcanic action; falling objects; weight of snow, ice or sleet; water damage.

    a. Sinkhole collapse means the sudden sinking or collapse of land into underground empty spaces created by the action of water on limestone or dolomite. This cause of loss does not include:

       (1) The cost of filling sinkholes; or

       (2) Sinking or collapse of land into man-made underground cavities.

    b. Falling objects does not include loss of or damage to:

       (1) Personal property in the open; or

       (2) The interior of a building or structure, or property inside a building or structure, unless the roof or an outside wall of the building or structure is first damaged by a falling object.

c. Water damage means accidental discharge or leakage of water or steam as the direct result of the breaking apart or cracking of any part of a system or appliance (other than a sump system including its related equipment and parts) containing water or steam.

12. "Stock" means merchandise held in storage or for sale, raw materials and in-process or finished goods, including supplies used in their packing or shipping.

13. "Valuable papers and records" means:

   a. Inscribed, printed or written:

   (1) Documents;

   (2) Manuscripts; and

   (3) Records;

   including abstracts, books, deeds, drawings, films, maps or mortgages; and

   b. "Electronic media and records".

   But "valuable papers and records" does not mean "money" or "securities".

SECTION II – LIABILITY

A. Coverages

1. Business Liability

   a. We will pay those sums that the insured becomes legally obligated to pay as damages because of "bodily injury", "property damage" or "personal and advertising injury" to which this insurance applies. We will have the right and duty to defend the insured against any "suit" seeking those damages. However, we will have no duty to defend the insured against any "suit" seeking damages for "bodily injury", "property damage" or "personal and advertising injury", to which this insurance does not apply. We may at our discretion, investigate any "occurrence" and settle any claim or "suit" that may result. But:

   (1) The amount we will pay for damages is limited as described in Paragraph **D** – Liability And Medical Expenses Limits Of Insurance in **Section II – Liability;** and

   (2) Our right and duty to defend end when we have used up the applicable limit of insurance in the payment of judgments or settlements or medical expenses.

   No other obligation or liability to pay sums or perform acts or services is covered unless explicitly provided for under Paragraph **f.** Coverage Extension – Supplementary Payments.

b. This insurance applies:

   (1) To "bodily injury" and "property damage" only if:

      (a) The "bodily injury" or "property damage" is caused by an "occurrence" that takes place in the "coverage territory";

      (b) The "bodily injury" or "property damage" occurs during the policy period; and

      (c) Prior to the policy period, no insured listed under Paragraph **C.1.** Who Is An Insured and no "employee" authorized by you to give or receive notice of an "occurrence" or claim, knew that the "bodily injury" or "property damage" had occurred, in whole or in part. If such a listed insured or authorized "employee" knew, prior to the policy period, that the "bodily injury" or "property damage" occurred, then any continuation, change or resumption of such "bodily injury" or "property damage" during or after the policy period will be deemed to have been known before the policy period.

   (2) To "personal and advertising injury" caused by an offense arising out of your business, but only if the offense was committed in the "coverage territory" during the policy period.

   c. "Bodily injury" or "property damage" which occurs during the policy period and was not, prior to the policy period, known to have occurred by any insured listed under Paragraph **C.1.** Who Is An Insured or any "employee" authorized by you to give or receive notice of an "occurrence" or claim, includes any continuation, change or resumption of "bodily injury" or "property damage" after the end of the policy period.

   d. "Bodily injury" or "property damage" will be deemed to have been known to have occurred at the earliest time when any insured listed under Paragraph **C.1.** Who Is An Insured or any "employee" authorized by you to give or receive notice of an "occurrence" or claim:

   (1) Reports all, or any part, of the "bodily injury" or "property damage" to us or any other insurer;

   (2) Receives a written or verbal demand or claim for damages because of the "bodily injury" or "property damage"; or

© ISO Properties, Inc., 2001

(3) Becomes aware by any other means that "bodily injury" or "property damage" has occurred or has begun to occur.

e. Damages because of "bodily injury" include damages claimed by any person or organization for care, loss of services or death resulting at any time from the "bodily injury".

f. **Coverage Extension – Supplementary Payments**

(1) In addition to the Limit of Insurance of **Section II – Liability** we will pay, with respect to any claim we investigate or settle, or any "suit" against an insured we defend:

(a) All expenses we incur.

(b) Up to $250 for cost of bail bonds required because of accidents or traffic law violations arising out of the use of any vehicle to which Business Liability Coverage for "bodily injury" applies. We do not have to furnish these bonds.

(c) The cost of bonds to release attachments, but only for bond amounts within our Limit of Insurance. We do not have to furnish these bonds.

(d) All reasonable expenses incurred by the insured at our request to assist us in the investigation or defense of the claim or "suit", including actual loss of earnings up to $250 a day because of time off from work.

(e) All costs taxed against the insured in the "suit".

(f) Prejudgment interest awarded against the insured on that part of the judgment we pay. If we make an offer to pay the Limit of Insurance, we will not pay any prejudgment interest based on that period of time after the offer.

(g) All interest on the full amount of any judgment that accrues after entry of the judgment and before we have paid, offered to pay, or deposited in court the part of the judgment that is within our Limit of Insurance.

(2) If we defend an insured against a "suit" and an indemnitee of the insured is also named as a party to the "suit", we will defend that indemnitee if all of the following conditions are met:

(a) The "suit" against the indemnitee seeks damages for which the insured has assumed the liability of the indemnitee in a contract or agreement that is an "insured contract";

(b) This insurance applies to such liability assumed by the insured;

(c) The obligation to defend, or the cost of the defense of, that indemnitee, has also been assumed by the insured in the same "insured contract";

(d) The allegations in the "suit" and the information we know about the "occurrence" are such that no conflict appears to exist between the interests of the insured and the interests of the indemnitee:

(e) The indemnitee and the insured ask us to conduct and control the defense of that indemnitee against such "suit" and agree that we can assign the same counsel to defend the insured and the indemnitee; and

(f) The indemnitee:

(i) Agrees in writing to:

i. Cooperate with us in the investigation, settlement or defense of the "suit";

ii. Immediately send us copies of any demands, notices, summonses or legal papers received in connection with the "suit";

iii. Notify any other insurer whose coverage is available to the indemnitee; and

iv. Cooperate with us with respect to coordinating other applicable insurance available to the indemnitee; and

(ii) Provides us with written authorization to:

i. Obtain records and other information related to the "suit"; and

ii. Conduct and control the defense of the indemnitee in such "suit".

(3) So long as the conditions in Paragraph **2.** are met, attorneys' fees incurred by us in the defense of that indemnitee, necessary litigation expenses incurred by us and necessary litigation expenses incurred by the indemnitee at our request will be paid as Supplementary Payments. Notwithstanding the provisions of Paragraph **B.1.b.(2)** Exclusions in **Section II – Liability,** such payments will not be deemed to be damages for "bodily injury" and "property damage" and will not reduce the limits of insurance.

Our obligation to defend an insured's indemnitee and to pay for attorneys' fees and necessary litigation expenses as Supplementary Payments ends when:

(a) We have used up the applicable limit of insurance in the payment of judgments or settlements; or

(b) The conditions set forth above, or the terms of the agreement described in Paragraph **2.f.** above are no longer met.

2. Medical Expenses

a. We will pay medical expenses as described below for "bodily injury" caused by an accident:

(1) On premises you own or rent;

(2) On ways next to premises you own or rent; or

(3) Because of your operations;

provided that:

(a) The accident takes place in the "coverage territory" and during the policy period;

(b) The expenses are incurred and reported to us within one year of the date of the accident; and

(c) The injured person submits to examination, at our expense, by physicians of our choice as often as we reasonably require.

b. We will make these payments regardless of fault. These payments will not exceed the Limits of Insurance of **Section II – Liability.** We will pay reasonable expenses for:

(1) First aid administered at the time of an accident;

(2) Necessary medical, surgical, x-ray and dental services, including prosthetic devices; and

(3) Necessary ambulance, hospital, professional nursing and funeral services.

B. Exclusions

1. Applicable To Business Liability Coverage

This insurance does not apply to:

a. Expected Or Intended Injury

"Bodily injury" or "property damage" expected or intended from the standpoint of the insured. This exclusion does not apply to "bodily injury" resulting from the use of reasonable force to protect persons or property.

b. Contractual Liability

"Bodily injury" or "property damage" for which the insured is obligated to pay damages by reason of the assumption of liability in a contract or agreement. This exclusion does not apply to liability for damages:

(1) That the insured would have in the absence of the contract or agreement; or

(2) Assumed in a contract or agreement that is an "insured contract", provided the "bodily injury" or "property damage" occurs subsequent to the execution of the contract or agreement. Solely for the purposes of liability assumed in an "insured contract", reasonable attorney fees and necessary litigation expenses incurred by or for a party other than an insured are deemed to be damages because of "bodily injury" or "property damage", provided:

(a) Liability to such party for, or for the cost of, that party's defense has also been assumed in the same "insured contract"; and

(b) Such attorney fees and litigation expenses are for defense of that party against a civil or alternative dispute resolution proceeding in which damages to which this insurance applies are alleged.

© ISO Properties, Inc., 2001   **BP 00 03 07 02**

c. Liquor Liability

"Bodily injury" or "property damage" for which any insured may be held liable by reason of:

(1) Causing or contributing to the intoxication of any person;

(2) The furnishing of alcoholic beverages to a person under the legal drinking age or under the influence of alcohol; or

(3) Any statute, ordinance or regulation relating to the sale, gift, distribution or use of alcoholic beverages.

This exclusion applies only if you are in the business of manufacturing, distributing, selling, serving or furnishing alcoholic beverages.

d. Workers' Compensation And Similar Laws

Any obligation of the insured under a workers' compensation, disability benefits or unemployment compensation law or any similar law.

e. Employer's Liability

"Bodily Injury" to:

(1) An "employee" of the insured arising out of and in the course of:

  (a) Employment by the insured; or

  (b) Performing duties related to the conduct of the insured's business; or

(2) The spouse, child, parent, brother or sister of that "employee" as a consequence of Paragraph **(1)** above.

This exclusion applies:

(1) Whether the insured may be liable as an employer or in any other capacity; and

(2) To any obligation to share damages with or repay someone else who must pay damages because of the injury.

This exclusion does not apply to liability assumed by the insured under an "insured contract".

f. Pollution

(1) "Bodily injury" or "property damage" arising out of the actual, alleged or threatened discharge, dispersal, seepage, migration, release or escape of "pollutants":

(a) At or from any premises, site or location which is or was at any time owned or occupied by, or rented or loaned to, any insured. However, this subparagraph does not apply to:

  (i) "Bodily injury" if sustained within a building and caused by smoke, fumes, vapor or soot from equipment used to heat that building;

  (ii) "Bodily injury" or "property damage" for which you may be held liable, if you are a contractor and the owner or lessee of such premises, site or location has been added to your policy as an additional insured with respect to your ongoing operations performed for that additional insured at that premises, site or location and such premises, site or location is not and never was owned or occupied by, or rented or loaned to, any insured, other than that additional insured; or

  (iii) "Bodily injury" or "property damage" arising out of heat, smoke or fumes from a "hostile fire";

(b) At or from any premises, site or location which is or was at any time used by or for any insured or others for the handling, storage, disposal, processing or treatment of waste;

(c) Which are or were at any time transported, handled, stored, treated, disposed of, or processed as waste by or for:

  (i) Any insured; or

  (ii) Any person or organization for whom you may be legally responsible; or

(d) At or from any premises, site or location on which any insured or any contractors or subcontractors working directly or indirectly on any insured's behalf are performing operations if the "pollutants" are brought on or to the premises, site or location in connection with such operations by such insured, contractor or subcontractor. However, this subparagraph does not apply to:

(i) "Bodily injury" or "property damage" arising out of the escape of fuels, lubricants or other operating fluids which are needed to perform the normal electrical, hydraulic or mechanical functions necessary for the operation of "mobile equipment" or its parts, if such fuels, lubricants or other operating fluids escape from a vehicle part designed to hold, store or receive them. This exception does not apply if the "bodily injury" or "property damage" arises out of the intentional discharge, dispersal or release of the fuels, lubricants or other operating fluids, or if such fuels, lubricants or other operating fluids are brought on or to the premises, site or location with the intent that they be discharged, dispersed or released as part of the operations being performed by such insured, contractor or subcontractor;

(ii) "Bodily injury" or "property damage" sustained within a building and caused by the release of gases, fumes or vapors from materials brought into that building in connection with operations being performed by you or on your behalf by a contractor or subcontractor; or

(iii) "Bodily injury" or "property damage" arising out of heat, smoke or fumes from a "hostile fire".

(e) At or from any premises, site or location on which any insured or any contractors or subcontractors working directly or indirectly on any insured's behalf are performing operations if the operations are to test for, monitor, clean up, remove, contain, treat, detoxify or neutralize, or in any way respond to, or assess the effects of, "pollutants".

(2) Any loss, cost or expense arising out of any:

(a) Request, demand, order or statutory or regulatory requirement that any insured or others test for, monitor, clean up, remove, contain, treat, detoxify or neutralize, or in any way respond to, or assess the effects of, "pollutants"; or

(b) Claim or "suit" by or on behalf of a governmental authority for damages because of testing for, monitoring, cleaning up, removing, containing, treating, detoxifying or neutralizing, or in any way responding to, or assessing the effects of, "pollutants".

However, this paragraph does not apply to liability for damages because of "property damage" that the insured would have in the absence of such request, demand, order or statutory or regulatory requirement or such claim or "suit" by or on behalf of a governmental authority.

g. Aircraft, Auto Or Watercraft

"Bodily injury" or "property damage" arising out of the ownership, maintenance, use or entrustment to others of any aircraft, "auto" or watercraft owned or operated by or rented or loaned to any insured. Use includes operation and "loading or unloading".

This exclusion applies even if the claims allege negligence or other wrongdoing in the supervision, hiring, employment, training or monitoring of others by an insured, if the "occurrence" which caused the "bodily injury" or "property damage" involved the ownership, maintenance, use or entrustment to others of any aircraft, "auto" or watercraft that is owned or operated by or rented or loaned to any insured.

This exclusion does not apply to:

(1) A watercraft while ashore on premises you own or rent;

(2) A watercraft you do not own that is:

(a) Less than 51 feet long; and

(b) Not being used to carry persons or property for a charge;

(3) Parking an "auto" on, or on the ways next to, premises you own or rent, provided the "auto" is not owned by or rented or loaned to you or the insured;

(4) Liability assumed under any "insured contract" for the ownership, maintenance or use of aircraft or watercraft; or

(5) "Bodily injury" or "property damage" arising out of the operation of any of the following equipment:

(a) Cherry pickers and similar devices mounted on automobile or truck chassis and used to raise or lower workers; and

(b) Air compressors, pumps and generators, including spraying, welding, building cleaning, geophysical exploration, lighting and well servicing equipment.

h. Mobile Equipment

"Bodily injury" or "property damage" arising out of:

(1) The transportation of "mobile equipment" by an "auto" owned or operated by or rented or loaned to any insured; or

(2) The use of "mobile equipment" in, or while in practice for, or while being prepared for, any prearranged racing, speed, demolition or stunting activity.

i. War

"Bodily injury" or "property damage" due to war, whether or not declared, or any act or condition incident to war. War includes civil war, insurrection, rebellion or revolution. This exclusion applies only to liability assumed under a contract or agreement.

j. Professional Services

"Bodily injury", "property damage", "personal and advertising injury" caused by the rendering or failure to render any professional service. This includes but is not limited to:

(1) Legal, accounting or advertising services;

(2) Preparing, approving, or failing to prepare or approve maps, drawings, opinions, reports, surveys, change orders, designs or specifications;

(3) Supervisory, inspection or engineering services;

(4) Medical, surgical, dental, x-ray or nursing services treatment, advice or instruction;

(5) Any health or therapeutic service treatment, advice or instruction;

(6) Any service, treatment, advice or instruction for the purpose of appearance or skin enhancement, hair removal or replacement or personal grooming;

(7) Optometry or optical or hearing aid services including the prescribing, preparation, fitting, demonstration or distribution of ophthalmic lenses and similar products or hearing aid devices;

(8) Body piercing services; and

(9) Services in the practice of pharmacy.

k. Damage To Property

"Property damage" to:

(1) Property you own, rent or occupy, including any costs or expenses incurred by you, or any other person, organization or entity, for repair, replacement, enhancement, restoration or maintenance of such property for any reason, including prevention of injury to a person or damage to another's property;

(2) Premises you sell, give away or abandon, if the "property damage" arises out of any part of those premises;

(3) Property loaned to you;

(4) Personal property in the care, custody or control of the insured;

(5) That particular part of real property on which you or any contractor or subcontractor working directly or indirectly on your behalf is performing operations, if the "property damage" arises out of those operations; or

(6) That particular part of any property that must be restored, repaired or replaced because "your work" was incorrectly performed on it.

Paragraphs **(1)**, **(3)** and **(4)** of this exclusion do not apply to "property damage" (other than damage by fire or explosion) to premises, including the contents of such premises, rented to you for a period of 7 or fewer consecutive days. A separate limit of insurance applies to Damage To Premises Rented To You as described in Paragraph **D.** Liability And Medical Expenses Limit Of Insurance in **Section II – Liability.**

Paragraph **(2)** of this exclusion does not apply if the premises are "your work" and were never occupied, rented or held for rental by you.

Paragraphs **(3)**, **(4)**, **(5)** and **(6)** of this exclusion do not apply to liability assumed under a sidetrack agreement.

Paragraph **(6)** of this exclusion does not apply to "property damage" included in the "products – completed operations hazard".

l. Damage To Your Product

"Property damage" to "your product" arising out of it or any part of it.

m. Damage To Your Work

"Property damage" to "your work" arising out of it or any part of it and included in the "products – completed operations hazard".

This exclusion does not apply if the damaged work or the work out of which the damage arises was performed on your behalf by a subcontractor.

n. Damage To Impaired Property Or Property Not Physically Injured

"Property damage" to "impaired property" or property that has not been physically injured, arising out of:

(1) A defect, deficiency, inadequacy or dangerous condition in "your product" or "your work"; or

(2) A delay or failure by you or anyone acting on your behalf to perform a contract or agreement in accordance with its terms.

This exclusion does not apply to the loss of use of other property arising out of sudden and accidental physical injury to "your product" or "your work" after it has been put to its intended use.

o. Recall Of Products, Work Or Impaired Property

Damages claimed for any loss, cost or expense incurred by you or others for the loss of use, withdrawal, recall, inspection, repair, replacement, adjustment, removal or disposal of:

(1) "Your product";

(2) "Your work"; or

(3) "Impaired property";

if such product, work or property is withdrawn or recalled from the market or from use by any person or organization because of a known or suspected defect, deficiency, inadequacy or dangerous condition in it.

p. Personal And Advertising Injury

"Personal and advertising injury":

(1) Caused by or at the direction of the insured with the knowledge that the act would violate the rights of another and would inflict "personal and advertising injury";

(2) Arising out of oral or written publication of material, if done by or at the direction of the insured with knowledge of its falsity;

(3) Arising out of oral or written publication of material whose first publication took place before the beginning of the policy period;

(4) Arising out of a criminal act committed by or at the direction of any insured;

(5) For which the insured has assumed liability in a contract or agreement. This exclusion does not apply to liability for damages that the insured would have in the absence of the contract or agreement;

(6) Arising out of a breach of contract, except an implied contract to use another's advertising idea in your "advertisement";

(7) Arising out of the failure of goods, products or services to conform with any statement of quality or performance made in your "advertisement";

(8) Arising out of the wrong description of the price of goods, products or services stated in your "advertisement";

(9) Committed by an insured whose business is:

(a) Advertising, broadcasting, publishing or telecasting;

(b) Designing or determining content of web-sites for others; or

(c) An Internet search, access, content or service provider.

However, this exclusion does not apply to Paragraphs **14.a., b.** and **c.** of "personal and advertising injury" under Paragraph **F.** Liability And Medical Expenses Definitions.

For the purposes of this exclusion, the placing of frames, borders or links, or advertising, for you or others anywhere on the Internet, by itself, is not considered the business of advertising, broadcasting, publishing or telecasting.

(10) Arising out of the actual, alleged or threatened discharge, dispersal, seepage, migration, release or escape of "pollutants" at any time.

(11) With respect to any loss, cost or expense arising out of any:

(a) Request, demand or order that any insured or others test for, monitor, clean-up, remove, contain, treat, detoxify or neutralize or in any way respond to, or assess the effects of, "pollutants"; or

(b) Claim or "suit" by or on behalf of a governmental authority for damages because of testing for, monitoring, cleaning up, removing, containing, treating, detoxifying or neutralizing or in any way responding to, or assessing the effects of, "pollutants".

BP 00 03 07 02

(12) Arising out of an electronic chatroom or bulletin board the insured hosts, owns or over which the insured exercises control.

(13) Arising out of the infringement of copyright, patent, trademark, trade secret or other intellectual property rights.

However, this exclusion does not apply to infringement, in your "advertisement", of copyright, trade dress or slogan.

(14) Arising out of the unauthorized use of another's name or product in your e-mail address, domain name or metatags, or any other similar tactics to mislead another's potential customers.

Exclusions **c., d., e., f., g., h., i., k., l., m., n.** and **o.** in **Section II – Liability** do not apply to damage by fire or explosion to premises while rented to you, or temporarily occupied by you with permission of the owner. A separate Damage To Premises Rented To You Limit of Insurance applies to this coverage as described in Paragraph **D.** Liability And Medical Expenses Limits of Insurance in **Section II – Liability.**

2. Applicable To Medical Expenses Coverage

We will not pay expenses for "bodily injury":

a. To any insured, except "volunteer workers".

b. To a person hired to do work for or on behalf of any insured or a tenant of any insured.

c. To a person injured on that part of premises you own or rent that the person normally occupies.

d. To a person, whether or not an "employee" of any insured, if benefits for the "bodily injury" are payable or must be provided under a workers' compensation or disability benefits law or a similar law.

e. To a person injured while taking part in athletics.

f. Included within the "products – completed operations hazard".

g. Excluded under Business Liability Coverage.

h. Due to war, whether or not declared, or any act or condition incident to war. War includes civil war, insurrection, rebellion or revolution.

3. Applicable To Both Business Liability Coverage And Medical Expenses Coverage – Nuclear Energy Liability Exclusion

This insurance does not apply:

a. Under Business Liability Coverage, to "bodily injury" or "property damage":

(1) With respect to which an insured under the policy is also an insured under a nuclear energy liability policy issued by the Nuclear Energy Liability Insurance Association, Mutual Atomic Energy Liability Underwriters or Nuclear Insurance Association of Canada, or would be an insured under any such policy but for its termination upon exhaustion of its limit of liability; or

(2) Resulting from the "hazardous properties" of "nuclear material" and with respect to which:

(a) Any person or organization is required to maintain financial protection pursuant to the Atomic Energy Act of 1954, or any law amendatory thereof; or

(b) The insured is, or had this policy not been issued would be, entitled to indemnity from the United States of America, or any agency thereof, under any agreement entered into by the United States of America, or any agency thereof, with any person or organization.

b. Under Medical Expenses Coverage, to expenses incurred with respect to "bodily injury" resulting from the "hazardous properties" of "nuclear material" and arising out of the operation of a "nuclear facility" by any person or organization.

c. Under Business Liability Coverage, to "bodily injury" or "property damage" resulting from the "hazardous properties" of the "nuclear material"; if:

(1) The "nuclear material":

(a) Is at any "nuclear facility" owned by, or operated by or on behalf of, an insured; or

(b) Has been discharged or dispersed therefrom;

(2) The "nuclear material" is contained in "spent fuel" or "waste" at any time possessed, handled, used, processed, stored, transported or disposed of by or on behalf of an insured; or

(3) The "bodily injury" or "property damage" arises out of the furnishing by an insured of services, materials, parts or equipment in connection with the planning, construction, maintenance, operation or use of any "nuclear facility"; but if such facility is located within the United States of America, its territories or possessions or Canada, this Exclusion **(3)** applies only to "property damage" to such "nuclear facility" and any property thereat.

d. As used in this exclusion:

(1) "By-product material" has the meaning given it in the Atomic Energy Act of 1954 or in any law amendatory thereof;

(2) "Hazardous properties" include radioactive, toxic or explosive properties;

(3) "Nuclear facility" means:

(a) Any "nuclear reactor";

(b) Any equipment or device designed or used for:

(i) Separating the isotopes of uranium or plutonium;

(ii) Processing or utilizing "spent fuel"; or

(iii) Handling, processing or packaging "waste";

(c) Any equipment or device used for the processing, fabricating or alloying of "special nuclear material" if at any time the total amount of such material in the custody of the insured at the premises where such equipment or device is located consists of or contains more than 25 grams of plutonium or uranium 233 or any combination thereof, or more than 250 grams of uranium 235;

(d) Any structure, basin, excavation, premises or place prepared or used for the storage or disposal of "waste";

and includes the site on which any of the foregoing is located, all operations conducted on such site and all premises used for such operations;

(4) "Nuclear material" means "source material", "special nuclear material" or "by-product material";

(5) "Nuclear reactor" means any apparatus designed or used to sustain nuclear fission in a self-supporting chain reaction or to contain a critical mass of fissionable material;

(6) "Property damage" includes all forms of radioactive contamination of property.

(7) "Source material" has the meaning given it in the Atomic Energy Act of 1954 or in any law amendatory thereof;

(8) "Special nuclear material" has the meaning given it in the Atomic Energy Act of 1954 or in any law amendatory thereof;

(9) "Spent fuel" means any fuel element or fuel component, solid or liquid, which has been used or exposed to radiation in a "nuclear reactor";

(10) "Waste" means any waste material:

(a) Containing "by-product material" other than the tailings or wastes produced by the extraction or concentration of uranium or thorium from any ore processed primarily for its "source material" content; and

(b) Resulting from the operation by any person or organization of any "nuclear facility" included under Paragraphs **(a)** and **(b)** of the definition of "nuclear facility".

C. Who Is An Insured

1. If you are designated in the Declarations as:

a. An individual, you and your spouse are insureds, but only with respect to the conduct of a business of which you are the sole owner.

b. A partnership or joint venture, you are an insured. Your members, your partners and their spouses are also insureds, but only with respect to the conduct of your business.

c. A limited liability company, you are an insured. Your members are also insureds, but only with respect to the conduct of your business. Your managers are insureds, but only with respect to their duties as your managers.

d. An organization other than a partnership, joint venture or limited liability company, you are an insured. Your "executive officers" and directors are insureds, but only with respect to their duties as your officers or directors. Your stockholders are also insureds, but only with respect to their liability as stockholders.

© ISO Properties, Inc., 2001 BP 00 03 07 02

2. Each of the following is also an insured:

a. Your "volunteer workers" only while performing duties related to the conduct of your business, or your "employees", other than either your "executive officers" (if you are an organization other than a partnership, joint venture or limited liability company) or your managers (if you are a limited liability company), but only for acts within the scope of their employment by you or while performing duties related to the conduct of your business. However, none of these "employees" or "volunteer workers" are insureds for:

(1) "Bodily injury" or "personal and advertising injury":

(a) To you, to your partners or members (if you are a partnership or joint venture), to your members (if you are a limited liability company), or to a co-"employee" while in the course of his or her employment or performing duties related to the conduct of your business, or to your other "volunteer workers" while performing duties related to the conduct of your business;

(b) To the spouse, child, parent, brother or sister of that co-"employee" as a consequence of Paragraph **(a)** above;

(c) For which there is any obligation to share damages with or repay someone else who must pay damages because of the injury described in Paragraphs **(a)** or **(b)**; or

(d) Arising out of his or her providing or failing to provide professional health care services.

(2) "Property damage" to property:

(a) Owned, occupied or used by,

(b) Rented to, in the care, custody or control of, or over which physical control is being exercised for any purpose by

you, any of your "employees", "volunteer workers", any partner or member (if you are a partnership or joint venture), or any member (if you are a limited liability company).

b. Any person (other than your "employee" or "volunteer worker"), or any organization while acting as your real estate manager.

c. Any person or organization having proper temporary custody of your property if you die, but only:

(1) With respect to liability arising out of the maintenance or use of that property; and

(2) Until your legal representative has been appointed.

d. Your legal representative if you die, but only with respect to duties as such. That representative will have all your rights and duties under this policy.

3. With respect to "mobile equipment" registered in your name under any motor vehicle registration law, any person is an insured while driving such equipment along a public highway with your permission. Any other person or organization responsible for the conduct of such person is also an insured, but only with respect to liability arising out of the operation of the equipment, and only if no other insurance of any kind is available to that person or organization for this liability. However, no person or organization is an insured with respect to:

a. "Bodily injury" to a co-"employee" of the person driving the equipment; or

b. "Property damage" to property owned by, rented to, in the charge of or occupied by you or the employer of any person who is an insured under this provision.

No person or organization is an insured with respect to the conduct of any current or past partnership, joint venture or limited liability company that is not shown as a Named Insured in the Declarations.

D. Liability And Medical Expenses Limits Of Insurance

1. The Limits of Insurance of **Section II – Liability** shown in the Declarations and the rules below fix the most we will pay regardless of the number of:

a. Insureds;

b. Claims made or "suits" brought; or

c. Persons or organizations making claims or bringing "suits".

2. The most we will pay for the sum of all damages because of all:

a. "Bodily injury", "property damage" and medical expenses arising out of any one "occurrence"; and

b. "Personal and advertising injury" sustained by any one person or organization;

is the Liability and Medical Expenses limit shown in the Declarations. But the most we will pay for all medical expenses because of "bodily injury" sustained by any one person is the Medical Expenses limit shown in the Declarations.

3. The most we will pay under Business Liability Coverage for damages because of "property damage" to premises while rented to you or temporarily occupied by you with permission of the owner, arising out of any one fire or explosion is the Damage To Premises Rented To You limit shown in the Declarations.

4. Aggregate Limits

The most we will pay for:

a. All "bodily injury" or "property damage" that is included in the "products-completed operations hazard" is twice the Liability and Medical Expenses limit; and

b. All:

(1) "Bodily injury" or "property damage" except damages because of "bodily injury" and "property damage" included in the "products-completed operations hazard";

(2) Plus medical expenses;

(3) Plus all "personal and advertising injury" caused by offenses committed;

is twice the Liability and Medical Expenses limit.

This Aggregate Limit does not apply to "property damage" to premises while rented to you or temporarily occupied by you with the permission of the owner, arising out of fire or explosion.

The Limits of Insurance of **Section II – Liability** apply separately to each consecutive annual period and to any remaining period of less than 12 months, starting with the beginning of the policy period shown in the Declarations, unless the policy period is extended after issuance for an additional period of less than 12 months. In that case, the additional period will be deemed part of the last preceding period for purposes of determining the Limits of Insurance.

E. Liability And Medical Expenses General Conditions

1. Bankruptcy

Bankruptcy or insolvency of the insured or of the insured's estate will not relieve us of our obligations under this policy.

2. Duties In The Event Of Occurrence, Offense, Claim Or Suit

a. You must see to it that we are notified as soon as practicable of an "occurrence" or an offense which may result in a claim. To the extent possible, notice should include:

(1) How, when and where the "occurrence" or offense took place;

(2) The names and addresses of any injured persons and witnesses; and

(3) The nature and location of any injury or damage arising out of the "occurrence" or offense.

b. If a claim is made or "suit" is brought against any insured, you must:

(1) Immediately record the specifics of the claim or "suit" and the date received; and

(2) Notify us as soon as practicable.

You must see to it that we receive written notice of the claim or "suit" as soon as practicable.

c. You and any other involved insured must:

(1) Immediately send us copies of any demands, notices, summonses or legal papers received in connection with the claim or "suit";

(2) Authorize us to obtain records and other information;

(3) Cooperate with us in the investigation, or settlement of the claim or defense against the "suit"; and

(4) Assist us, upon our request, in the enforcement of any right against any person or organization that may be liable to the insured because of injury or damage to which this insurance may also apply.

d. No insured will, except at that insured's own cost, voluntarily make a payment, assume any obligation, or incur any expense, other than for first aid, without our consent.

3. Financial Responsibility Laws

a. When this policy is certified as proof of financial responsibility for the future under the provisions of any motor vehicle financial responsibility law, the insurance provided by the policy for "bodily injury" liability and "property damage" liability will comply with the provisions of the law to the extent of the coverage and limits of insurance required by that law.

       BP 00 03 07 02

   b. With respect to "mobile equipment" to which this insurance applies, we will provide any liability, uninsured motorists, underinsured motorists, no-fault or other coverage required by any motor vehicle law. We will provide the required limits for those coverages.

4. Legal Action Against Us

No person or organization has a right under this policy:

   a. To join us as a party or otherwise bring us into a "suit" asking for damages from an insured; or

   b. To sue us on this policy unless all of its terms have been fully complied with.

A person or organization may sue us to recover on an agreed settlement or on a final judgment against an insured; but we will not be liable for damages that are not payable under the terms of this policy or that are in excess of the applicable limit of insurance. An agreed settlement means a settlement and release of liability signed by us, the insured and the claimant or the claimant's legal representative.

5. Separation Of Insureds

Except with respect to the Limits of Insurance of **Section II – Liability,** and any rights or duties specifically assigned in this policy to the first Named Insured, this insurance applies:

   a. As if each Named Insured were the only Named Insured; and

   b. Separately to each insured against whom claim is made or "suit" is brought.

F. Liability And Medical Expenses Definitions

1. "Advertisement" means a notice that is broadcast or published to the general public or specific market segments about your goods, products or services for the purpose of attracting customers or supporters. For the purposes of this definition:

   a. Notices that are published include material placed on the Internet or on similar electronic means of communication; and

   b. Regarding web-sites, only that part of a web-site that is about your goods, products or services for the purposes of attracting customers or supporters is considered an advertisement.

2. "Auto" means a land motor vehicle, trailer or semitrailer designed for travel on public roads, including any attached machinery or equipment. But "auto" does not include "mobile equipment".

3. "Bodily injury" means bodily injury, sickness or disease sustained by a person, including death resulting from any of these at any time.

4. "Coverage territory" means:

   a. The United States of America (including its territories and possessions), Puerto Rico and Canada;

   b. International waters or airspace, but only if the injury or damage occurs in the course of travel or transportation between any places included in Paragraph **a.** above; or

   c. All other parts of the world if the injury or damage arises out of:

     (1) Goods or products made or sold by you in the territory described in Paragraph **a.** above;

     (2) The activities of a person whose home is in the territory described in Paragraph **a.** above, but is away for a short time on your business; or

     (3) "Personal and advertising injury" offenses that take place through the Internet or similar electronic means of communication;

   provided the insured's responsibility to pay damages is determined in a "suit" on the merits in the territory described in Paragraph **a.** above or in a settlement we agree to.

5. "Employee" includes a "leased worker". "Employee" does not include a "temporary worker".

6. "Executive officer" means a person holding any of the officer positions created by your charter, constitution, by-laws or any other similar governing document.

7. "Hostile fire" means one which becomes uncontrollable or breaks out from where it was intended to be.

8. "Impaired property" means tangible property, other than "your product" or "your work", that cannot be used or is less useful because:

   a. It incorporates "your product" or "your work" that is known or thought to be defective, deficient, inadequate or dangerous; or

   b. You have failed to fulfill the terms of a contract or agreement;

   if such property can be restored to use by:

     (1) The repair, replacement, adjustment or removal of "your product" or "your work"; or

     (2) Your fulfilling the terms of the contract or agreement.

9. "Insured contract" means:

a. A contract for a lease of premises. However, that portion of the contract for a lease of premises that indemnifies any person or organization for damage by fire to premises while rented to you or temporarily occupied by you with permission of the owner is not an "insured contract";

b. A sidetrack agreement;

c. Any easement or license agreement, except in connection with construction or demolition operations on or within 50 feet of a railroad;

d. An obligation, as required by ordinance, to indemnify a municipality, except in connection with work for a municipality;

e. An elevator maintenance agreement;

f. That part of any other contract or agreement pertaining to your business (including an indemnification of a municipality in connection with work performed for a municipality) under which you assume the tort liability of another party to pay for "bodily injury" or "property damage" to a third person or organization. Tort liability means a liability that would be imposed by law in the absence of any contract or agreement.

Paragraph f. does not include that part of any contract or agreement:

(1) That indemnifies a railroad for "bodily injury" or "property damage" arising out of construction or demolition operations, within 50 feet of any railroad property and affecting any railroad bridge or trestle, tracks, road beds, tunnel, underpass or crossing;

(2) That indemnifies an architect, engineer or surveyor for injury or damage arising out of:

(a) Preparing, approving or failing to prepare or approve maps, drawings, opinions, reports, surveys, change orders, designs or specifications; or

(b) Giving directions or instructions, or failing to give them, if that is the primary cause of the injury or damage; or

(3) Under which the insured, if an architect, engineer or surveyor, assumes liability for an injury or damage arising out of the insured's rendering or failure to render professional services, including those listed in Paragraph (2) above and supervisory, inspection or engineering services.

10. "Leased worker" means a person leased to you by a labor leasing firm under an agreement between you and the labor leasing firm, to perform duties related to the conduct of your business. "Leased worker" does not include a "temporary worker".

11. "Loading or unloading" means the handling of property:

a. After it is moved from the place where it is accepted for movement into or onto an aircraft, watercraft or "auto";

b. While it is in or on an aircraft, watercraft or "auto"; or

c. While it is being moved from an aircraft, watercraft or "auto" to the place where it is finally delivered;

but "loading or unloading" does not include the movement of property by means of a mechanical device, other than a hand truck, that is not attached to the aircraft, watercraft or "auto".

12. "Mobile equipment" means any of the following types of land vehicles, including any attached machinery or equipment:

a. Bulldozers, farm machinery, forklifts and other vehicles designed for use principally off public roads;

b. Vehicles maintained for use solely on or next to premises you own or rent;

c. Vehicles that travel on crawler treads;

d. Vehicles, whether self-propelled or not, on which are permanently mounted:

(1) Power cranes, shovels, loaders, diggers or drills; or

(2) Road construction or resurfacing equipment such as graders, scrapers or rollers;

e. Vehicles not described in Paragraphs a., b., c. or d. above that are not self-propelled and are maintained primarily to provide mobility to permanently attached equipment of the following types:

(1) Air compressors, pumps and generators, including spraying, welding, building cleaning, geophysical exploration, lighting and well servicing equipment; or

© ISO Properties, Inc., 2001 **BP 00 03 07 02**

(2) Cherry pickers and similar devices used to raise or lower workers;

f. Vehicles not described in Paragraphs **a.**, **b.**, **c.** or **d.** above maintained primarily for purposes other than the transportation of persons or cargo.

However, self-propelled vehicles with the following types of permanently attached equipment are not "mobile equipment" but will be considered "autos":

(1) Equipment designed primarily for:

(a) Snow removal;

(b) Road maintenance, but not construction or resurfacing; or

(c) Street cleaning;

(2) Cherry pickers and similar devices mounted on automobile or truck chassis and used to raise or lower workers; and

(3) Air compressors, pumps and generators, including spraying, welding, building cleaning, geophysical exploration, lighting and well servicing equipment.

13. "Occurrence" means an accident, including continuous or repeated exposure to substantially the same general harmful conditions.

14. "Personal and advertising injury" means injury, including consequential "bodily injury", arising out of one or more of the following offenses:

a. False arrest, detention or imprisonment;

b. Malicious prosecution;

c. The wrongful eviction from, wrongful entry into, or invasion of the right of private occupancy of a room, dwelling or premises that a person occupies, committed by or on behalf of its owner, landlord or lessor;

d. Oral or written publication, in any manner, of material that slanders or libels a person or organization or disparages a person's or organization's goods, products or services;

e. Oral or written publication, in any manner, of material that violates a person's right of privacy;

f. The use of another's advertising idea in your "advertisement"; or

g. Infringing upon another's copyright, trade dress or slogan in your "advertisement".

15. "Pollutants" mean any solid, liquid, gaseous or thermal irritant or contaminant, including smoke, vapor, soot, fumes, acids, alkalis, chemicals and waste. Waste includes materials to be recycled, reconditioned or reclaimed.

16. "Products – completed operations hazard":

a. Includes all "bodily injury" and "property damage" occurring away from premises you own or rent and arising out of "your product" or "your work" except:

(1) Products that are still in your physical possession; or

(2) Work that has not yet been completed or abandoned. However, "your work" will be deemed completed at the earliest of the following times:

(a) When all of the work called for in your contract has been completed.

(b) When all of the work to be done at the job site has been completed if your contract calls for work at more than one job site.

(c) When that part of the work done at the job site has been put to its intended use by any other person or organization other than another contractor or subcontractor working on the same project.

Work that may need service, maintenance, correction, repair or replacement, but which is otherwise complete, will be treated as completed.

The "bodily injury" or "property damage" must occur away from premises you own or rent, unless your business includes the selling, handling or distribution of "your product" for consumption on premises you own or rent.

b. Does not include "bodily injury" or "property damage" arising out of:

(1) The transportation of property, unless the injury or damage arises out of a condition in or on a vehicle not owned or operated by you, and that condition was created by the "loading or unloading" of that vehicle by any insured; or

(2) The existence of tools, uninstalled equipment or abandoned or unused materials.

17. "Property damage" means:

a. Physical injury to tangible property, including all resulting loss of use of that property. All such loss of use shall be deemed to occur at the time of the physical injury that caused it; or

b. Loss of use of tangible property that is not physically injured. All such loss of use shall be deemed to occur at the time of the "occurrence" that caused it.

For the purposes of this insurance, electronic data is not tangible property.

As used in this definition, electronic data means information, facts or programs stored as, created or used on, or transmitted to or from computer software, including systems and applications software, hard or floppy disks, CD-ROMs, tapes, drives, cells, data processing devices or any other media which are used with electronically controlled equipment.

18. "Suit" means a civil proceeding in which damages because of "bodily injury", "property damage", "personal and advertising injury" to which this insurance applies are alleged. "Suit" includes:

   a. An arbitration proceeding in which such damages are claimed and to which the insured must submit or does submit with our consent; or

   b. Any other alternative dispute resolution proceeding in which such damages are claimed and to which the insured submits with our consent.

19. "Temporary worker" means a person who is furnished to you to substitute for a permanent "employee" on leave or to meet seasonal or short-term workload conditions.

20. "Volunteer worker" means a person who is not your "employee", and who donates his or her work and acts at the direction of and within the scope of duties determined by you, and is not paid a fee, salary or other compensation by you or anyone else for their work performed for you.

21. "Your product":

   a. Means:

     (1) Any goods or products, other than real property, manufactured, sold, handled, distributed or disposed of by:

       (a) You;

       (b) Others trading under your name; or

       (c) A person or organization whose business or assets you have acquired; and

     (2) Containers (other than vehicles), materials, parts or equipment furnished in connection with such goods or products.

   b. Includes:

     (1) Warranties or representations made at any time with respect to the fitness, quality, durability, performance or use of "your product"; and

     (2) The providing of or failure to provide warnings or instructions.

   c. Does not include vending machines or other property rented to or located for the use of others but not sold.

22. "Your work":

   a. Means:

     (1) Work or operations performed by you or on your behalf; and

     (2) Materials, parts or equipment furnished in connection with such work or operations.

   b. Includes:

     (1) Warranties or representations made at any time with respect to the fitness, quality, durability, performance or use of "your work"; and

     (2) The providing of or failure to provide warnings or instructions.

SECTION III – COMMON POLICY CONDITIONS (APPLICABLE TO SECTION I – PROPERTY AND SECTION II – LIABILITY)

A. Cancellation

1. The first Named Insured shown in the Declarations may cancel this policy by mailing or delivering to us advance written notice of cancellation.

2. We may cancel this policy by mailing or delivering to the first Named Insured written notice of cancellation at least:

   a. 5 days before the effective date of cancellation if any one of the following conditions exists at any building that is Covered Property in this policy.

     (1) The building has been vacant or unoccupied 60 or more consecutive days. This does not apply to:

       (a) Seasonal unoccupancy; or

       (b) Buildings in the course of construction, renovation or addition.

       Buildings with 65% or more of the rental units or floor area vacant or unoccupied are considered unoccupied under this provision.

     (2) After damage by a covered cause of loss, permanent repairs to the building:

       (a) Have not started, and

       (b) Have not been contracted for,

       within 30 days of initial payment of loss.

(3) The building has:

    (a) An outstanding order to vacate;

    (b) An outstanding demolition order; or

    (c) Been declared unsafe by governmental authority.

(4) Fixed and salvageable items have been or are being removed from the building and are not being replaced. This does not apply to such removal that is necessary or incidental to any renovation or remodeling.

(5) Failure to:

    (a) Furnish necessary heat, water, sewer service or electricity for 30 consecutive days or more, except during a period of seasonal unoccupancy; or

    (b) Pay property taxes that are owing and have been outstanding for more than one year following the date due, except that this provision will not apply where you are in a bona fide dispute with the taxing authority regarding payment of such taxes.

b. 10 days before the effective date of cancellation if we cancel for nonpayment of premium.

c. 30 days before the effective date of cancellation if we cancel for any other reason.

3. We will mail or deliver our notice to the first Named Insured's last mailing address known to us.

4. Notice of cancellation will state the effective date of cancellation. The policy period will end on that date.

5. If this policy is cancelled, we will send the first Named Insured any premium refund due. If we cancel, the refund will be pro rata. If the first Named Insured cancels, the refund may be less than pro rata. The cancellation will be effective even if we have not made or offered a refund.

6. If notice is mailed, proof of mailing will be sufficient proof of notice.

B. Changes

This policy contains all the agreements between you and us concerning the insurance afforded. The first Named Insured shown in the Declarations is authorized to make changes in the terms of this policy with our consent. This policy's terms can be amended or waived only by endorsement issued by us and made a part of this policy.

C. Concealment, Misrepresentation Or Fraud

This policy is void in any case of fraud by you as it relates to this policy at any time. It is also void if you or any other insured, at any time, intentionally conceal or misrepresent a material fact concerning:

1. This policy;

2. The Covered Property;

3. Your interest in the Covered Property; or

4. A claim under this policy.

D. Examination Of Your Books And Records

We may examine and audit your books and records as they relate to this policy at any time during the policy period and up to three years afterward.

E. Inspections And Surveys

1. We have to right to:

    a. Make inspections and surveys at any time;

    b. Give you reports on the conditions we find; and

    c. Recommend changes.

2. We are not obligated to make any inspections, surveys, reports or recommendations and any such actions we do undertake relate only to insurability and the premiums to be charged. We do not make safety inspections. We do not undertake to perform the duty of any person or organization to provide for the health or safety of workers or the public. And we do not warrant that conditions:

    a. Are safe and healthful; or

    b. Comply with laws, regulations, codes or standards.

3. Paragraphs **1.** and **2.** of this condition apply not only to us, but also to any rating, advisory, rate service or similar organization which makes insurance inspections, surveys, reports or recommendations.

4. Paragraph **2.** of this condition does not apply to any inspections, surveys, reports or recommendations we may make relative to certification, under state or municipal statutes, ordinances or regulations, of boilers, pressure vessels or elevators.

F. Insurance Under Two Or More Coverages

If two or more of this policy's coverages apply to the same loss or damage, we will not pay more than the actual amount of the loss or damage.

G. Liberalization

If we adopt any revision that would broaden the coverage under this policy without additional premium within 45 days prior to or during the policy period, the broadened coverage will immediately apply to this policy.

H. Other Insurance

1. If there is other insurance covering the same loss or damage, we will pay only for the amount of covered loss or damage in excess of the amount due from that other insurance, whether you can collect on it or not. But we will not pay more than the applicable Limit of Insurance of **Section I – Property.**

2. Business Liability Coverage is excess over:

   a. Any other insurance that insures for direct physical loss or damage; or

   b. Any other primary insurance available to you covering liability for damages arising out of the premises or operations for which you have been added as an additional insured by attachment of an endorsement.

3. When this insurance is excess, we will have no duty under Business Liability Coverage to defend any claim or "suit" that any other insurer has a duty to defend. If no other insurer defends, we will undertake to do so; but we will be entitled to the insured's rights against all those other insurers.

I. Premiums

1. The first Named Insured shown in the Declarations:

   a. Is responsible for the payment of all premiums; and

   b. Will be the payee for any return premiums we pay.

2. The premium shown in the Declarations was computed based on rates in effect at the time the policy was issued. On each renewal, continuation or anniversary of the effective date of this policy, we will compute the premium in accordance with our rates and rules then in effect.

3. With our consent, you may continue this policy in force by paying a continuation premium for each successive one-year period. The premium must be:

   a. Paid to us prior to the anniversary date; and

   b. Determined in accordance with Paragraph 2. above.

   Our forms then in effect will apply. If you do not pay the continuation premium, this policy will expire on the first anniversary date that we have not received the premium.

4. Undeclared exposures or change in your business operation, acquisition or use of locations may occur during the policy period that are not shown in the Declarations. If so, we may require an additional premium. That premium will be determined in accordance with our rates and rules then in effect.

J. Premium Audit

1. This policy is subject to audit if a premium designated as an advance premium is shown in the Declarations. We will compute the final premium due when we determine your actual exposures.

2. Premium shown in this policy as advance premium is a deposit premium only. At the close of each audit period we will compute the earned premium for that period and send notice to the first Named Insured. The due date for audit premiums is the date shown as the due date on the bill. If the sum of the advance and audit premiums paid for the policy period is greater than the earned premium, we will return the excess to the first Named Insured.

3. The first Named Insured must keep records of the information we need for premium computation, and send us copies at such times as we may request.

K. Transfer Of Rights Of Recovery Against Others To Us

1. Applicable to Businessowners Property Coverage:

   If any person or organization to or for whom we make payment under this policy has rights to recover damages from another, those rights are transferred to us to the extent of our payment. That person or organization must do everything necessary to secure our rights and must do nothing after loss to impair them. But you may waive your rights against another party in writing:

   a. Prior to a loss to your Covered Property.

   b. After a loss to your Covered Property only if, at time of loss, that party is one of the following:

      (1) Someone insured by this insurance;

      (2) A business firm:

         (a) Owned or controlled by you; or

         (b) That owns or controls you; or

      (3) Your tenant.

   You may also accept the usual bills of lading or shipping receipts limiting the liability of carriers.

   This will not restrict your insurance.

2. Applicable to Businessowners Liability Coverage:

If the insured has rights to recover all or part of any payment we have made under this policy, those rights are transferred to us. The insured must do nothing after loss to impair them. At our request, the insured will bring "suit" or transfer those rights to us and help us enforce them. This condition does not apply to Medical Expenses Coverage.

L. Transfer Of Your Rights And Duties Under This Policy

Your rights and duties under this policy may not be transferred without our written consent except in the case of death of an individual Named Insured.

If you die, your rights and duties will be transferred to your legal representative but only while acting within the scope of duties as your legal representative. Until your legal representative is appointed, anyone having proper temporary custody of your property will have your rights and duties but only with respect to that property.

COMMERCIAL PROPERTY COVERAGE PART
DECLARATIONS PAGE

POLICY NO. 1234	**EFFECTIVE DATE:** 4/1/X1	☐ *"X" IF SUPPLEMENTAL DECLARATIONS IS ATTACHED*

NAMED INSURED

April Winslow and Ben Trainer
    doing business as: Campus Book Store

DESCRIPTION OF PREMISES

PREM. NO.	BLDG. NO.	LOCATION , CONSTRUCTION, AND OCCUPANCY
1	1	1234 University Avenue, Collegetown, OI 1-story building of ordinary construction occupied as book store

COVERAGES PROVIDED   INSURANCE AT THE DESCRIBED PREMISES APPLIES ONLY FOR COVERAGES FOR WHICH A LIMIT OF INSURANCE IS SHOWN.

PREM NO	BLDG NO	COVERAGE	LIMIT OF INSURANCE	COVERED CAUSES OF LOSS	COINSURANCE*	RATES
1	1	Building	$200,000	Special	90	.XX
1	1	Your Business Personal Prop.	$300,000	Special	90	.XX

OPTIONAL COVERAGES   APPLICABLE ONLY WHEN ENTRIES ARE MADE IN THE SCHEDULE BELOW

PREM. NO.	BLDG. NO.	AGREED VALUE EXPIRATION DATE	COVERAGE	AMOUNT	REPLACEMENT COST 00 BUILDING	PERSONAL PROPERTY	INCLUDING STOCK
					X		

INFLATION GUARD BUILDING	(Percentage) PERSONAL PROPERTY	*MONTHLY LIMIT OF INDEMNITY (Fraction)	*MAXIMUM PERIOD OF INDEMNITY 00	*EXTENDED PERIOD OF INDEMNITY (Days)

*APPLIES TO BUSINESS INCOME ONLY

MORTGAGE HOLDERS

PREM. NO.	BLDG. NO.	MORTGAGE HOLDER NAME AND MAILLING ADDRESS
1	1	Piggy Bank and Trust, Collegetown, OI

DEDUCTIBLE

$250.

FORMS APPLICABLE

CP 00 90, CP 00 10, CP 10 30

IL 00 17 11 98

COMMON POLICY CONDITIONS

All Coverage Parts included in this policy are subject to the following conditions.

A. Cancellation

1. The first Named Insured shown in the Declarations may cancel this policy by mailing or delivering to us advance written notice of cancellation.

2. We may cancel this policy by mailing or delivering to the first Named Insured written notice of cancellation at least:

   a. 10 days before the effective date of cancellation if we cancel for nonpayment of premium; or

   b. 30 days before the effective date of cancellation if we cancel for any other reason.

3. We will mail or deliver our notice to the first Named Insured's last mailing address known to us.

4. Notice of cancellation will state the effective date of cancellation. The policy period will end on that date.

5. If this policy is cancelled, we will send the first Named Insured any premium refund due. If we cancel, the refund will be pro rata. If the first Named Insured cancels, the refund may be less than pro rata. The cancellation will be effective even if we have not made or offered a refund.

6. If notice is mailed, proof of mailing will be sufficient proof of notice.

B. Changes

This policy contains all the agreements between you and us concerning the insurance afforded. The first Named Insured shown in the Declarations is authorized to make changes in the terms of this policy with our consent. This policy's terms can be amended or waived only by endorsement issued by us and made a part of this policy.

C. Examination Of Your Books And Records

We may examine and audit your books and records as they relate to this policy at any time during the policy period and up to three years afterward.

D. Inspections And Surveys

1. We have the right to:

   a. Make inspections and surveys at any time;

   b. Give you reports on the conditions we find; and

   c. Recommend changes.

2. We are not obligated to make any inspections, surveys, reports or recommendations and any such actions we do undertake relate only to insurability and the premiums to be charged. We do not make safety inspections. We do not undertake to perform the duty of any person or organization to provide for the health or safety of workers or the public. And we do not warrant that conditions:

   a. Are safe or healthful; or

   b. Comply with laws, regulations, codes or standards.

3. Paragraphs **1.** and **2.** of this condition apply not only to us, but also to any rating, advisory, rate service or similar organization which makes insurance inspections, surveys, reports or recommendations.

4. Paragraph **2.** of this condition does not apply to any inspections, surveys, reports or recommendations we may make relative to certification, under state or municipal statutes, ordinances or regulations, of boilers, pressure vessels or elevators.

E. Premiums

The first Named Insured shown in the Declarations:

1. Is responsible for the payment of all premiums; and

2. Will be the payee for any return premiums we pay.

F. Transfer Of Your Rights And Duties Under This Policy

Your rights and duties under this policy may not be transferred without our written consent except in the case of death of an individual named insured.

If you die, your rights and duties will be transferred to your legal representative but only while acting within the scope of duties as your legal representative. Until your legal representative is appointed, anyone having proper temporary custody of your property will have your rights and duties but only with respect to that property.

IL 00 17 11 98   Copyright, Insurance Services Office, Inc., 1998   **Page 1 of 1**

COMMERCIAL PROPERTY

COMMERCIAL PROPERTY CONDITIONS

This Coverage Part is subject to the following conditions, the Common Policy Conditions and applicable Loss Conditions and Additional Conditions in Commercial Property Coverage Forms.

A. CONCEALMENT, MISREPRESENTATION OR FRAUD

This Coverage Part is void in any case of fraud by you as it relates to this Coverage Part at any time. It is also void if you or any other insured, at any time, intentionally conceal or misrepresent a material fact concerning:

1. This Coverage Part;

2. The Covered Property;

3. Your interest in the Covered Property; or

4. A claim under this Coverage Part.

B. CONTROL OF PROPERTY

Any act or neglect of any person other than you beyond your direction or control will not affect this insurance.

The breach of any condition of this Coverage Part at any one or more locations will not affect coverage at any location where, at the time of loss or damage, the breach of condition does not exist.

C. INSURANCE UNDER TWO OR MORE COVERAGES

If two or more of this policy's coverages apply to the same loss or damage, we will not pay more than the actual amount of the loss or damage.

D. LEGAL ACTION AGAINST US

No one may bring a legal action against us under this Coverage Part unless:

1. There has been full compliance with all of the terms of this Coverage Part; and

2. The action is brought within 2 years after the date on which the direct physical loss or damage occurred.

E. LIBERALIZATION

If we adopt any revision that would broaden the coverage under this Coverage Part without additional premium within 45 days prior to or during the policy period, the broadened coverage will immediately apply to this Coverage Part.

F. NO BENEFIT TO BAILEE

No person or organization, other than you, having custody of Covered Property will benefit from this insurance.

G. OTHER INSURANCE

1. You may have other insurance subject to the same plan, terms, conditions and provisions as the insurance under this Coverage Part. If you do, we will pay our share of the covered loss or damage. Our share is the proportion that the applicable Limit of Insurance under this Coverage Part bears to the Limits of Insurance of all insurance covering on the same basis.

2. If there is other insurance covering the same loss or damage, other than that described in 1. above, we will pay only for the amount of covered loss or damage in excess of the amount due from that other insurance, whether you can collect on it or not. But we will not pay more than the applicable Limit of Insurance.

H. POLICY PERIOD, COVERAGE TERRITORY

Under this Coverage Part:

1. We cover loss or damage commencing:

   a. During the policy period shown in the Declarations; and

   b. Within the coverage territory.

2. The coverage territory is:

   a. The United States of America (including its territories and possessions);

   b. Puerto Rico; and

   c. Canada.

I. TRANSFER OF RIGHTS OF RECOVERY AGAINST OTHERS TO US

If any person or organization to or for whom we make payment under this Coverage Part has rights to recover damages from another, those rights are transferred to us to the extent of our payment. That person or organization must do everything necessary to secure our rights and must do nothing after loss to impair them. But you may waive your rights against another party in writing:

1. Prior to a loss to your Covered Property or Covered Income.

2. After a loss to your Covered Property or Covered Income only if, at time of loss, that party is one of the following:

   a. Someone insured by this insurance;

   b. A business firm:

      (1) Owned or controlled by you; or

      (2) That owns or controls you; or

   c. Your tenant.

This will not restrict your insurance.

COMMERCIAL PROPERTY
CP 00 10 04 02

BUILDING AND PERSONAL PROPERTY COVERAGE FORM

Various provisions in this policy restrict coverage. Read the entire policy carefully to determine rights, duties and what is and is not covered.

Throughout this policy the words "you" and "your" refer to the Named Insured shown in the Declarations. The words "we", "us" and "our" refer to the Company providing this insurance.

Other words and phrases that appear in quotation marks have special meaning. Refer to Section **H. – Definitions.**

A. Coverage

We will pay for direct physical loss of or damage to Covered Property at the premises described in the Declarations caused by or resulting from any Covered Cause of Loss.

1. Covered Property

Covered Property, as used in this Coverage Part, means the type of property described in this Section, **A.1.**, and limited in **A.2.**, Property Not Covered, if a Limit of Insurance is shown in the Declarations for that type of property.

a. Building, meaning the building or structure described in the Declarations, including:

(1) Completed additions;

(2) Fixtures, including outdoor fixtures;

(3) Permanently installed:

   (a) Machinery and

   (b) Equipment;

(4) Personal property owned by you that is used to maintain or service the building or structure or its premises, including:

   (a) Fire extinguishing equipment;

   (b) Outdoor furniture;

   (c) Floor coverings; and

   (d) Appliances used for refrigerating, ventilating, cooking, dishwashing or laundering;

(5) If not covered by other insurance:

   (a) Additions under construction, alterations and repairs to the building or structure;

   (b) Materials, equipment, supplies and temporary structures, on or within 100 feet of the described premises, used for making additions, alterations or repairs to the building or structure.

b. Your Business Personal Property located in or on the building described in the Declarations or in the open (or in a vehicle) within 100 feet of the described premises, consisting of the following unless otherwise specified in the Declarations or on the Your Business Personal Property – Separation of Coverage form:

(1) Furniture and fixtures;

(2) Machinery and equipment;

(3) "Stock";

(4) All other personal property owned by you and used in your business;

(5) Labor, materials or services furnished or arranged by you on personal property of others;

(6) Your use interest as tenant in improvements and betterments. Improvements and betterments are fixtures, alterations, installations or additions:

   (a) Made a part of the building or structure you occupy but do not own; and

   (b) You acquired or made at your expense but cannot legally remove;

(7) Leased personal property for which you have a contractual responsibility to insure, unless otherwise provided for under Personal Property of Others.

c. Personal Property Of Others that is:

   (1) In your care, custody or control; and

   (2) Located in or on the building described in the Declarations or in the open (or in a vehicle) within 100 feet of the described premises.

   However, our payment for loss of or damage to personal property of others will only be for the account of the owner of the property.

2. Property Not Covered

Covered Property does not include:

   a. Accounts, bills, currency, food stamps or other evidences of debt, money, notes or securities. Lottery tickets held for sale are not securities;

   b. Animals, unless owned by others and boarded by you, or if owned by you, only as "stock" while inside of buildings;

   c. Automobiles held for sale;

   d. Bridges, roadways, walks, patios or other paved surfaces;

   e. Contraband, or property in the course of illegal transportation or trade;

   f. The cost of excavations, grading, backfilling or filling;

   g. Foundations of buildings, structures, machinery or boilers if their foundations are below:

   (1) The lowest basement floor; or

   (2) The surface of the ground, if there is no basement;

   h. Land (including land on which the property is located), water, growing crops or lawns;

   i. Personal property while airborne or waterborne;

   j. Bulkheads, pilings, piers, wharves or docks;

   k. Property that is covered under another coverage form of this or any other policy in which it is more specifically described, except for the excess of the amount due (whether you can collect on it or not) from that other insurance;

   l. Retaining walls that are not part of a building;

   m. Underground pipes, flues or drains;

   n. Electronic data, except as provided under Additional Coverages – Electronic Data. Electronic data means information, facts or computer programs stored as or on, created or used on, or transmitted to or from computer software (including systems and applications software), on hard or floppy disks, CD-ROMs, tapes, drives, cells, data processing devices or any other repositories of computer software which are used with electronically controlled equipment. The term computer programs, referred to in the foregoing description of electronic data, means a set of related electronic instructions which direct the operations and functions of a computer or device connected to it, which enable the computer or device to receive, process, store, retrieve or send data. This Paragraph **n.,** does not apply to your "stock" of prepackaged software.

   o. The cost to replace or restore the information on valuable papers and records, including those which exist as electronic data. Valuable papers and records include but are not limited to proprietary information, books of account, deeds, manuscripts, abstracts, drawings and card index systems. Refer to the Coverage Extension for Valuable Papers And Records (Other Than Electronic Data) for limited coverage for valuable papers and records other than those which exist as electronic data.

   p. Vehicles or self-propelled machines (including aircraft or watercraft) that:

   (1) Are licensed for use on public roads; or

   (2) Are operated principally away from the described premises.

   This paragraph does not apply to:

   (a) Vehicles or self-propelled machines or autos you manufacture, process or warehouse;

   (b) Vehicles or self-propelled machines, other than autos, you hold for sale;

   (c) Rowboats or canoes out of water at the described premises; or

   (d) Trailers, but only to the extent provided for in the Coverage Extension for Non-Owned Detached Trailers.

       CP 00 10 04 02

q. The following property while outside of buildings:

(1) Grain, hay, straw or other crops;

(2) Fences, radio or television antennas (including satellite dishes) and their lead-in wiring, masts or towers, signs (other than signs attached to buildings), trees, shrubs or plants (other than "stock" of trees, shrubs or plants), all except as provided in the Coverage Extensions.

3. Covered Causes Of Loss

See applicable Causes of Loss Form as shown in the Declarations.

4. Additional Coverages

a. Debris Removal

(1) Subject to Paragraphs (3) and (4), we will pay your expense to remove debris of Covered Property caused by or resulting from a Covered Cause of Loss that occurs during the policy period. The expenses will be paid only if they are reported to us in writing within 180 days of the date of direct physical loss or damage.

(2) Debris Removal does not apply to costs to:

(a) Extract "pollutants" from land or water; or

(b) Remove, restore or replace polluted land or water.

(3) Subject to the exceptions in Paragraph (4), the following provisions apply:

(a) The most we will pay for the total of direct physical loss or damage plus debris removal expense is the Limit of Insurance applicable to the Covered Property that has sustained loss or damage.

(b) Subject to (a) above, the amount we will pay for debris removal expense is limited to 25% of the sum of the deductible plus the amount that we pay for direct physical loss or damage to the Covered Property that has sustained loss or damage.

(4) We will pay up to an additional $10,000 for debris removal expense, for each location, in any one occurrence of physical loss or damage to Covered Property, if one or both of the following circumstances apply:

(a) The total of the actual debris removal expense plus the amount we pay for direct physical loss or damage exceeds the Limit of Insurance on the Covered Property that has sustained loss or damage.

(b) The actual debris removal expense exceeds 25% of the sum of the deductible plus the amount that we pay for direct physical loss or damage to the Covered Property that has sustained loss or damage.

Therefore, if (4)(a) and/or (4)(b) apply, our total payment for direct physical loss or damage and debris removal expense may reach but will never exceed the Limit of Insurance on the Covered Property that has sustained loss or damage, plus $10,000.

(5) Examples

The following examples assume that there is no coinsurance penalty.

Example #1

Limit of Insurance	$ 90,000
Amount of Deductible	$ 500
Amount of Loss	$ 50,000
Amount of Loss Payable	$ 49,500
	($50,000 - $500)
Debris Removal Expense	$ 10,000
Debris Removal Expense Payable	$ 10,000
($10,000 is 20% of $50,000)	

The debris removal expense is less than 25% of the sum of the loss payable plus the deductible. The sum of the loss payable and the debris removal expense ($49,500 + $10,000 = $59,500) is less than the Limit of Insurance. Therefore the full amount of debris removal expense is payable in accordance with the terms of Paragraph (3).

Example #2

Limit of Insurance	$ 90,000
Amount of Deductible	$ 500
Amount of Loss	$ 80,000
Amount of Loss Payable	$ 79,500
	($80,000 - $500)
Debris Removal Expense	$ 30,000
Debris Removal Expense Payable	
Basic Amount	$ 10,500
Additional Amount	$ 10,000

The basic amount payable for debris removal expense under the terms of Paragraph **(3)** is calculated as follows: $80,000 ($79,500 + $500) x .25 = $20,000; capped at $10,500. The cap applies because the sum of the loss payable ($79,500) and the basic amount payable for debris removal expense ($10,500) cannot exceed the Limit of Insurance ($90,000).

The additional amount payable for debris removal expense is provided in accordance with the terms of Paragraph **(4),** because the debris removal expense ($30,000) exceeds 25% of the loss payable plus the deductible ($30,000 is 37.5% of $80,000), and because the sum of the loss payable and debris removal expense ($79,500 + $30,000 = $109,500) would exceed the Limit of Insurance ($90,000). The additional amount of covered debris removal expense is $10,000, the maximum payable under Paragraph **(4).** Thus the total payable for debris removal expense in this example is $20,500; $9,500 of the debris removal expense is not covered.

b. Preservation Of Property

If it is necessary to move Covered Property from the described premises to preserve it from loss or damage by a Covered Cause of Loss, we will pay for any direct physical loss or damage to that property:

(1) While it is being moved or while temporarily stored at another location; and

(2) Only if the loss or damage occurs within 30 days after the property is first moved.

c. Fire Department Service Charge

When the fire department is called to save or protect Covered Property from a Covered Cause of Loss, we will pay up to $1,000 for your liability for fire department service charges:

(1) Assumed by contract or agreement prior to loss; or

(2) Required by local ordinance.

No Deductible applies to this Additional Coverage.

d. Pollutant Clean Up And Removal

We will pay your expense to extract "pollutants" from land or water at the described premises if the discharge, dispersal, seepage, migration, release or escape of the "pollutants" is caused by or results from a Covered Cause of Loss that occurs during the policy period. The expenses will be paid only if they are reported to us in writing within 180 days of the date on which the Covered Cause of Loss occurs.

This Additional Coverage does not apply to costs to test for, monitor or assess the existence, concentration or effects of "pollutants". But we will pay for testing which is performed in the course of extracting the "pollutants" from the land or water.

The most we will pay under this Additional Coverage for each described premises is $10,000 for the sum of all covered expenses arising out of Covered Causes of Loss occurring during each separate 12 month period of this policy.

e. Increased Cost Of Construction

(1) This Additional Coverage applies only to buildings to which the Replacement Cost Optional Coverage applies.

(2) In the event of damage by a Covered Cause of Loss to a building that is Covered Property, we will pay the increased costs incurred to comply with enforcement of an ordinance or law in the course of repair, rebuilding or replacement of damaged parts of that property, subject to the limitations stated in **e.(3)** through **e.(9)** of this Additional Coverage.

(3) The ordinance or law referred to in **e.(2)** of this Additional Coverage is an ordinance or law that regulates the construction or repair of buildings or establishes zoning or land use requirements at the described premises, and is in force at the time of loss.

(4) Under this Additional Coverage, we will not pay any costs due to an ordinance or law that:

(a) You were required to comply with before the loss, even when the building was undamaged; and

(b) You failed to comply with.

(5) Under this Additional Coverage, we will not pay for:

(a) The enforcement of any ordinance or law which requires demolition, repair, replacement, reconstruction, remodeling or remediation of property due to contamination by "pollutants" or due to the presence, growth, proliferation, spread or any activity of "fungus", wet or dry rot or bacteria; or

(b) Any costs associated with the enforcement of an ordinance or law which requires any insured or others to test for, monitor, clean up, remove, contain, treat, detoxify or neutralize, or in any way respond to, or assess the effects of "pollutants", "fungus", wet or dry rot or bacteria.

(6) The most we will pay under this Additional Coverage, for each described building insured under this Coverage Form, is $10,000 or 5% of the Limit of Insurance applicable to that building, whichever is less. If a damaged building is covered under a blanket Limit of Insurance which applies to more than one building or item of property, then the most we will pay under this Additional Coverage, for that damaged building, is the lesser of: $10,000 or 5% times the value of the damaged building as of the time of loss times the applicable coinsurance percentage.

The amount payable under this Additional Coverage is additional insurance.

(7) With respect to this Additional Coverage:

(a) We will not pay for the Increased Cost of Construction:

(i) Until the property is actually repaired or replaced, at the same or another premises; and

(ii) Unless the repairs or replacement are made as soon as reasonably possible after the loss or damage, not to exceed two years. We may extend this period in writing during the two years.

(b) If the building is repaired or replaced at the same premises, or if you elect to rebuild at another premises, the most we will pay for the Increased Cost of Construction, subject to the provisions of **e.(6)** of this Additional Coverage, is the increased cost of construction at the same premises.

(c) If the ordinance or law requires relocation to another premises, the most we will pay for the Increased Cost of Construction, subject to the provisions of **e.(6)** of this Additional Coverage, is the increased cost of construction at the new premises.

(8) This Additional Coverage is not subject to the terms of the Ordinance or Law Exclusion, to the extent that such Exclusion would conflict with the provisions of this Additional Coverage.

(9) The costs addressed in the Loss Payment and Valuation Conditions, and the Replacement Cost Optional Coverage, in this Coverage Form, do not include the increased cost attributable to enforcement of an ordinance or law. The amount payable under this Additional Coverage, as stated in **e.(6)** of this Additional Coverage, is not subject to such limitation.

f. Electronic Data

(1) Under this Additional Coverage, electronic data has the meaning described under Property Not Covered – Electronic Data.

(2) Subject to the provisions of this Additional Coverage, we will pay for the cost to replace or restore electronic data which has been destroyed or corrupted by a Covered Cause of Loss. To the extent that electronic data is not replaced or restored, the loss will be valued at the cost of replacement of the media on which the electronic data was stored, with blank media of substantially identical type.

(3) The Covered Causes of Loss applicable to Your Business Personal Property apply to this Additional Coverage – Electronic Data, subject to the following:

(a) If the Causes Of Loss – Special Form applies, coverage under this Additional Coverage – Electronic Data is limited to the "specified causes of loss" as defined in that form, and Collapse as set forth in that form.

(b) If the Causes Of Loss – Broad Form applies, coverage under this Additional Coverage – Electronic Data includes Collapse as set forth in that form.

(c) If the Causes Of Loss Form is endorsed to add a Covered Cause of Loss, the additional Covered Cause of Loss does not apply to the coverage provided under this Additional Coverage – Electronic Data.

(d) The Covered Causes of Loss include a virus, harmful code or similar instruction introduced into or enacted on a computer system (including electronic data) or a network to which it is connected, designed to damage or destroy any part of the system or disrupt its normal operation. But there is no coverage for loss or damage caused by or resulting from manipulation of a computer system (including electronic data) by any employee, including a temporary or leased employee, or by an entity retained by you or for you to inspect, design, install, modify, maintain, repair or replace that system.

(4) The most we will pay under this Additional Coverage – Electronic Data is $2,500 for all loss or damage sustained in any one policy year, regardless of the number of occurrences of loss or damage or the number of premises, locations or computer systems involved. If loss payment on the first occurrence does not exhaust this amount, then the balance is available for subsequent loss or damage sustained in but not after that policy year. With respect to an occurrence which begins in one policy year and continues or results in additional loss or damage sustained in a subsequent policy year(s), all loss or damage is deemed to be sustained in the policy year in which the occurrence began.

5. Coverage Extensions

Except as otherwise provided, the following Extensions apply to property located in or on the building described in the Declarations or in the open (or in a vehicle) within 100 feet of the described premises.

If a Coinsurance percentage of 80% or more or, a Value Reporting period symbol, is shown in the Declarations, you may extend the insurance provided by this Coverage Part as follows:

a. Newly Acquired Or Constructed Property

(1) Buildings

If this policy covers Building, you may extend that insurance to apply to:

(a) Your new buildings while being built on the described premises; and

(b) Buildings you acquire at locations, other than the described premises, intended for:

(i) Similar use as the building described in the Declarations; or

(ii) Use as a warehouse.

The most we will pay for loss or damage under this Extension is $250,000 at each building.

(2) Your Business Personal Property

(a) If this policy covers Your Business Personal Property, you may extend that insurance to apply to:

(i) Business personal property, including such property that you newly acquire, at any location you acquire other than at fairs, trade shows or exhibitions;

(ii) Business personal property, including such property that you newly acquire, located at your newly constructed or acquired buildings at the location described in the Declarations; or

(iii) Business personal property that you newly acquire, located at the described premises.

The most we will pay for loss or damage under this Extension is $100,000 at each building.

(b) This Extension does not apply to:

(i) Personal property of others that is temporarily in your possession in the course of installing or performing work on such property; or

    © ISO Properties, Inc., 2001   **CP 00 10 04 02**

(ii) Personal property of others that is temporarily in your possession in the course of your manufacturing or wholesaling activities.

(3) Period Of Coverage

With respect to insurance on or at each newly acquired or constructed property, coverage will end when any of the following first occurs:

(a) This policy expires;

(b) 30 days expire after you acquire the property or begin construction of that part of the building that would qualify as covered property; or

(c) You report values to us.

We will charge you additional premium for values reported from the date you acquire the property or begin construction of that part of the building that would qualify as covered property.

b. Personal Effects And Property Of Others

You may extend the insurance that applies to Your Business Personal Property to apply to:

(1) Personal effects owned by you, your officers, your partners or members, your managers or your employees. This extension does not apply to loss or damage by theft.

(2) Personal property of others in your care, custody or control.

The most we will pay for loss or damage under this Extension is $2,500 at each described premises. Our payment for loss of or damage to personal property of others will only be for the account of the owner of the property.

c. Valuable Papers And Records (Other Than Electronic Data)

(1) You may extend the insurance that applies to Your Business Personal Property to apply to the cost to replace or restore the lost information on valuable papers and records for which duplicates do not exist. But this Extension does not apply to valuable papers and records which exist as electronic data. Electronic data has the meaning described under Property Not Covered – Electronic Data.

(2) If the Causes Of Loss – Special Form applies, coverage under this Extension is limited to the "specified causes of loss" as defined in that form, and Collapse as set forth in that form.

(3) If the Causes Of Loss – Broad Form applies, coverage under this Extension includes Collapse as set forth in that form.

(4) Under this Extension, the most we will pay to replace or restore the lost information is $2,500 at each described premises, unless a higher limit is shown in the Declarations. Such amount is additional insurance. We will also pay for the cost of blank material for reproducing the records (whether or not duplicates exist), and (when there is a duplicate) for the cost of labor to transcribe or copy the records. The costs of blank material and labor are subject to the applicable Limit of Insurance on Your Business Personal Property and therefore coverage of such costs is not additional insurance.

d. Property Off-Premises

(1) You may extend the insurance provided by this Coverage Form to apply to your Covered Property while it is away from the described premises, if it is:

(a) Temporarily at a location you do not own, lease or operate;

(b) In storage at a location you lease, provided the lease was executed after the beginning of the current policy term; or

(c) At any fair, trade show or exhibition.

(2) This Extension does not apply to property:

(a) In or on a vehicle; or

(b) In the care, custody or control of your salespersons, unless the property is in such care, custody or control at a fair, trade show or exhibition.

(3) The most we will pay for loss or damage under this Extension is $10,000.

e. Outdoor Property

You may extend the insurance provided by this Coverage Form to apply to your outdoor fences, radio and television antennas (including satellite dishes), signs (other than signs attached to buildings), trees, shrubs and plants (other than "stock" of trees, shrubs or plants), including debris removal expense, caused by or resulting from any of the following causes of loss if they are Covered Causes of Loss:

(1) Fire;

(2) Lightning;

(3) Explosion;

(4) Riot or Civil Commotion; or

(5) Aircraft.

The most we will pay for loss or damage under this Extension is $1,000, but not more than $250 for any one tree, shrub or plant. These limits apply to any one occurrence, regardless of the types or number of items lost or damaged in that occurrence.

f. Non-Owned Detached Trailers

(1) You may extend the insurance that applies to Your Business Personal Property to apply to loss or damage to trailers that you do not own, provided that:

(a) The trailer is used in your business;

(b) The trailer is in your care, custody or control at the premises described in the Declarations; and

(c) You have a contractual responsibility to pay for loss or damage to the trailer.

(2) We will not pay for any loss or damage that occurs:

(a) While the trailer is attached to any motor vehicle or motorized conveyance, whether or not the motor vehicle or motorized conveyance is in motion;

(b) During hitching or unhitching operations, or when a trailer becomes accidentally unhitched from a motor vehicle or motorized conveyance.

(3) The most we will pay for loss or damage under this Extension is $5,000, unless a higher limit is shown in the Declarations.

(4) This insurance is excess over the amount due (whether you can collect on it or not) from any other insurance covering such property.

Each of these Extensions is additional insurance unless otherwise indicated. The Additional Condition, Coinsurance, does not apply to these Extensions.

B. Exclusions And Limitations

See applicable Causes of Loss Form as shown in the Declarations.

C. Limits Of Insurance

The most we will pay for loss or damage in any one occurrence is the applicable Limit of Insurance shown in the Declarations.

The most we will pay for loss or damage to outdoor signs attached to buildings is $1,000 per sign in any one occurrence.

The limits applicable to the Fire Department Service Charge and Pollutant Clean Up and Removal Additional Coverages are in addition to the Limits of Insurance.

Payments under the Preservation of Property Additional Coverage will not increase the applicable Limit of Insurance.

D. Deductible

In any one occurrence of loss or damage (hereinafter referred to as loss), we will first reduce the amount of loss if required by the Coinsurance Condition or the Agreed Value Optional Coverage. If the adjusted amount of loss is less than or equal to the Deductible, we will not pay for that loss. If the adjusted amount of loss exceeds the Deductible, we will then subtract the Deductible from the adjusted amount of loss, and will pay the resulting amount or the Limit of Insurance, whichever is less.

When the occurrence involves loss to more than one item of Covered Property and separate Limits of Insurance apply, the losses will not be combined in determining application of the Deductible. But the Deductible will be applied only once per occurrence.

Example No. 1:

(This example assumes there is no coinsurance penalty.)

Deductible:	$ 250
Limit of Insurance – Bldg. 1:	$ 60,000
Limit of Insurance – Bldg. 2:	$ 80,000
Loss to Bldg. 1:	$ 60,100
Loss to Bldg. 2:	$ 90,000

The amount of loss to Bldg. 1 ($60,100) is less than the sum ($60,250) of the Limit of Insurance applicable to Bldg. 1 plus the Deductible.

The Deductible will be subtracted from the amount of loss in calculating the loss payable for Bldg. 1:

$ 60,100

– 250

$ 59,850 Loss Payable – Bldg. 1

The Deductible applies once per occurrence and therefore is not subtracted in determining the amount of loss payable for Bldg. 2. Loss payable for Bldg. 2 is the Limit of Insurance of $80,000.

Total amount of loss payable: $59,850 + 80,000 = $139, 850

Example No. 2:

(This example, too, assumes there is no coinsurance penalty.)

The Deductible and Limits of Insurance are the same as those in Example No. 1.

Loss to Bldg. 1: $ 70,000

(exceeds Limit of Insurance plus Deductible)

Loss to Bldg. 2: $ 90,000

(exceeds Limit of Insurance plus Deductible)

Loss Payable – Bldg. 1: $60,000

(Limit of Insurance)

Loss Payable – Bldg. 2: $80,000

(Limit of Insurance)

Total amount of loss payable:

$140,000

E. Loss Conditions

The following conditions apply in addition to the Common Policy Conditions and the Commercial Property Conditions.

1. Abandonment

There can be no abandonment of any property to us.

2. Appraisal

If we and you disagree on the value of the property or the amount of loss, either may make written demand for an appraisal of the loss. In this event, each party will select a competent and impartial appraiser. The two appraisers will select an umpire. If they cannot agree, either may request that selection be made by a judge of a court having jurisdiction. The appraisers will state separately the value of the property and amount of loss. If they fail to agree, they will submit their differences to the umpire. A decision agreed to by any two will be binding. Each party will:

a. Pay its chosen appraiser; and

b. Bear the other expenses of the appraisal and umpire equally.

If there is an appraisal, we will still retain our right to deny the claim.

3. Duties In The Event Of Loss Or Damage

a. You must see that the following are done in the event of loss or damage to Covered Property:

(1) Notify the police if a law may have been broken.

(2) Give us prompt notice of the loss or damage. Include a description of the property involved.

(3) As soon as possible, give us a description of how, when and where the loss or damage occurred.

(4) Take all reasonable steps to protect the Covered Property from further damage, and keep a record of your expenses necessary to protect the Covered Property, for consideration in the settlement of the claim. This will not increase the Limit of Insurance. However, we will not pay for any subsequent loss or damage resulting from a cause of loss that is not a Covered Cause of Loss. Also, if feasible, set the damaged property aside and in the best possible order for examination.

(5) At our request, give us complete inventories of the damaged and undamaged property. Include quantities, costs, values and amount of loss claimed.

(6) As often as may be reasonably required, permit us to inspect the property proving the loss or damage and examine your books and records.

Also permit us to take samples of damaged and undamaged property for inspection, testing and analysis, and permit us to make copies from your books and records.

(7) Send us a signed, sworn proof of loss containing the information we request to investigate the claim. You must do this within 60 days after our request. We will supply you with the necessary forms.

(8) Cooperate with us in the investigation or settlement of the claim.

b. We may examine any insured under oath, while not in the presence of any other insured and at such times as may be reasonably required, about any matter relating to this insurance or the claim, including an insured's books and records. In the event of an examination, an insured's answers must be signed.

4. Loss Payment

a. In the event of loss or damage covered by this Coverage Form, at our option, we will either:

(1) Pay the value of lost or damaged property;

(2) Pay the cost of repairing or replacing the lost or damaged property, subject to **b.** below;

(3) Take all or any part of the property at an agreed or appraised value; or

(4) Repair, rebuild or replace the property with other property of like kind and quality, subject to **b.** below.

We will determine the value of lost or damaged property, or the cost of its repair or replacement, in accordance with the applicable terms of the Valuation Condition in this Coverage Form or any applicable provision which amends or supersedes the Valuation Condition.

b. The cost to repair, rebuild or replace does not include the increased cost attributable to enforcement of any ordinance or law regulating the construction, use or repair of any property.

c. We will give notice of our intentions within 30 days after we receive the sworn proof of loss.

d. We will not pay you more than your financial interest in the Covered Property.

e. We may adjust losses with the owners of lost or damaged property if other than you. If we pay the owners, such payments will satisfy your claims against us for the owners' property. We will not pay the owners more than their financial interest in the Covered Property.

f. We may elect to defend you against suits arising from claims of owners of property. We will do this at our expense.

g. We will pay for covered loss or damage within 30 days after we receive the sworn proof of loss, if you have complied with all of the terms of this Coverage Part and:

(1) We have reached agreement with you on the amount of loss; or

(2) An appraisal award has been made.

5. Recovered Property

If either you or we recover any property after loss settlement, that party must give the other prompt notice. At your option, the property will be returned to you. You must then return to us the amount we paid to you for the property. We will pay recovery expenses and the expenses to repair the recovered property, subject to the Limit of Insurance.

6. Vacancy

a. Description Of Terms

(1) As used in this Vacancy Condition, the term building and the term vacant have the meanings set forth in **(1)(a)** and **(1)(b)** below:

(a) When this policy is issued to a tenant, and with respect to that tenant's interest in Covered Property, building means the unit or suite rented or leased to the tenant. Such building is vacant when it does not contain enough business personal property to conduct customary operations.

(b) When this policy is issued to the owner or general lessee of a building, building means the entire building. Such building is vacant unless at least 31% of its total square footage is:

(i) Rented to a lessee or sub-lessee and used by the lessee or sub-lessee to conduct its customary operations; and/or

(ii) Used by the building owner to conduct customary operations.

(2) Buildings under construction or renovation are not considered vacant.

b. Vacancy Provisions

If the building where loss or damage occurs has been vacant for more than 60 consecutive days before that loss or damage occurs:

(1) We will not pay for any loss or damage caused by any of the following even if they are Covered Causes of Loss:

(a) Vandalism;

(b) Sprinkler leakage, unless you have protected the system against freezing;

(c) Building glass breakage;

(d) Water damage;

(e) Theft; or

(f) Attempted theft.

(2) With respect to Covered Causes of Loss other than those listed in **b.(1)(a)** through **b.(1)(f)** above, we will reduce the amount we would otherwise pay for the loss or damage by 15%.

7. Valuation

We will determine the value of Covered Property in the event of loss or damage as follows:

a. At actual cash value as of the time of loss or damage, except as provided in **b., c., d.** and **e.** below.

b. If the Limit of Insurance for Building satisfies the Additional Condition, Coinsurance, and the cost to repair or replace the damaged building property is $2,500 or less, we will pay the cost of building repairs or replacement.

The cost of building repairs or replacement does not include the increased cost attributable to enforcement of any ordinance or law regulating the construction, use or repair of any property. However, the following property will be valued at the actual cash value even when attached to the building:

(1) Awnings or floor coverings;

(2) Appliances for refrigerating, ventilating, cooking, dishwashing or laundering; or

(3) Outdoor equipment or furniture.

c. "Stock" you have sold but not delivered at the selling price less discounts and expenses you otherwise would have had.

d. Glass at the cost of replacement with safety glazing material if required by law.

e. Tenant's Improvements and Betterments at:

(1) Actual cash value of the lost or damaged property if you make repairs promptly.

(2) A proportion of your original cost if you do not make repairs promptly. We will determine the proportionate value as follows:

(a) Multiply the original cost by the number of days from the loss or damage to the expiration of the lease; and

(b) Divide the amount determined in **(a)** above by the number of days from the installation of improvements to the expiration of the lease.

If your lease contains a renewal option, the expiration of the renewal option period will replace the expiration of the lease in this procedure.

(3) Nothing if others pay for repairs or replacement.

F. Additional Conditions

The following conditions apply in addition to the Common Policy Conditions and the Commercial Property Conditions.

1. Coinsurance

If a Coinsurance percentage is shown in the Declarations, the following condition applies.

a. We will not pay the full amount of any loss if the value of Covered Property at the time of loss times the Coinsurance percentage shown for it in the Declarations is greater than the Limit of Insurance for the property.

Instead, we will determine the most we will pay using the following steps:

(1) Multiply the value of Covered Property at the time of loss by the Coinsurance percentage;

(2) Divide the Limit of Insurance of the property by the figure determined in Step **(1)**;

(3) Multiply the total amount of loss, before the application of any deductible, by the figure determined in Step **(2)**; and

(4) Subtract the deductible from the figure determined in Step **(3)**.

We will pay the amount determined in Step **(4)** or the limit of insurance, whichever is less. For the remainder, you will either have to rely on other insurance or absorb the loss yourself.

Example No. 1 (Underinsurance):

When:	The value of the property is	$	250,000
	The Coinsurance percentage for it is		80%
	The Limit of Insurance for it is	$	100,000
	The Deductible is	$	250
	The amount of loss is	$	40,000

Step **(1):**	$250,000 x 80% = $200,000 (the minimum amount of insurance to meet your Coinsurance requirements)
Step **(2):**	$100,000 ÷ $200,000 = .50
Step **(3):**	$40,000 x .50 = $20,000
Step **(4):**	$20,000 – $250 = $19,750

We will pay no more than $19,750. The remaining $20,250 is not covered.

Example No. 2 (Adequate Insurance):

When:	The value of the property is	$	250,000
	The Coinsurance percentage for it is		80%
	The Limit of Insurance for it is	$	200,000
	The Deductible is	$	250
	The amount of loss is	$	40,000

The minimum amount of insurance to meet your Coinsurance requirement is $200,000 ($250,000 x 80%). Therefore, the Limit of Insurance in this Example is adequate and no penalty applies. We will pay no more than $39,750 ($40,000 amount of loss minus the deductible of $250).

b. If one Limit of Insurance applies to two or more separate items, this condition will apply to the total of all property to which the limit applies.

Example No. 3:

When:	The value of property is:		
	Bldg. at Location No. 1	$	75,000
	Bldg. at Location No. 2	$	100,000
	Personal Property at Location No. 2	$	75,000
		$	250,000
	The Coinsurance percentage for it is		90%
	The Limit of Insurance for Buildings and Personal Property at Location Nos. 1 and 2 is	$	180,000
	The Deductible is	$	1,000
	The amount of loss is:		
	Bldg. at Location No. 2	$	30,000
	Personal Property at Location No. 2.	$	20,000
		$	50,000

Step **(1):**	$250,000 x 90% = $225,000 (the minimum amount of insurance to meet your Coinsurance requirements and to avoid the penalty shown below)
Step **(2):**	$180,000 ÷ $225,000 = .80
Step **(3):**	$50,000 x .80 = $40,000
Step **(4):**	$40,000 – $1,000 = $39,000

We will pay no more than $39,000. The remaining $11,000 is not covered.

2. Mortgageholders

a. The term mortgageholder includes trustee.

b. We will pay for covered loss of or damage to buildings or structures to each mortgageholder shown in the Declarations in their order of precedence, as interests may appear.

c. The mortgageholder has the right to receive loss payment even if the mortgageholder has started foreclosure or similar action on the building or structure.

d. If we deny your claim because of your acts or because you have failed to comply with the terms of this Coverage Part, the mortgageholder will still have the right to receive loss payment if the mortgageholder:

(1) Pays any premium due under this Coverage Part at our request if you have failed to do so;

(2) Submits a signed, sworn proof of loss within 60 days after receiving notice from us of your failure to do so; and

CP 00 10 04 02

(3) Has notified us of any change in ownership, occupancy or substantial change in risk known to the mortgageholder.

All of the terms of this Coverage Part will then apply directly to the mortgageholder.

e. If we pay the mortgageholder for any loss or damage and deny payment to you because of your acts or because you have failed to comply with the terms of this Coverage Part:

(1) The mortgageholder's rights under the mortgage will be transferred to us to the extent of the amount we pay; and

(2) The mortgageholder's right to recover the full amount of the mortgageholder's claim will not be impaired.

At our option, we may pay to the mortgageholder the whole principal on the mortgage plus any accrued interest. In this event, your mortgage and note will be transferred to us and you will pay your remaining mortgage debt to us.

f. If we cancel this policy, we will give written notice to the mortgageholder at least:

(1) 10 days before the effective date of cancellation if we cancel for your non-payment of premium; or

(2) 30 days before the effective date of cancellation if we cancel for any other reason.

g. If we elect not to renew this policy, we will give written notice to the mortgageholder at least 10 days before the expiration date of this policy.

G. Optional Coverages

If shown as applicable in the Declarations, the following Optional Coverages apply separately to each item.

1. Agreed Value

a. The Additional Condition, Coinsurance, does not apply to Covered Property to which this Optional Coverage applies. We will pay no more for loss of or damage to that property than the proportion that the Limit of Insurance under this Coverage Part for the property bears to the Agreed Value shown for it in the Declarations.

b. If the expiration date for this Optional Coverage shown in the Declarations is not extended, the Additional Condition, Coinsurance, is reinstated and this Optional Coverage expires.

c. The terms of this Optional Coverage apply only to loss or damage that occurs:

(1) On or after the effective date of this Optional Coverage; and

(2) Before the Agreed Value expiration date shown in the Declarations or the policy expiration date, whichever occurs first.

2. Inflation Guard

a. The Limit of Insurance for property to which this Optional Coverage applied will automatically increase by the annual percentage shown in the Declarations.

b. The amount of increase will be:

(1) The Limit of Insurance that applied on the most recent of the policy inception date, the policy anniversary date, or any other policy change amending the Limit of Insurance, times

(2) The percentage of annual increase shown in the Declarations, expressed as a decimal (example: 8% is .08), times

(3) The number of days since the beginning of the current policy year or the effective date of the most recent policy change amending the Limit of Insurance, divided by 365.

Example:

If:			
	The applicable Limit of Insurance is	$	100,000
	The annual percentage increase is		8%
	The number of days since the beginning of the policy year (or last policy change) is		146
	The amount of increase is $100,000 x .08 x 146 ÷ 365 =	$	3,200

3. Replacement Cost

a. Replacement Cost (without deduction for depreciation) replaces Actual Cash Value in the Loss Condition, Valuation, of this Coverage Form.

b. This Optional Coverage does not apply to:

(1) Personal property of others;

(2) Contents of a residence;

(3) Works of art, antiques or rare articles, including etchings, pictures, statuary, marbles, bronzes, porcelains and bric-a-brac; or

(4) "Stock", unless the Including "Stock" option is shown in the Declarations.

Under the terms of this Replacement Cost Optional Coverage, tenants' improvements and betterments are not considered to be the personal property of others.

c. You may make a claim for loss or damage covered by this insurance on an actual cash value basis instead of on a replacement cost basis. In the event you elect to have loss or damage settled on an actual cash value basis, you may still make a claim for the additional coverage this Optional Coverage provides if you notify us of your intent to do so within 180 days after the loss or damage.

d. We will not pay on a replacement cost basis for any loss or damage:

(1) Until the lost or damaged property is actually repaired or replaced; and

(2) Unless the repairs or replacement are made as soon as reasonably possible after the loss or damage.

With respect to tenants' improvements and betterments, the following also apply:

(3) If the conditions in **d.(1)** and **d.(2)** above are not met, the value of tenants' improvements and betterments will be determined as a proportion of your original cost, as set forth in the Valuation Condition of this Coverage Form; and

(4) We will not pay for loss or damage to tenants' improvements and betterments if others pay for repairs or replacement.

e. We will not pay more for loss or damage on a replacement cost basis than the least of **(1)**, **(2)** or **(3)**, subject to **f.** below:

(1) The Limit of Insurance applicable to the lost or damaged property;

(2) The cost to replace the lost or damaged property with other property:

(a) Of comparable material and quality; and

(b) Used for the same purpose; or

(3) The amount actually spent that is necessary to repair or replace the lost or damaged property.

If a building is rebuilt at a new premises, the cost described in **e.(2)** above is limited to the cost which would have been incurred if the building had been rebuilt at the original premises.

f. The cost of repair or replacement does not include the increased cost attributable to enforcement of any ordinance or law regulating the construction, use or repair of any property.

4. Extension Of Replacement Cost To Personal Property Of Others

a. If the Replacement Cost Optional Coverage is shown as applicable in the Declarations, then this Extension may also be shown as applicable. If the Declarations show this Extension as applicable, then Paragraph **3.b.(1)** of the Replacement Cost Optional Coverage is deleted and all other provisions of the Replacement Cost Optional Coverage apply to replacement cost on personal property of others.

b. With respect to replacement cost on the personal property of others, the following limitation applies:

If an item(s) of personal property of others is subject to a written contract which governs your liability for loss or damage to that item(s), then valuation of that item(s) will be based on the amount for which you are liable under such contract, but not to exceed the lesser of the replacement cost of the property or the applicable Limit of Insurance.

H. Definitions

1. "Fungus" means any type or form of fungus, including mold or mildew, and any mycotoxins, spores, scents or by-products produced or released by fungi.

2. "Pollutants" means any solid, liquid, gaseous or thermal irritant or contaminant, including smoke, vapor, soot, fumes, acids, alkalis, chemicals and waste. Waste includes materials to be recycled, reconditioned or reclaimed.

3. "Stock" means merchandise held in storage or for sale, raw materials and in-process or finished goods, including supplies used in their packing or shipping.

       CP 00 10 04 02

About the Code of Professional Ethics

This is a brief summary of information appearing in greater detail in the Code of Professional Ethics, which is among the CPCU 510 study materials.

All CPCU candidates and CPCUs are bound by the Code of Professional Ethics of the American Institute for CPCU. The Code describes both high goals and minimum standards of conduct.

1.   The high goals described in the Canons challenge all CPCUs and CPCU candidates to aspire to the highest level of ethical performance in all of their professional activities.

2.   The minimum standards of conduct, described in the Rules, maintain the integrity of the CPCU designation. CPCUs and CPCU candidates are obligated to at least meet the minimum standards in the Rules, and failure to do so may subject a CPCU—or a CPCU candidate—to disciplinary measures.

CPCU candidates study the Code and are tested in CPCU 510 to ensure that all CPCUs understand their ethical obligations. The ultimate goal of the Code is to foster highly ethical conduct on the part of all CPCUs.

The Canons and Rules of the Code of Professional Ethics

Canon 1—CPCUs should endeavor at all times to place the public interest above their own.

Rule R1.1—A CPCU has a duty to understand and abide by all *Rules* of conduct which are prescribed in the *Code of Professional Ethics of the American Institute*.

Rule R1.2—A CPCU shall not advocate, sanction, participate in, cause to be accomplished, otherwise carry out through another, or condone any act which the CPCU is prohibited from performing by the *Rules* of this *Code*.

Canon 2—CPCUs should seek continually to maintain and improve their professional knowledge, skills, and competence.

Rule R2.1—A CPCU shall keep informed on those technical matters that are essential to the maintenance of the CPCU's professional competence in insurance, risk management, or related fields.

Canon 3—CPCUs should obey all laws and regulations, and should avoid any conduct or activity which would cause unjust harm to others.

Rule R3.1—In the conduct of business or professional activities, a CPCU shall not engage in any act or omission of a dishonest, deceitful, or fraudulent nature.

Rule R3.2—A CPCU shall not allow the pursuit of financial gain or other personal benefit to interfere with the exercise of sound professional judgment and skills.

Rule R3.3—A CPCU shall not violate any law or regulation relating to professional activities or commit any felony.

Canon 4—CPCUs should be diligent in the performance of their occupational duties and should continually strive to improve the functioning of the insurance mechanism.

Rule R4.1—A CPCU shall competently and consistently discharge his or her occupational duties.

Rule R4.2—A CPCU shall support efforts to effect such improvements in claims settlement, contract design, investment, marketing, pricing, reinsurance, safety engineering, underwriting, and other insurance operations as will both inure to the benefit of the public and improve the overall efficiency with which the insurance mechanism functions.

Canon 5—CPCUs should assist in maintaining and raising professional standards in the insurance business.

Rule R5.1—A CPCU shall support personnel policies and practices which will attract qualified individuals to the insurance business, provide them with ample and equal opportunities for advancement, and encourage them to aspire to the highest levels of professional competence and achievement.

Rule R5.2—A CPCU shall encourage and assist qualified individuals who wish to pursue CPCU or other studies which will enhance their professional competence.

Rule R5.3—A CPCU shall support the development, improvement, and enforcement of such laws, regulations, and codes as will foster competence and ethical conduct on the part of all insurance practitioners and inure to the benefit of the public.

Rule R5.4—A CPCU shall not withhold information or assistance officially requested by appropriate regulatory authorities who are investigating or prosecuting any alleged violation of the laws or regulations governing the qualifications or conduct of insurance practitioners.

Canon 6—CPCUs should strive to establish and maintain dignified and honorable relationships with those whom they serve, with fellow insurance practitioners, and with members of other professions.

Rule R6.1—A CPCU shall keep informed on the legal limitations imposed upon the scope of his or her professional activities.

Rule R6.2—A CPCU shall not disclose to another person any confidential information entrusted to, or obtained by, the CPCU in the course of the CPCU's business or professional activities, unless a disclosure of such information is required by law or is made to a person who necessarily must have the information in order to discharge legitimate occupational or professional duties.

Rule R6.3—In rendering or proposing to render professional services for others, a CPCU shall not knowingly misrepresent or conceal any limitations on the CPCU's ability to provide the quantity or quality of professional services required by the circumstances.

Canon 7—CPCUs should assist in improving the public understanding of insurance and risk management.

Rule R7.1—A CPCU shall support efforts to provide members of the public with objective information concerning their risk management and insurance needs and the products, services, and techniques which are available to meet their needs.

Rule R7.2—A CPCU shall not misrepresent the benefits, costs, or limitations of any risk management technique or any product or service of an insurer.

Canon 8—CPCUs should honor the integrity of the CPCU designation and respect the limitations placed on its use.

Rule R8.1—A CPCU shall use the CPCU designation and the CPCU key only in accordance with the relevant *Guidelines* promulgated by the American Institute.

Rule R8.2—A CPCU shall not attribute to the mere possession of the designation depth or scope of knowledge, skills, and professional capabilities greater than those demonstrated by successful completion of the CPCU program.

Rule R8.3—A CPCU shall not make unfair comparisons between a person who holds the CPCU designation and one who does not.

Rule R8.4—A CPCU shall not write, speak, or act in such a way as to lead another to reasonably believe the CPCU is officially representing the American Institute, unless the CPCU has been duly authorized to do so by the American Institute.

Canon 9—CPCUs should assist in maintaining the integrity of the *Code of Professional Ethics*.

Rule R9.1—A CPCU shall not initiate or support the CPCU candidacy of any individual known by the CPCU to engage in business practices which violate the ethical standards prescribed by this *Code*.

Rule R9.2—A CPCU possessing unprivileged information concerning an alleged violation of this *Code* shall, upon request, reveal such information to the tribunal or other authority empowered by the American Institute to investigate or act upon the alleged violation.

Rule R9.3—A CPCU shall report promptly to the American Institute any information concerning the use of the CPCU designation by an unauthorized person.